Dissecting Antismokers' Brains

DISSECTING

ANTISMOKERS'

BRAINS

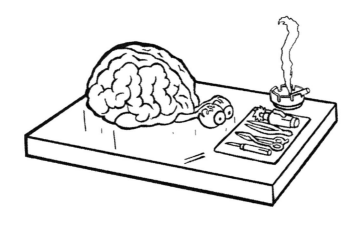

Michael J. McFadden

Published by:
AEthna Press
15 Loockerman Street
P.O. Box 841
Dover, DE 19904

ISBN 0-9744979-0-8

www.Antibrains.com

To my mother, Ethna, for teaching me the importance
of tolerance and of having love and respect for all living things.
To my father, Joseph, for teaching me the importance of right
and wrong and of knowing and acting upon that knowledge.
And finally, to my brother Joseph, his wife Eileen, and my
two wonderful nieces, Karen and Maureen, for the love
and support that have energized and sustained me.

I also must thank all those who proofread, edited, and
offered the encouragement that made this book not just possible,
but even fairly good. People like Spinner, Samantha, Audrey, Lockjaw,
Bayla, Martha, Gian, Jessica, Tman, Stephen, Darlene, Morgan, Linda,
Carol, Andy, Mike, Wanda, Ashley, Terry, Kenny, Elizabeth, Marty,
Barb, Kimmie, Craig, Karyn, Wiel, Ted, Tom, John, Dave, Joy,
Bob, Dan, Archie, Jack, Jon, Debbie, Hunter, Otto, Sam,
Warren, Irma, Joe, Don, Larry, Randi, and Laura,
all of whom energized and inspired me to write.
People like Gabz and Charlie who edited above and beyond the
call of duty and saved my wet soul from stormy and deserted bus stops.
People like Hallie, Joanie, Phil, and Owen, good friends who
slogged through drafts and gave me wonderful advice.
To all these people, and any whom I have missed:
Many thanks indeed.

Antibrains could not have been born in a vacuum.

The true horror of 1984 is not what was done to Winston Smith. The true horror was that the vast majority of the populace was happy, content, and believed that what their government was doing was "right."

-- David MacLean, alt.smokers FAQ, 1998

Author's Preface

I am not now, nor have I ever, been a member of the Communist Party.

I am also not now, nor have I ever, been affiliated with Big Tobacco or their stocks, nor do I have any plans to be.

I also do not now, nor have I ever, tried to claim smoking is good for you, although many may enjoy it enough to justify its risks. I do claim, and support the claim, that long-term risk from normal contact with other's smoke is virtually nonexistent. *Dissecting Antismokers' Brains* will show clearly that fears of secondary smoke have been exaggerated beyond all reason purely for purposes of social engineering.

Even the infamous EPA Report of 1993 testified more to the safety of secondary smoke than to its danger. According to the EPA figures themselves, a nonsmoker living with a smoker for 30 to 40 years would have better than a 99.9% chance of **not** getting lung cancer from such long-term, constant exposure (based on the claimed 19% increase over the base rate of .4%).

Now that those preliminaries are out of the way...

This book provides insight into what motivates the activists of the "Great American Antismoking Crusade," and examines the techniques and tricks used to mold political opinion and action around this issue. Understanding how these methods have been used in government hearings, in clever television ads, and on highway billboards will help us all resist future efforts by special interest groups seeking to control our thoughts and behaviors.

For issues both small and large, whether smoking bans or declarations of war, citizens of a democracy need a defense against those who would control them with deep pockets and sophisticated use of the media.

I wrote this book to help those seeking to cut through the forest of lies and half-truths about smoking bans and secondary smoke and to help smokers understand why they have been so stridently attacked, so grossly overtaxed, and so callously cast out into the elements to enjoy a previously quite acceptable social activity. Additionally, I hope to give nonsmokers insight into their own manipulation and exploitation as weapons in this "War on Smokers" and show them how and why they have been lied to.

Dissecting Antismokers' Brains has an openly admitted point of view but is honest in its facts and presentation. It flows from a strong belief that smokers are being unjustly discriminated against personally, financially, and societally, and argues that this is largely the result of an intense and well-funded campaign by a small group of activists and agencies thriving on an endless ocean of smokers' tax dollars. We will see that this campaign brought both injustice to smokers and harm to our larger society.

I focus more upon the psychological and the scientific aspects of this debate than the political: the Recommended Bibliography at the end presents some excellent choices for those seeking to expand more into the political history of the Antismoking Crusade. Prime choices for such reading include Don Oakley's *Slow Burn* (Eyrie Press. 1999), and Jacob Sullum's *For Your Own Good* (Simon & Schuster. 1999). Internet users should check FORCES.org, NYCCLASH.com, and Dave Hitt's outstanding reference: "The Facts."

A final note: "Antismokers" and the "Antismoking Crusade" are capitalized to emphasize the fact that many of these activists are formally connected and coordinated with each other under coherent and organized plans and programs. "Antismokers vs. Big Tobacco" is no longer David vs. Goliath: today's Crusading groups have multi-million dollar international conferences where thousands of activists gather to plan campaigns reaching decades into the future.

Your Antismoking neighbor next door may not be on the payroll of an organized group, but the information that inspired his or her feelings came from those who are: as documented later, over 880 million dollars a year is being spent on "tobacco control" just by state governments alone.

Table of Contents

APPENDICES:

Psychological Aspects of the Antismoking Crusade

Not so long ago there was basically one type of person in the United States: that type was called an American. You could go to a restaurant, advertise for a lover, apply for a job, and even run for President without further differentiating yourself. About 30 years ago, under pressure from a small but vocal pressure group, this basic indivisibility of our national identity began to change.

Although there had rarely been much attention paid to formally labeling oneself, there were indeed two large subgroups that made up the bulk of the population. The labels attached to the two groups were "smokers" and "nonsmokers," but the difference between the two was generally regarded as profoundly unimportant. Actually it was a rather soft difference, as many nonsmokers would occasionally smoke during festivities or celebrations.

Smokers generally lit tubes or bowls of tobacco and puffed the resulting smoke into the air in pretty much every location where it was physically possible to do so, and non-smokers generally ignored the resulting smoke unless it reached visibly uncomfortable levels or was blown directly in their faces. In some restricted situations, such as eating breakfast between two smokers at a diner counter or having an assigned seat next to a heavy smoker during a long flight, many nonsmokers would find the smoke somewhat annoying and some would go to the effort of seeking another seat or asking the smoker(s) to desist for a while. Most smokers in such situations were sympathetic to nonsmokers' discomforts and would make a conscious effort to restrict or redirect their smoke production.

Certainly there were exceptions. There have always been individuals who were obnoxious and insensitive to the feelings of those around them. There were smokers who'd blow **more** smoke when asked to refrain, and there were nonsmokers who'd go out of their way to complain to and about smokers even if the scent of smoke was barely or even totally non-detectable. Such antisocial people made up a small minority of the general population.

Today this has all changed. Today Americans seem locked into a state of war between two supposedly hostile camps, smokers and nonsmokers. In truth these two groups are not as antagonistic as usually pictured: the **real** antagonism lies between smokers and a much smaller third group: the Antismokers.

Antismokers have become powerful within America and American-influenced countries worldwide. What once was seen as a personality flaw -- the inability to tolerate a minor social annoyance -- is now considered a virtue throughout a small but growing portion of the world's nonsmoking population.

Antismokers have a voice far louder and more organized than that of either smokers or nonsmokers despite their far smaller numbers. This is largely due to massive infusions of money from regular cigarette taxes and the special "invisible tax" levied directly upon American smokers through the MSA (Master Settlement Agreement). The MSA is nothing more than a sweet deal made by a coalition of States with Big Tobacco to double or triple the government's take from smokers without forcing the politicians to pass an unpopular tax hike. The tobacco companies liked the agreement because it gave them large-scale immunity from lawsuits. Smokers simply paid the bill whether they liked it or not: they were never consulted.

This taxpayer-magnified voice has been amplified due to incredible expenditures of energy by a few highly driven subgroups of individuals. It also benefits from a successful effort by the core Antismoking Crusaders to portray themselves as being truly representative of a much larger population grouping: nonsmokers in general.

Antismokers are not simply nonsmokers, nor even simply people who don't like smoking or believe smoking to be unhealthful... most nonsmokers are not Antismokers. Antismokers are those who take it upon themselves to actively militate against the entire habit of smoking and seek to reduce its practice through such things as excessive taxes and unreasonable smoking bans.

Who are these Crusaders? Why have they become this way? What means have been used by government and by activist organizations to promote the goals of those who have been called "Smoke-Nazis" by their detractors and "Clean-Air Advocates" by their supporters? This book seeks to answer these questions largely through focusing on their psychological aspects but it is obviously impossible to completely isolate them from the larger societal framework; thus social and financial aspects of the Antismoking Crusade are also touched upon throughout.

Finally, the concluding sections gather some observations about the hidden costs of this movement and looks at why it should be and at how it can be fought by ordinary concerned citizens, whether smokers or nonsmokers. Several Appendices deal with important side issues and present technical information and arguments that do not properly fit within the body of the book itself although still having a significant impact upon the issue.

The Antismokers

To start out, let's differentiate between a simple nonsmoker and an Antismoker.

Nonsmokers do not smoke and may find tobacco smoke at least mildly offensive at times. For most nonsmokers the smell of burning tobacco is generally shunted into the background of their consciousness unless it is noticed in an unusual location, in an unusual quantity, or at a particular time when such a smell interferes with the nonsmoker's enjoyment of other smells or tastes. For most Antismokers even a slight tinge of smoke in the air, even if detectable only by eye and not by nose, becomes instantly attention getting and triggers a response of annoyance, avoidance, and perhaps even anger or fear.

Nonsmokers will sometimes avoid sitting directly next to an active smoker while eating, but will only occasionally concern themselves with whether a healthy friend or relative smokes or not. Antismokers will almost always avoid sitting anywhere near a smoker at any time whether that smoker is upwind, downwind, or out in an open field, although sometimes that rule is broken when an activist Antismoker will deliberately locate him or her self so as to have an excuse for a confrontation.

As for friends and relatives, the more extreme Antismokers will usually find a person's smoking status to be paramount in terms of personal relationships. They will associate almost exclusively with nonsmokers and will go out of their way to constantly demonstrate discomfort, disapproval, and a loudly exaggerated concern for the health of any smokers who have somehow moved within their circle of intimacy.

Unless they are asked, nonsmokers will generally not think twice about whether an otherwise clean, fresh hotel room or taxicab might have been previously occupied by a smoker.

Antismokers however will usually demand accommodations that make special recognition of their nonsmoking status and are specifically certified to be "clean" from any possible taint of past smoking, no matter how undetectable such taint might be. They will push private management and public officials to guarantee such accommodations as an important and fundamental right of human existence, and then go on to insist that **all** nonsmokers want such a guarantee.

Ordinary nonsmokers generally ignore smoking as a social issue unless they believe it impacts themselves or their loved ones personally in a seriously negative way. Antismokers will generally rank the importance of smoking very high as a social concern and will often allow a politician's smoking status or stands on tobacco taxes and smoking bans to have an important influence on their voting decisions.   Whereas the nonsmoker usually sees smoking as a somewhat negative activity that lies in the general realm of personal freedom and choice, the Antismoker will see it as a highly negative activity with a social impact so severe that it lies well beyond the parameters of personal freedoms.

While no good statistics exist as to how many people fall into these categories it's pretty clear to most people over forty that the proportion of Antismokers has grown enormously since the 1970s. Throughout my own high school and college years I had some degree of personal acquaintance with perhaps several thousand people. As a "sensitive smoker," one who had as a child been very much against smoking myself, I was very aware of people's reactions to smoking.

Of the thousands of nonsmokers I knew in my educational career I cannot think of more than a half dozen or so who would today be called Antismokers. Of the three who come most clearly to mind, one was an obsessively neat and orderly individual, one was highly nervous and played constantly with worry beads throughout classes, and one actually had occasionally severe asthmatic reactions when exposed to unusual levels of smoke in the air.

If it were possible to get actual statistics, I believe they would show that perhaps as little as one percent of the general population would have fit the profile of an Antismoker in the decades prior to the 1980s. Before the mid 1970s the concern was so rare that it was difficult to convince colleges to even bother offering a choice of "smoking or nonsmoking" on dorm-itory roommate preference cards: students were far more concerned about the many other facets of life with a roommate than they were about the roommate's smoking status. Indeed, smoking was often accepted and allowed in college classrooms! (Don Matchan. *We Mind If You Smoke.* Pyramid 1977)

Today the figure may be as much as five or ten times that size. It would not be unreasonable to estimate that five percent or more of today's adult population could be called or would consider themselves to be Antismokers. The reason for this growth will be made clear as we look at the types of people who make up this bloc of Antismokers and at the campaigns and tools that have been used to create and fan their fears.

While the following breakdown is somewhat arbitrary, the major groupings of those most active in the Antismoking Crusade might best be broken down into nine distinct categories. These categories are largely based upon the motivations of the individuals within them and many of them overlap others to some extent. These groupings will be labeled as follows:

1) The Innocents
2) The Neurotics
3) The Truly Affected
4) The Bereaved
5) The Ex-Smokers and The Victims
6) The Controllers
7) The Idealists
8) The Moralists
9) The Greedy

They are listed roughly in order of their likely sizes, though the details of that order could be argued. The Innocents comprise the largest grouping and The Greedy make up the smallest. The impact of each group upon the effectiveness of the Crusade is largely independent of size: The Greedy, although numbering perhaps only ten or twenty thousand individuals, have had a major impact; while The Innocents, with perhaps several million members, have generally had less influence except when an appeal to and a magnification of their size is used as the basis of a political effort by one of the other groups.

1) The Innocents

Why would they lie to us?

-- Anonymous

The voices of "Innocent" Antismokers are sometimes quite strident but are also sometimes little louder than those of many ordinary nonsmokers when it comes to expressing distaste for tobacco smoke. The Innocents would ordinarily have been simply nonsmokers throughout their lives: people who might object to extremely smoky conditions or to smoke in particular circumstances, but who would otherwise have generally accepted smoking and smokers as part and parcel of the world around them without much further concern or thought.

However, due to the efforts of those in the groups examined later, and provoked by massive media campaigns proclaiming dire dangers from even casual contact with wisps of tobacco smoke, The Innocents have come to believe that their long-term health is at least moderately endangered by those who smoke around them.   Despite this, most of them will generally not preach to smokers about their habit and will generally not seek confrontations with smokers. However many of them will significantly alter aspects of their routine daily activities in order to reduce their direct exposure to tobacco smoke.

Usually those decisions will have little impact on their lives or those of smokers. The Innocent Antismoker will simply choose to sit away from smokers and will dutifully opt for nonsmoking accommodations in hotels and restaurants. If such accommodations are unavailable, many of those in this category will more or less diffidently accept what is available without much complaint and with little degree of health concern.

Sometimes Innocents will favor a particular restaurant or entertainment venue because it does not allow smoking, but generally the quality of the food or fun will take primacy. While they accept the tone of the media proclamations about the dangers of secondary tobacco smoke they generally temper that acceptance with a more realistic belief that moderate or occasional exposure is not going to have any real effect on their lives or health.

While many Innocents will prefer a love relationship with someone who does not smoke, most will usually look beyond simple smoking status in deciding such things. He or she will usually accept a moderate smoker as a partner with only a minimum of reservation while putting only a small amount of pressure upon the partner to give up their "nasty habit." The hundred and one other aspects of life that create a supportive relationship will usually take far greater precedence.

When voting time comes, many Innocents may feel that a candidate's stand on smoking bans and taxes is worth noting, but is not as important as their other positions. The Innocent will rarely refuse to vote for someone simply because the person is a smoker. On the other hand, they may vote for increased cigarette taxes or more restrictions on smoking: it's a rare population that will refuse to take the opportunity of voting in its own favor if given even the slightest moral justification for doing so, and most Innocents are no exception. In this regard they are often joined by the more neutral masses of ordinary nonsmokers.

Two of the earliest groups in the Antismoking Crusade were ASH (Action on Smoking and Health) and GASP (Group Against Smokers' Pollution). They fought on both legal and social fronts to challenge the acceptability of smoking. One of their earliest victories was the widespread implementation of their demand that public facilities go beyond simple provision of nonsmoking spaces for those requesting such. ASH and GASP sought to create a situation in which all people entering commercial establishments would be confronted with the need to identify themselves as desiring smoking or nonsmoking accommodations regardless of whether they actually cared about that distinction. By thus constantly encouraging ordinary nonsmokers to identify themselves as such, Antismokers created a constant barrage of situations where nonsmokers would feel separated from smokers as a distinctly important group.

Ultimately this also provided a basis for Antismokers to demand that establishments mandate nonsmoking sections at least as large as the statistically nonsmoking population, despite the fact that many customer groups are likely to be mixed and would often prefer accommodations that would allow their smoking members to smoke in comfort. An additional perceived benefit of this forced self-identification was a reinforcement of the message being broadcast by the Crusaders that smokers were different and needed to be seen as and treated differently than "normal" people... a concept more recently enshrined in their stated goal of achieving the "Denormalization" of smokers (ReutersHealth.com/wellconnected/doc41.html).

Surprisingly, a number of doctors and medical professionals would find themselves listed as being among The Innocent. The foundations upon which most claims about the health effects of secondary smoke are built come from the field of epidemiology, the study of large population groupings and the impact of environment, organisms, and behavior upon the statistical health of such groupings. Most doctors have little training or expertise in this field but still have a general negative feeling about smoking because of what they believe to be the harm it has done to some of their smoking patients.

Given the demands upon their time and energy in keeping up with their own areas of expertise it is hardly surprising that many doctors have simply accepted the highly publicized press releases about the effects of secondary smoke without giving them much scrutiny. Most of them have not paid much attention to the background motivations of the Anti-smoking Crusade and see little reason to question news about harms connected with a habit they already believe to be bad.

As the largest group of Antismokers, The Innocents are responsible for much of the Crusade's raw political power. They act as a loose voting bloc, making up perhaps as much as five percent or more of the voting population. The more strident activists often portray their Innocent supporters as being single-issue voters, and that image has given this grouping significant political strength. Activist Crusaders further magnify the size and power of this group as they deliberately redefine and blur the difference between Antismokers and ordinary non-smokers.

Antismoking political activists always seek to portray the 70 percent or so of adults who don't smoke as all being politically aware of and strongly opposed to smoking at every level. While such a claim is patently ridiculous when given some thought, the assertion is usually jumbled in with a bunch of other background statistics that serve as a base for whatever campaign is currently being pursued: it winds up delivering its political punch while never being properly singled out for critical examination. The mere existence of the comparatively large though relatively inactive group of Innocent Antismokers serves as a foundation upon which the smaller groups can magnify their perceived size and support; thus building the power of their Crusade.

2) The Neurotics

The title of this chapter has not been chosen for its derogatory connotations, but because it seems to be an accurate description of one of the largest subsets of Antismokers. A good general definition of a neurotic is "a person who has markedly and significantly more than average psychological difficulty in dealing contentedly and productively with one or more commonly encountered aspects of life."

Those whose difficulties become sufficiently debilitating and whose perceptions of those difficulties migrate sufficiently far from what is considered reality may find themselves considered as being more than simply neurotic and could be labeled psychotic. This is particularly true if they are seen as posing an active threat to themselves or others because of their behaviors and beliefs.

Before the 1970s, if someone who was not clearly suffering extreme physical distress found themselves getting fired or quitting jobs because of conflicts over colleagues' smoking habits; if they had overwhelming fears of disease due to contact with normally encountered levels of tobacco smoke; or if they found themselves unable to enjoy restaurants or hotels because of possible encounters with smokers or undetectable traces of past smoking; that person would likely have been referred to counseling for help in dealing with their neurotic fear.

If it reached a level where violent confrontations occurred, where the nonsmoker felt so assaulted or offended by someone else's smoke that they actually assaulted that person, the line would clearly have been crossed into psychosis. One case in point was noted by a New York reporter who had been one of the first victims of the anthrax terrorist a year earlier. In late 2002, fully recovered, she stepped outside her office building for a smoke only to meet another type of budding terrorist: a woman physically attacked her, hitting and kicking at her, while screaming about her "cancer stick" (Johanna Huden. "Antismokers Get Physical." *New York Post* 11/19/02).

There are few cases of outright Antismoking psychosis, though news stories of a mother deliberately torturing a daughter with a hot iron for smoking or a husband repeatedly stabbing a wife who refused to quit are not unknown (*Ananova* 03/30/01; Nigel Bunyan. *London Telegraph* 04/21/00). One Internet activist outlined the idea and a method for injecting anthrax into cigarette packs: he reasoned that ultimately the number of people who would quit out of fear of anthrax might more than compensate for those killed by it, though he was careful not to officially endorse such an idea (roedy@mindprod.com, alt.current-events.wtc-explosion, 10/20/01).

Over the past 20 years or so we've seen an increasing acceptance of what would once have been considered a neurotic fear or phobia centered around tobacco smoke, and a similar acceptance of an obsessive-compulsive attitude toward cleansing one's environment from possible contamination by undetectable amounts of such smoke. Many such Neurotics are simply more extreme members of The Innocent: people who have absorbed, believed, and internally exaggerated the statements about the dangers of tobacco smoke to such an extent that they have developed what is sometimes an almost life-destroying neurosis centered around such smoke. That phobia is expressed in many ways, but one of the most common is a type of obsessive-compulsion.

The National Institute of Mental Health estimates that between two and three percent of the adult American population suffers from at least some form of non-substance-related obsessive-compulsive behavior that is beyond their ability to control. In its mildest form it can consist of actions as innocent as always going back to double-check a locked door a couple of times, or giving one's hands a second thorough washing before eating despite having washed them quite sufficiently the first time.

In its more severe forms an individual can feel forced to spend most of his or her waking hours performing dozens of checks of simple unimportant actions to see that they have been properly performed or that certain conditions have been adequately met. The cleaning and avoidance manifestations of Obsessive Compulsive Disorder often tie closely to phobic neuroses centered on contamination (www.nimh.nih.gov/anxiety/ocdfacts.cfm).

One common manifestation of obsessive-compulsive behavior takes the form of cleaning or purification rituals. The individual fears contamination of some type, usually caused by invisible germs, and the only way to be free of that feeling of dirtiness is by repeated and extreme cleansing despite having religiously avoided contact with offending objects and substances in the first place.

The Antismoking media campaign has played right into this type of neurosis by suggesting that casual and normal levels of contact with wisps of tobacco smoke in public places will result not only in contamination but in a slow and horrible death for those exposed. The more clever approaches to this incorporate an element of humor (e.g. the billboards asking "Mind if I smoke?" followed by the answer "Care if I die?") but the image meant to be conveyed is far more serious.

While 30 years ago a healthy individual who was afraid to go into a restaurant or hotel room for fear of "breathing someone else's smoke" would have been considered a prime candidate for counseling and therapy, today that individual finds not only a wellspring of support among respected members of both the general and the medical communities, but the complete reassurance that such fear, no matter how preposterously exaggerated, is not only normal but outright commendable. The traditional graduated exposure type therapy where individuals are encouraged to deliberately expose themselves to the triggering situation/substance/item while building emotional tolerance to it is no longer even considered with regard to tobacco smoke!

Individuals consumed with obsessive fears of contamination by germs were always plagued by the fact that they couldn't really **see** the germs... they just had to take it on faith that they existed and that the contamination was real. People fearing tobacco smoke can not only see the offending substance, but they can **smell** it, all the way down to concentrations of a few parts in a trillion. When this exposure combines with physical symptoms (sometimes or even often psychologically based and exaggerated in this subgroup) the perceived need to protect oneself from such contact can be extreme and provoke intense anxiety and activity.

One of the more zealous Antismokers in the public eye is a Mr. James Repace. Repace is a self-styled "Second-Hand Smoke Consultant" and generally refers to himself as a "Health Physicist" although he holds no doctoral degree. He claims that smoking sections would need winds of up to 300 miles per hour ("tornado-like levels") blowing through them to adequately protect those in nonsmoking sections. Anyone who has experienced or seen video of hurricane winds of far less than half that speed would immediately recognize how laughable such an assertion is (James Repace. Testimony at New York City Council Hearing, Feb. 2000).

The fact that negative air pressures equating to airflow of perhaps a hundredth of that amount are considered sufficient protection in biological weapons laboratories is conveniently ignored by this "Health Physicist" in his appeals to The Neurotics. He and other activists are now trying to whip this vulnerable segment of the population to an even greater frenzy of fear by talking about invisible contamination from microscopic levels of tobacco smoke long after a smoker has left a room.

Some extremists have even claimed that a dangerous threat exists from the "toxic particles" that might burrow into the clothing of a smoker's friend or hide in a room where someone had smoked and then jump out and attack someone else at a later time. One Crusader, a registered nurse who should know better, put it this way: "...carcinogens from smoking linger up to a week in the environment. They are not the part of the smoke that you can smell or see, but the insidious, dangerous parts you can't smell or see" (Wanda Chomilo, RN. *Eden Prairie News* 07/17/02).

Even more frightening, we've reached a point where Crusaders have actually convinced a New York Supreme Court Judge that these invisible but insidious particles in a mother's house or car were deadly enough that she should be denied visitation rights with her son even if she refrained from smoking during such visits! This was not a case of a child being made sick in any way: the judge simply decided that the time was ripe to make smoking a general consideration in custody and visitation cases! (Bryan Robinson. ABCNews.com 04/04/02)

Ordinarily the energy of an obsessive-compulsive personality is directed into personal rituals such as repetitive washing, item checking, or door locking. But for those whose neurosis is centered on tobacco smoke the energy can be channeled directly into political action. Writing hundreds of letters to papers and politicians, going to multiple City Council and Town Hall meetings hundreds of miles from one's home, and volunteering countless hours for Antismoking political candidates are all behaviors that can relieve the stress brought on by a compulsion to fight the smoky invader and contaminator of one's vital space.

Politicians usually figure one letter represents about a hundred constituents.

People don't realize it, but ten letters to a congressman or senator or governor will often get real results.

--David Siegel, What Is Worth Doing

Figure 1

The presence of such a volatile element within their ranks has furthered the cause of Antismoking Crusaders in another way as well. It is partly the fear of nasty confrontations with the pent-up emotional instabilities of such people that has prompted many smokers to accept unreasonable restrictions on their smoking behavior. Despite the Antismokers' claims about smokers' addiction to nicotine, most smokers will choose to abstain for a while rather than risk a public confrontation with an out of control fanatic.

In their literature and Internet messages it is common to see Crusading instigators urging such folks to speak up and confront smokers publicly at every available opportunity without regard for normal standards of politeness or propriety. The standardized and carefully prepared sound bite type attacks later noted in the chapter on Language are sometimes inflammatory enough to even invite violent confrontations, as witnessed by the shooting of a pregnant smoker in an outdoor parking lot by an angry Crusader in Louisiana (Michael Perlstein. *Times-Picayune* 10/05/02).

As noted earlier, the National Institute for Mental Health estimates that roughly two and a half percent of the population suffers from some degree of general obsessive-compulsive disorder. If just one tenth of them suffer it severely, and just one tenth of **those** sufferers have a phobic focus on tobacco smoke as the prime contaminant that they must devote their lives to avoiding, cleansing, and fighting, we are dealing with one 4,000[th] of roughly 220 million adult Americans. If those estimates are at all correct, that equates to a pool of over 50,000 psychologically troubled individuals who may now be devoting significant parts of their lives and manic energy to the Antismoking Crusade (http://www.nimh.nih.gov/anxiety/ocdfacts.cfm).

No wonder the voice of the Antismoker seems so loud to politicians and business owners. One obsessive compulsive, being encouraged in his or her neurosis rather than being treated for it, can have the political voice of a thousand more normal citizens. As in the above cited example of the nurse whipping up fears of "invisible particles," the courting of this mentally troubled segment of the population has become a prime objective of some activist Crusaders in recent years. Callous Antismokers who prey upon the fears of these people are at least as heartless as the tobacco companies that historically refused to address the health issues of smoking itself out of concern over reduced profits.

A particularly unfortunate subset of Antismoking neurotics are parents who exhibit symptoms of a condition known as Munchausen's Syndrome By Proxy. In this disorder parents seek attention, sympathy, and self-affirmation by exaggerating or outright fantasizing illnesses and conditions in their children. Parents suffering from its most extreme forms may even unconsciously injure their children in the effort to support their beliefs and claims that those children need special medical attention.

For an extremist Antismoker with a child it can be a small step from worrying that constant exposure to tobacco smoke will harm that child to imagining that a wisp of smoke from across a large room or even outdoors is going to send that child to the hospital. Another small step and the parent will begin dressing the child up in air masks whenever they go out in public just in case a smoker happens to appear nearby. As that child grows and reacts to the parent's concerns it's only natural that a full-blown case of psychosomatic hysterical reactions will develop that actually **does** send the child into panic attacks and hospitalizations when a smoker appears on the horizon. The psychological harm to such children can last throughout their lives.

While the majority of Antismokers are probably not phobic, paranoid, or obsessive-compulsive in the clinical sense, it would seem certain that such people are disproportionately represented among those who are most active. The visibility of the supposed threat combined with its constant repetition and exaggeration in the media form a recipe that's hard to resist for this type of personality, particularly when the compulsive behavior itself is actually applauded rather than being derided by those who become aware of it.

3) The Truly Affected

There does exist a small segment of the overall population that exhibits strong negative physical reactions to even small amounts of tobacco smoke. This group has two subcategories: those with true physical reactions, and those whose physical reactions flow largely or entirely from psychosomatic bases.

On a practical level it is difficult to distinguish between these two since true psychosomatic reactions can produce physical effects that are almost impossible to separate from purely physiological reactions. Doctors have falsely told many people that they are allergic to tobacco smoke on the basis of skin patch or skin scratch tests that show them to be allergic to unburned tobacco. However most elements present in a tobacco leaf undergo enormous change in the process of being burned. Even the US Surgeon General has stated: "*Evidence that tobacco smoke is antigenic in man, however, is meager and contro-versial...*" (*1979 Report of the Surgeon General.* p. 10-9).

To the best of my knowledge that evidence has not grown significantly since that report. It should be noted nevertheless that tobacco smoke can act as an irritant that can trigger non-allergic respiratory reactions, particularly in individuals psychogenically predisposed toward such reactions. It should also be noted that such predisposition can be created entirely by an atmosphere of fear fostered by propaganda.

An allergy to tobacco is NOT an allergy to tobacco smoke. Double blind tests in which patients were put into situations where they believed they were being exposed to tobacco smoke, while in reality only being exposed to warm air and hypoallergenic aromatics, could help differentiate between the two types of reaction, but there has been no push by Antismoking organizations to grant funding for such studies. If such research were carried out honestly it might very well show that there are few, if any, truly allergic individuals... obviously not a desired result for those devoted to the Antismoking Crusade and thus unlikely to be the basis of a study design that would receive a research grant from any credible (i.e. non-tobacco company) source. The Report cited above also decried the lack of properly controlled double-blind protocols in these sorts of studies and the situation has not improved much since then (*1979 SGR* p. 10-7).

However, it is of extreme importance to note that people experiencing such reactions will often have no way themselves of knowing what the true cause is and will often strongly resent any implication that the reaction is based within the psyche rather than the body. When people feel they can't breathe, they don't care whether it's psychological or physical... they simply want to be able to breathe! When Antismokers take advantage of those in such distressed condition to make them believe that their suffering is caused by the acts of another who might be a friend or family member, it's not only heartless, but outright cruel to all involved.

Unfortunately, the Antismoking Crusaders have greatly swelled the number of people who experience psychosomatic physical reactions to even trace amounts of smoke. As discussed above in the chapter on Neurotics such reactions and the fears they flow from can be quite intense and can serve strongly as a motivator for political action.

There has been little if any attempt to actually investigate the extent to which such psychosomatic reactions have increased in the last decade or two. The tobacco companies themselves have backed away from any but the most fundamentally defensive research out of fear of negative publicity and lawsuits and, as noted above, no researcher proposing such a study would be likely to get a grant from the funds politically dedicated to Antismoking research and activities. Such research would simply not pass the "Glantz Test" outlined later in Figure 2.

It seems safe to say that those who are Truly Affected have grown from perhaps a mere fraction of a percent in years past to perhaps as much as two or three percent of the adult population today.   This growth may all be psychosomatically based, but as noted above, the physical effects as manifested are no less real or scary.   It would require a great amount of media attention to the true nature of the "risks" of secondary smoke and a large scale relaxing of general concerns about it before this number would be likely to go down. Until then these people will not be relieved of the constant burden that has been placed upon them by the Antismoking Crusade, a burden that has grown to haunt many of their lives.

The Truly Affected are both the most fortunate bene-ficiaries and the most unfortunate victims of the Antismoking Crusade.   Those with actual antigenic physically based reactions (an unknown but probably very small fraction of the whole) would normally be thought to have benefited greatly from the enormous expansion of smoke-free venues offered over the last 15 years.

Ironically it could be argued that they have not benefited as much as it first appears. The Truly Affected used to have at least some venues that were filled almost exclusively with nonsmokers and had no smokers clustering in the bathroom or outside the doorway. Nowadays those venues, being no different than others that have simply been forced to enact bans, attract a sizeable percentage of smokers and possible encounters with smoke! With the advent of universal bans came the loss of true smoke-free meccas for those most strongly concerned.

Meanwhile, those with psychosomatic reactions have had their lives strongly impacted in a negative sense by the propaganda that has engendered or magnified these reactions. The recruitment of this cadre of Crusaders by extremists playing upon their fears has probably had far more of a real cost to human well being than any benefits it may have conferred.

And, as we noted in the chapter on Neurotics, even more tragic is the effect such parents can eventually have upon their children.   Imagine the earliest memories of a child as it is snatched frantically from the arms of a smoking relative while being warned of the "deadly poisons" in the air. Such children may even be armed with inhalers and face masks from an early age and conditioned to use them instantly upon the sight of anyone smoking.

Lives that might have been happy and normal will instead be filled by battles with and escapes from people who could have been friends. Overnight trips or even afternoon visits to homes of friends where parents have not agreed to similar stringent smoke-free requirements become off-limits and the child's social life and development are even further damaged. Such situations may be uncommon, but are nonetheless real.

Related to those who are Truly Affected, but usually much milder in their reaction and much less likely to translate their feelings into a desire for political control, is a much larger group that simply objects to the smell of burning tobacco. While a great many nonsmokers object strongly to the smell of a cheap cigar, far fewer object to a nice pipe tobacco.

Somewhere in between these two extremes lies the reaction to cigarette smoke, and even within that category there are those who only mind the smell of "light cigarettes" that have been fortified with flavor enhancers. Some who strongly object to commercial filter cigarettes will actually claim to like the smell of hand rolled pure tobacco cigarettes.

I am hesitant to include this category of what might be called "smellers" into the more general realm of Antismokers since so few of them take their objections beyond the home front, and many are quite tolerant of some degree of olfactory annoyance as long as it's not too extreme. In most situations this group will applaud effective ventilation as a solution to a smoky environment as readily or even more readily than they would applaud an outright ban on smoking: their interest is personal comfort, not behavioral control or societal change.

The Truly Affected get their political power from two bases: First, when testifying at public hearings or in television interviews, they fall into the general category of the handicapped. Just as politicians found the power of the handicapped daunting when it came to issues of care and access despite whatever costs were involved, so too do they find themselves helpless in the face of demands to provide "clean air" for those who claim to be Truly Affected by wisps of tobacco smoke. The power of language in this case is immense: who can deny the desirability of "air that is safe to breathe"? As pointed out in more detail later, Anti-smokers squeeze even more power from these words by cobbling together the statement that "ALL workers deserve safe, clean, smokefree air!" as though absolutely "smoke-free air" was a strict and necessary precondition for air that is safe and clean: goodbye to scented candles, morning toast and a roaring fireplace!

While such requirements certainly do not require air that is 100% free of all scents, dusts, or smoke, true Crusaders never make such a distinction. OSHA and the EPA have set safety standards for virtually all the potentially dangerous elements of tobacco smoke that come into question, and these official safety standards are hardly ever approached even in the smokiest bar environment (See Appendix B for more detailed figures on this.)

However, the power of simply demanding "clean air" for "those who need to breathe" translates directly into political action. No politician can allow him or her self to be seen as being against the handicapped: those with disabilities are all too powerful as a voting bloc, their grievances are often all too real, and their sympathetic appeal to the general voting population is all too great to be ignored.

Secondly, on a more personal level, no compassionate human being is likely to forget the rare instances they encounter where someone actually **does** seem to experience a strong negative physical reaction to tobacco smoke. Although most such instances may not be based on true physiology they are still scary for all involved.

Younger smokers (those under 40 or so) in particular will almost always feel profound guilt if they think they have triggered such a reaction. Older smokers however will often tend to remember the virtual nonexistence of such reactions before the mid-1970s, and are more likely to show annoyance at symptoms they feel are not real; particularly if the level of exposure is extremely low or could have been easily avoided. This difference of reaction is not based upon levels of humanity or degree of caring, but rather simply upon the tendency of many older smokers not to believe in something which didn't seem to exist before it was so highly publicized and promoted.

4) The Bereaved

When a loved one dies, we all ask "Why?" Such a question is a normal and almost unavoidable part of the bereavement process and people frequently find some comfort in having an answer other than the vagaries of fate. Being able to say "Uncle Bob died from the dust he inhaled in the factory." or "Aunt Thelma got cancer from smoking." somehow reassures many of those who are left that they themselves are not soon slated for the Grim Reaper since they don't share that particular characteristic with the deceased. There are also some who draw comfort from feeling that a death was due to a "punishment" for some undesirable aspect of the dead one's life, or who simply find that their worldview is more complete when every misfortune can be ascribed to a cause.

   Since smoking is almost universally accepted as a prime cause of lung cancer, it seems natural to assume that when a smoker suffers such a death it had to be due to their smoking. Of course, scientifically, no such assumption can be made with certitude: it's always quite possible (though perhaps unlikely) that the person would have contracted cancer at that time even if they had never smoked. Even Michael Thun, head of epidemiological research at the ACS has admitted that:

> There's no definitive way of establishing the cause of a cancer in an individual. Are there people that develop lung cancer without exposures [to any of the known cancer-causing agents]? No one knows. (*Washington Post*. 02/16/03).

Still, it's safe to say that, at least in America, almost every living relative of any smoker who has died of lung cancer will point to smoking as the absolutely indisputable cause. While deaths from heart disease or other cancers are far less heavily correlated with smoking, many, prompted by the media campaigns of the Antismoking Crusade, will ascribe those deaths with certainty to smoking as well.

When a loved one is killed, the desire for revenge is a common emotion. Revenge against Big Tobacco has taken on the holy mantle of serving society by helping to destroy "those who have killed and continue to kill." The fact that Evil Big Tobacco hasn't behaved much differently from Evil Big Auto (which spent years covering up the dangers of such things as leaded gasoline and the lack of seat belts and air bags) when it comes to concerns about consumer good versus company profit is lost amid the emotional upwelling at the loss of a loved one.

Big Auto has taken its lumps over issues like the Corvair or the more recent spate of tire tread and SUV related accidents, but it's never been called to task for decades of promoting its product as safe while those products clearly continue to kill and maim tens of thousands of children (while they **are** still children!) every year. The ultimate cost to our society of our dependence on Big Auto has never been properly tabulated and published; and of course no serious effort has ever been made to recoup those costs through taxation aimed at drivers. While automobiles may serve a clearer purpose and impart a greater benefit to our society than cigarettes, the reality of their cost cannot be denied.

For some odd reason no other "evil" corporate entity has ever garnered quite the same degree of public enmity as tobacco... perhaps partly because no other entity has ever had as well funded an enemy as the Antismoking Crusade. It's important to remember that Antismokers now have actual access to not just millions, but many hundreds of millions of dollars for their "public education" and vilification efforts. Added to that are the many years of seemingly poor policy choices recommended to Big Tobacco by its expensive cadre of corporate lawyers.

Aside from occasional one-page ads in major newspapers and even more occasional lawsuits, the tobacco companies in recent years have largely refrained from aggressively defending themselves against their multitude of attackers. "Joe Chemo" posters were quite widespread in our educational systems for a number of years... can you imagine the lawsuits that would have sprung from McDonald's if a similar promotion with public funds was given to "BigMacHeartAttack" posters?

Tobacco company lawyers have never understood or appreciated the strength of the underlying psychological drives of so many of their opponents. Ignoring and placating the enemy seemed fiscally safer in the long run than opposition that could form the basis for future lawsuits. If those lawyers had truly understood the nature of what they were up against, they would have realized that no concession would ever be enough to quiet the cry for the total destruction of their clients.

While most of The Bereaved tend to focus their anger and energy against the faceless Big Tobacco corporations, many of them feel frustration at attacking such an immaterial opponent. A significant portion of these activists move over into the wider arena of interpersonal Antismoking activity when they perceive that such activity is an effective way to hit back at those corporations. Indeed, one of the commonly heard justifications made by those pushing for bans is that tobacco industry memos express concern about such actions.

Again, just as with the Truly Affected, the testimonies of The Bereaved are heard frequently at hearings on smoking bans despite the fact that secondary smoke itself is seldom seen as the cause of the bereavement. Sadly enough though, there have even been examples of widows who firmly believe that secondary smoke at business meetings killed their husbands in spite of the fact that the deceased husbands had been heavy smokers them-selves for decades (e.g., see CBS Early Edition 07/27/01).

The Bereaved are a particularly powerful group in repre-senting the Antismoking Lobby at public hearings because to argue with them in any way is instantly seen by most as cruel and callous behavior, similar to attacking someone in a wheelchair or kicking a small helpless animal. Rational arguments are given little weight when posed against the grief of a bereaved friend or family member.

5) The Ex-Smokers And The Victims

While Antismokers from Ireland to New Zealand have proclaimed tobacco to be "more addictive than heroin" (Senator Glynn, Irish sub-committee on Health and Smoking, 5/30/01; The Cancer Society of New Zealand) the fact remains that there are upwards of 50 million Americans who have given up smoking without hospitalization, convulsions, or forced incarceration. Millions more have smoked for a little while or experimented with social smoking and then went on to give it up.

In addition, there are tens of millions of smokers out there who either smoke very little, deliberately choose light cigarettes (some smokers compensate for that with their smoking style, some do not), or smoke without inhaling. The image of an addict in withdrawal, writhing in agony upon the floor, has been played upon by the Crusaders (see the section on addiction in the chapter on Language), but the reality that such symptoms simply don't generally exist in smokers is indisputable.

Although the addictiveness of tobacco has been exaggerated it is still true that many smokers have difficulty in quitting the habit. This should not be surprising: smoking is something one engages in repetitively over a long period, feeling a small "reward" with each puff as the familiar pattern of smoking, the perceived enjoyment of the taste and feeling as one inhales and exhales the smoke, and nicotine's pharmacological effect all work together to make it an experience one wishes to repeat.

The purely physical withdrawal effects of nicotine, similar in many ways to those of caffeine, also prompt one to seek to smoke as one's body senses the level of nicotine decreasing in the bloodstream. The instant effectiveness of smoking as a means of delivering the enjoyable sensation to the partaker magnifies this effect. This frequent "self rewarding medication" has been a potent (though largely undocumented) self-treatment used by many to alleviate mild depression. According to psychiatry professor Dr. Gregory Ordway, "*Chronic smoking produces 'antidepressant-like' effects on the human brain.*" Of course the good Doctor quickly followed this statement with the standard caution that "*this is no reason to take up a smoking career*" (*Archives of General Psychiatry* 2001; 58:821-827).

It may be a coincidence that, as smoking rates have gone down, the rates of dependency upon anti-depressants such as Prozac and the profits to their companies have gone up: those of a more cynical bent may feel differently. Recent research by FORCES indicates that Big Pharmaceutical interests may well have replaced Big Tobacco interests in financial political lobbying power ("Big Pharma's Power." www.forces.org).

Big Pharma's advertising and marketing punch has certainly outstripped that of Big Tobacco. As will be detailed below in the chapter on the Media, Big Pharma today has almost double the advertising/marketing budget of Big Tobacco. And in terms of politics: at just one event, a June 2002 GOP fundraiser at Washington's Mayflower Hotel, the major pharmaceutical companies contributed well over three quarters of a million dollars to the politicians (*Washington Post* 06/19/02).

If a person truly desires to quit smoking of his or her own free will, the experience of quitting does not seem as traumatic as when such a decision is being forced upon them by external persons or circumstance. We've all heard tales of the fellow who just decided to quit cold turkey and claims, "It was nothing... I just stopped and never went back." We've also heard of those who have gone through multiple attempts and failures after becoming convinced that they had to stop for reasons of health or under pressures from family, friends, or doctors.

The quitting motivation is only part of the story. Each individual has different physiological and psychological tendencies with regard to various potentially addictive substances or behaviors. Quite apart from other considerations, some people will, just by their own nature, have a harder time quitting smoking than some other people will. This should be no more surprising than the realization that some people are more likely to become alcoholics or compulsive gamblers than others.

With activities like gambling, computer gaming, or even excessive amounts of praying, such behavior falls almost purely into the psychological realm of compulsions. I say "almost" because indulging in these behaviors may at times actually trigger the release of substances in the blood that can act as natural physiological reinforcers.

A CNN report in the fall of 2001 examined the way that some people are now seeking treatment for a disorder involving prayer compulsion: they felt compelled to spend so much of their time performing multiple prayer rituals before and after every normal daily activity that their lives were in ruins! They were, according to the psychiatrist being interviewed, "addicted" to prayer, although the "addiction" may in fact have been more of an obsessive-compulsion.

When it comes to nicotine, caffeine, alcohol, cocaine, or any other ingested substance the physical component and motivation becomes clearer and stronger. Smoking, having strong components in both the physical and the psychological areas, can be a particularly difficult activity to give up in the long-term, especially in cases where the prime motivation for quitting comes mainly from external sources and pressures that are fundamentally resented by the smoker.

While there are no clear cut standards for studies that would seek to quantify the number of ex-smokers who had a truly difficult time giving up the habit, it is likely that the number who have experienced such is significant. Depending upon what one defines as "a truly difficult time" the number could be anywhere from the thousands up into the tens of millions. The reasons behind the current stress on smoking as an "addiction" are explored more fully in the later chapter on Language.

For a portion of these ex-smokers a vital part of their success in quitting has lain in demonizing tobacco and their entire experience with it. Unable to simply give it up and get on with their lives, they have had to make the quitting experience an ongoing element of daily consciousness and have become active supporters, proselytizers and activists within the Antismoking Crusade.

Unlike those rare drivers who kill another or suffer a severe injury and decide never to drive again, many of these ex-smokers feel a need to justify their decision to quit by visualizing tobacco as so evil that it's necessary to make everyone else quit as well. To pacify the devil inside that urges them to take up smoking again, they put their energies, often quite enormous, into eliminating the sight and smell of smoke from the entire world around them. Every time they can feel that they've convinced or forced another person to quit, it justifies the decision that they themselves felt they were forced to make and convinces them of its rightness.

A special subset of Ex-Smokers is that which I call The Victims: individuals who have quit smoking only after suffering some specific medical event that they ascribe, rightly or wrongly, to smoking. Their anger at Big Tobacco springs from a natural unwillingness to blame their own behavior for their misfortunes, and their dedication to any and all activities designed to reduce smoking among others often flows from a sincere desire to help them avoid similar fates.

Some of The Victims may not be so altruistic in their motivations: there are certainly at least a few out there who will be acting out of resentment that **they** were singled out for "punishment" and who further resent no longer being able to enjoy smoking while others continue in that pleasure. This particular subset is probably quite small, but in fairness it must be mentioned: it may in fact be larger than one might at first think.

One often hears smokers say that "ex-smokers are the worst" in terms of their Antismoking fervor. While that's only true for a small minority, for that minority it is sometimes true to the extreme. Thus it's a common sight and ploy at City Council hearings on smoking bans for Antismoking organizations to urge those with laryngectomies to bring their electronic microphones and testify repeatedly, in voices sadly and eerily reminiscent of Darth Vader, how "tobacco smoke did this to me." In a very real sense activist Crusaders have preyed upon these already unfortunate people, using them as tools for their own ends (NY City Council Health Committee Hearing 02/23/00).

While extraordinarily effective as a propaganda technique because of the compassion one has to feel for them, it is usually overlooked that many of these victims were quite heavy smokers themselves for many years. If smoking had anything to do with their present condition it was likely the result of their own 2 or 3 pack a day habit... not the curls of smoke from those around them. Still, the political power of The Victims, even when misapplied to the discussion of concerns about secondary smoke, is often very effective in advancing the goals of the Antismoking Crusade as a whole.

6) The Controllers

While usually not as noticeable in their efforts as other subgroups of Antismokers, the Controllers are just as persistent. We've all known people who, often due to background insecurities of their own, feel a need to exert more than the normal level of control over the people near them and the world around them. This becomes most self evident in relationships with lovers or spouses and has formed the basis for many unhappy marriages.

Those Controllers who are nonsmokers and are either bothered by smoke or have been convinced by the media that secondary smoke is a real health threat are likely to make the lives of smokers around them miserable. Controllers who fit in neither category may simply notice this golden opportunity for extra control that has been presented to them by circumstance and use it to their advantage anyway!

If it's within the context of a love relationship, the Controller may confiscate cigarettes or sniff their partner's breath or fingers for telltale signs of smoking. If the partner is found "guilty" the Controller may then demand submission in the form of promises to quit smoking, promises to "undergo treatment," or willingness to submit to some form of punishment or deprivation for their misdeed.   If this cycle repeats itself endlessly, it's all the more to the Controller's satisfaction since it gives them continual power to play the superior role in relation to the weak and addicted partner. The London man mentioned earlier who repeatedly stabbed his wife because she wouldn't quit for him may not be the norm, but scenarios with lower levels of physical and psychological violence are probably played out far too commonly behind closed doors.

In domestic relationships Controllers will usually demand that a smoker smoke outdoors, regardless of whether they are in fact bothered by the smoke, and will take great satisfaction when the smoker actually goes outside in inclement weather to smoke. In addition, the Controller is likely to wait for the smoker to head for a smoke break and then take that opportunity to make some other demand that will interfere with or interrupt such a break. The acquiescence of the smoker once again satisfies the needs of the Controlling personality. If a child is present in the family and The Controller is able to point to "The Threat To Our Child" his or her power is clearly multiplied many fold... particularly if the power of family court can be brought to bear.

For the most part, such Controllers play the part of being an Antismoker on a personal and direct level, but some of them gravitate toward political or activist groups that will give them an even greater sense of power. And, since the issue is smoking, they can rest assured that no matter how extreme their urge to control others becomes, it will be seen as a virtue as they work to advance the cause of good health and clean air.

The final satisfaction for those Controllers who take their efforts beyond interactions in the personal sphere lies in the creation of laws and official regulations embodying the Controller's desires. Once their "will" has been made "the law" they can then go out into public with impunity and demand that others bend to their dictums or suffer repercussions such as fines or even possible jail time. Instead of being viewed as bullies, they will now be viewed as steadfast defenders of children and as champions of the right to breathe.

In some sections of California, Crusading groups seem to have actively sought after Controllers to act as "smoking cops," traveling undercover to bars and reporting those places where an employee or customer tries to sneak a smoke! As noted in more detail later, one cop has actually been quoted as saying: "*What we want to do is create paranoia.*" In the Waterloo Region of Canada, a law has been proposed that would allow for roving bands of Antismokers to have bar owners sent to jail if they refused to physically throw a smoking customer out in the snow (Jeff Outhit. *The Waterloo Record* 06/18/02).

In New York, things almost went even further as government funds were set to go out to bands of Antismokers who would go up to smokers in public places and confront them with "information" and "persuasion" to encourage them to quit their evil habit. At the last minute Governor Pataki rightly decided that such state-funded goon squad tactics should not be countenanced in today's America. ("Gov Tells Cig Activists To Butt Out," Fredric U. Dicker, *NY Post*, 05/19/01)

This hasn't stopped the new fascists from putting children in harm's way though: on June 1st 2003, Syracuse Post reporter Jennifer Jacobs revealed that government-funded youth gangs in something called the Reality Check movement were staging raids where the kids go into smoky bars and blatantly steal ashtrays, relying on their youth for protection. Even so, one child reported a case where she thought a particular bar staffer was "*going to pull a shotgun on us – for real!*" Historians familiar with the use of youth "bully gangs" will shudder at the parallels (*New York Post* 05/19/01; *Syracuse Post* 06/01/03).

Portraying themselves as battling Big Tobacco rather than individual smokers fortifies the Controllers' self-image of doing good for those they control and encourages them to expand their efforts. This reinforcement of a psychologically unhealthy behavior is similar to that experienced by the Obsessive Compulsives. While it can be difficult to spot Controllers testifying at such things as City Council hearings, it's almost certainly true that some of them must make that wider effort to buttress their need for power and control over others.

7) The Idealists

*A strong conviction that something must be done
is the parent of many bad measures.*

-- Daniel Webster

This group is most heavily represented among those in the medical profession and those who work or volunteer with non-profit groups that have extensive contact with the victims of diseases blamed on smoking. Having to face such suffering on a daily basis makes it inevitable that such people will have a tendency to demonize what they see as its cause.

To start off the discussion of this group, it should be made clear that there is indeed a subgroup of truly faultless Idealists. These are the people who, believing that smoking causes disease and suffering, seek in quiet and constructive ways to help people who want to quit smoking or seek through educa-tion and information to persuade people not to take it up in the first place. Many of this subgroup would generally not be considered Antismokers at all if one were to take the initial guidelines defining Antismokers as a basis.

However, many of The Idealists go beyond such simple goals and tactics. The desire to eliminate the perceived suffering due to smoking is obviously good, and if the means of such elimination involves activities that might be less than good, that can be seen as an acceptable price to pay. For those Idealists involved in the Antismoking Crusade, the awareness that the case against secondary smoke is certainly by no means as airtight or as scientifically compelling as that against smoking itself is subordinated to the awareness of the political power of smoking bans and the emotional reminders that *"Young lungs are tender and pink"* (Mike Thomas. *Orlando Sentinel* 05/22/01).

Idealists are quick to put the label of "Big Tobacco Front or Ally" upon **any** group or individual who opposes the notion of the deadliness of secondary smoke or any who question the funding or motivation of Crusading groups. Conjoining the term "Front" with the term "Ally" in the same phrase allows Antismokers to confuse the popular sense of groups paid by and secretly affiliated with Big Tobacco with true grassroots groups made up of citizens opposing the Antismoking agenda on their own. In the battle over the 2003 New York ban on smoking in bars Antismokers referred to the smokers, waitresses, and bartenders who opposed the ban as "disgruntled tobacco interests," again making it seem as though the opposition con-sisted of nothing but bought-and-paid-for industry mouthpieces (http://www.nietrokers.nl/e2/n02073.html).

Idealists will accept almost any study or survey that supports the Crusade without applying to it the normal level of scientific criticism or questioning. Secure in the belief that they are ultimately right in their cause, they are willing to be sloppy about the means used to achieve their noble end.

They don't even have to feel too guilty about it: some-times the path to greater research grants lies simply in choosing the proper questions to pursue and ignoring those that might give "undesirable" answers. The selective design of studies and data gathering or the deliberate structuring of a study to ensure a properly acceptable result are easily justified by those who see science more as a means to justify political movements than as a search for actual truth (See Figure 2).

Idealists can be difficult to argue against because most smokers would agree with their view that smoking can cause illness and death and are afraid that fighting against bans or questioning other aspects of the Antismoking Crusade is tantamount to promoting future illnesses and deaths. The fact that opposing extremist Antismokers may make sense in terms of the personal freedoms, choices, and overall life enjoyment of individuals can form the basis for some opposition; but a level of guilt at the side effects of such efforts will often remain and will surface when confronted with true Idealism.

The power of The Idealists generally comes not from their numbers, but from their credentials. As noted above, many Idealists are medical doctors, and as such their testimony is given considerable weight by politicians trying to reach decisions on health issues. Since smoking bans are almost always presented to politicians as a vital and urgent health issue by those advocating them, doctors have a lot of power at such public hearings even when their actual testimony focuses largely on matters such as comfort or even just purely on the harms of primary smoking itself.

"...and that's the question that I have applied to my research relating to tobacco. If this comes out the way I think, will it make a difference? And if the answer is yes, then we do it, and if the answer is I don't know then we don't bother. Okay? And that's the criteria."

- Stanton Glantz. "Revolt Against Tobacco." 10/2/92
Transcript p. 14

Figure 2

Even though few of these doctors have much training in the field of epidemiology, their testimony on what is largely an epidemiological issue is listened to by politicians because of their possession of a medical degree. In reality, the training and expertise a gastroenterologist brings to a discussion of the validity of something like the EPA report would actually be far less valuable than that of a competent statistician. As Crusaders know all too well, the label of "Dr." when it refers to an actual medical degree is far more idolized by politicians and the general public than the label of "Dr." when it refers merely to a Ph.D. in statistics.

A particularly egregious misuse of this English language quirk is seen in the case of Stanton Glantz, a man with a Ph.D. in mechanical engineering. Despite having no M.D., Stanton Glantz has been named a "professor of medicine" at the University of California. He has become a favorite son of the University as he brings in many millions of dollars in grants ($15 million recently just from the MSA-funded American Legacy Foundation!), and produces a significant quantity of research with his students that always seems specifically chosen and tailored to produce "favorable" Antismoking results (see Figure 2). Stanton Glantz seems to always be referred to as "Dr." Glantz without further qualification whenever he is in the media spotlight discussing the health effects of smoking or secondary smoke (Schevitz T. "UCSF to establish...." *San Francisco Chronicle* 01/31/01).

The built-in ambiguity of English in this regard allows for most of his nationwide audiences to believe he is an M.D. and that his pronouncements are based upon years of medical school and hospital training despite the fact that they are not. While ABC News goes to great lengths to expose this sort of duplicity when looking at Doctors of Chiropractic or Dental Medicine who promote such things as herbal breast enhancement treatments, they seem strangely silent about the issue when quoting "Dr." Glantz's opinion of the latest research on the health effects of secondary smoke (*20/20*. ABC News 06/21/02).

Many of The Idealists are medical doctors and theoretically adherents to the Hippocratic Oath. Given the potential repercussions of some of the propaganda they espouse on behalf of the Antismoking Crusade some of them should step back and evaluate whether they can truly be certain that they *"first do no harm."*

8) The Moralists

When the Puritan righteous among us get their hands on the levers of the state, the property and liberty of all of us are likely soon to be at risk.
                    -- Robert H. Nelson (*Reason* 06/96)

Nowadays, The Moralists are a small segment of the Crusade. Back in the days of Lucy Page Gaston's Anti-Cigarette League (ca. 1899 - 1920) when the sale of cigarettes was totally outlawed in over a dozen states because of their "corrupting influence" on women and children, this group was in fashion; but from the 1920s until quite recently such moral appeals packed little punch in America (Gene Borio. *Tobacco Timeline*. www.tobacco.org).

In recent years however, the cries about the corruption and addiction of innocent children have shown a lot of power, particularly since President Clinton's focus groups showed that concentration on this issue would boost his electoral opportunities despite his own special fondness for playing with his cigars. In addition, the imagery of cigarette smoking as an activity appropriate only to the depraved and disreputable still plucks some emotional chords among those who have had deeply religious or morally conservative upbringing.

A related but less sharply defined group within the Crusade is comprised of people who are sometimes called the Aunties (an unsubtle play on "Antis") or the Nannies. Lucy Page Gaston was the archetypal Auntie: a prissy and unhappy person who looks out at the world, sees others having a good time, and jumps in to interfere -- since obviously they **must** be doing something wrong if they're enjoying themselves!

Aunties and Nannies are terms frequently used by Free-Choice advocates to describe activists in any of the Antismoker subcategories. Such people are often active as well in seeking bans and restrictions on all manner of additional activities, substances, and products that others find enjoyable in their lives.

One particular Nanny currently quite active in Philadelphia politics (Councilman Michael Nutter) has seemingly tried to hype his political career not only by seeking to ban smoking in bar-restaurants and on many city sidewalks, but also by banning skateboarding on public property, including the world renowned haven of skateboarding, Love Park itself! The old adage about the Puritan applies here: An Auntie is someone who cannot sleep if they have the sneaking suspicion that someone, somewhere, is having fun.

The last great upsurge of The Moralists came not in America, but in Germany during the late 1930s. Hitler was unique and somewhat notorious among world leaders of the time for his Antismoking views and, as part of the Reich's overall efforts to assert control over the minutia of German life, he instituted many of the same sorts of bans and limitations on smoking that we have seen taking root in America today.

Laws forbidding cigarette sales to pregnant women and teens, smoking bans on public transit, in public buildings and the Reichstag, and even rallies of German Youth Groups dressed up in special outfits and pledging themselves to a nonsmoking lifestyle were all part of the plan to preserve the purity of Aryan blood and separate the undesirables. Posters adorned the walls of pre-war streets in Berlin proclaiming that "The German Woman Does Not Smoke!" while ads presaging those of Truth.com showed cigarettes raining out of the sky. Special licenses were required to sell tobacco products, taxes on them were raised, and unregulated vending machines were prohibited.

Although it was the scientists of the Reich who were the first to develop persuasive statistical evidence linking smoking to lung cancer, politicians of the Reich must also be credited (or blamed) as they were the first to develop sound social engineering techniques for effectively combating smoking. The Germans were in fact the first to invent the term "Passive Smoking." A detailed account of the entire German Antismoking campaign complete with references for all the above information can be found in Dr. Robert Proctor's excellent book *The Nazi War on Cancer* (Princeton University Press. 1999).

The book outlines parallels to today's American Antismoking movement that are both amazing and disturbing. It should be noted that Dr. Proctor is by no means a tobacco company spokesperson: in December 2000 he sought to redeem his image on the ASH website with a proclamation that tobacco would kill a billion people in the 21st century! (http://nosmoking.org/dec01/12-03-01-2.html)

Although rather superficial, one of the more emotionally disturbing parallels between current Crusaders and those of the Reich that I have myself encountered came in the form of officially presented testimony at the February 2000 New York City Council hearings on a bar/restaurant ban. James Repace, the "secondhand smoke consultant" mentioned earlier, used a smoking devil figure to illustrate smokers in his printed testimony. Compare that cartoon to the smoking devil mascot in Figure 3 taken from the Nazi Antismoking newspaper *Reine Luft* (Pure Air) and the anti-Semitic caricatures used as part of the 1930s' German Antismoking propaganda campaign (*Reine Luft.* 23 (1941): 145) <From Robert Proctor op.cit. p.188>.

Propagation of the idea that the Jews and Gypsies were corrupting the innocence of Aryan women and children with vices such as drinking and smoking was a powerful tool for the Reich. Repace's devilish caricature of smokers combined with his constant use of pejorative language in describing them and their habit would have found a warm and comfortable berth in the smoke-free Reichstag.

While my references to the Nazi campaign against smoking may appear as something of a "cheap shot" at Antismokers, the information is factual and the justification for the reference is real and will be explored further in the chapter examining the role of hate in the Antismoking Crusade. In one way today's Antismoking Crusade actually trumps the German model: The Germans never suggested that German parents must stop smoking in their own homes or used smoking as an excuse to decide child custody disputes, an experience becoming increasingly common in today's America. Further reading on this can be found at http://davehitt.com /nov02/nicotine.html.

1999 Repace Smoking Devil   **1941 Nazi Smoking Devil**

Smokers in 1940s German Antismoking Poster

Figure 3

Perhaps the most commonly encountered Moralists today come from the ranks of The Ex-Smokers, seemingly "born-again" and anxious to expunge the guilt of their smoky days.   In addition many Moralists blend into the ranks of the Controllers, seeking to impose their beliefs upon others and condemn (punish) nonconformists who refuse to reform.   Idealists and Neurotics are also likely to share traits with the Moralists. Indeed Moralists can be found in almost any of the Antismoker categories with the possible exception of the last... The Greedy.

9) The Greedy

The truly Greedy are few in number but have become great in power in recent years. The Bereaved and The Victims have been besieged by lawyers urging them to seek a revenge measured in dollars and cents against the makers of the products they blame. Lawyers have spent huge amounts of time and effort fighting to ensure that their own payments are not limited to a paltry few thousand dollars per hour in class actions against Big Tobacco. Congressional attempts to limit such lawyer's fees have been soundly rejected by the lawyers who make up so much of our government. Judges seeking such limitations are fought tooth and nail. ("N.Y. Judge Calls Tobacco Pact Legal Bills 'Offensive'." *Bloomberg News Service* 07/25/01).

A judgment found against Big Tobacco is the crown jewel of legal prizes: a single case can yield a lawyer literally millions of dollars for a few months of questionably honest work.   In Florida, an anti-tobacco judge denounced these fees, noting that *"(If) the attorneys worked 24 hours per day, 7 days per week, for 42 months, they would earn ...$7,716 per hour for each of the 12 lawyers."* If we assumed a more reasonable 8 hour a day, 5 day a week schedule, each lawyer working on the case would take home well over $25,000 per hour... not bad! (Robert A. Levy. "The Great Tobacco Robbery." *The Legal Times* 02/01/99)

With such incentives available, it's not surprising that many of the best and brightest legal minds in America have decided to devote their lives to fighting tobacco and its smoky product. ASH.org has an entire section devoted to Antismoking Lawyers for folks who wish to jump on the money train. Indeed, some Crusading lawyers have become so brazen in their grabs for money that they set up a conference specifically titled "How To Win A Giant Tobacco Settlement," though they later backed down and changed the word "Giant" to "Just."

Of course those really paying for such settlements are never the companies themselves, nor even their profiting share-holders. The bills are paid by smokers, and smokers alone. The money will flow from smokers making $30k/year straight into the pockets of lawyers making well over $300k/year with just a slight tip of the campaign funding hat to the wonderful politicians who make it all possible (www.tobacco.neu.edu/ conference/index.html;Lockjaw002@worldnet.att.net).

Naturally the lawyers didn't simply go it alone in their battles with the tobacco companies. In a truly amazing admission in a country where all are supposedly treated equally under the law, during the course of a battle over fees for one of the lawyers (a Mr. Angelos), Maryland Senate President Miller noted that **the legislature changed state law specifically for the tobacco case to make the lawyer's job easier!** According to Senator Miller:

> *Mr. Angelos, in my opinion, agreed to accept 12.5 percent if and only if we agreed to change tort law, which was no small feat. We changed centuries of precedent to ensure a win in this case.* (Daniel LeDue. "Angelos, Maryland Feud..." *Washington Post* 10/15/99).

This story might have been more appropriately titled: "Equal Justice Meets Greed... Greed Wins."

The Greedy are not just limited to the ranks of the legal profession. Researchers and nonprofit groups have also scrambled to get slices of the Antismoking money pie as it has swollen in a wild spurt of growth far beyond anything else in the world's economy. These funds have grown from mere millions of dollars a year to many **hundreds** of millions a year in the span of a single decade.

Amazingly enough, as the new millennium dawned, the annual funding to prepare for bioterrorism in the U.S. was actually dwarfed by the funds spent to fight the evil of smoking. The DHHS regular budget for bioterrorism was under 7 million dollars a year: less than one percent of the state money granted to Antismoking Crusaders! (www.fda.gov/oc/bioterrorism/budget.html)

The sight of the various Antismoking activist groups jostling to get in on this largess is almost comical at times. After all the lawsuits against tobacco companies, we are now seeing a new wave of suits: Antismokers suing each other in claims that they have not gotten their fair share of the kill! One notable example of such is the case of Richard Daynard, the founder of The Tobacco Liability Project. He has now sued anti-tobacco attorneys Motley and Scruggs, claiming that he is owed 5% of the $3,000,000,000 they received (*LA Times* 05/20/01).

That translates into one hundred and fifty million dollars for this particular public spirited Antismoker who has likely often, and without blinking an eye, joined his fellows in portraying hard working minimum-wage waitresses testifying against him at public hearings as "tobacco company shills" or "mouthpieces of the industry." In fairness though, he is not alone: Massachusetts law firm Brown, Rudnick, Freed, and Gesmer is suing to get $282 million from smokers for its work as well (McElhenny. "Law Firms Suing..." *Associated Press* –NY-12/27/01).

The Wall Street Journal on the MSA:

"What we have here is a legal system rapidly being corrupted into a legal extortion racket, one that mocks the constitutional separation of powers. As a result of the tobacco lawsuits the country got a new, unlegislated tax on smokers designed to enrich a small group of lawyers as well as state budgets."

- *WSJ*, Review & Outlook, 02/20/01

Figure 4

Speaking of industries, the Antismoking industries spawned out of MSA monies in individual states have exploded onto the scene with less than spectacular success in terms of using their funding as intended. According to an extensive investigative series in Minnesota's Star Tribune, the Minnesota Partnership for Action Against Tobacco (MPAAT) received over 200 million dollars in public money, focused a good part of its energies on advertising campaigns designed to stir up divisions within communities over smoking ban issues, and gave **over 80%** of its grant money to people and groups with ties to its board or advisory committees. The court order creating MPAAT had originally directed that it spend that $200 million primarily on helping people quit smoking, education of children, and research (David Phelps and Deborah Rybak, *Minnesota Star Tribune* 11/18/01).

In response to the public pressure generated by Phelps and Rybak's research, Attorney General Mike Hatch of Minnesota took MPAAT to court for its misuse of public money and succeeded in getting a scathing decision from Judge Michael Fetsch. The judge directed MPAAT to spend no more of its funds on public banning efforts until it caught up with spending an equal amount on its properly appointed activities. He also directed MPAAT to radically restructure its grant appropriations process to ensure that future monies were disbursed fairly. In a follow-up article David Phelps noted:

> *'MPAAT has departed from and has ignored one of [its] primary missions,' Fetsch wrote. The judge's sharply worded order also told MPAAT ... to draft new guidelines for avoiding conflicts of interest among its board members and grant recipients.* (David Phelps. *Minnesota Star Tribune* 06/28/02)

Minnesota's citizens have reacted strongly to these revelations: strong Crusading movements for widespread bans in Beltrami County and Eden Prairie were completely derailed after these stories came out as politicians decided that public sympathies could no longer support them (Terry Fiedler. *Star Tribune* 10/20/02).

This particular case of The Greedy getting caught does not to stand in isolation. In 1994, Texas Attorney General Morales, claiming that secondary smoke was hazardous "particularly to youngsters," led the way in suing to ban smoking at fast food restaurants (William Pack "Morales Sues..." *Houston Post* 02/17/94). He then went more directly after Big Tobacco in what would eventually result in the enormous Master Settlement Agreement.

According to Reuters, Morales is now being accused by federal prosecutors of "scheming with a friend... to get $520 million of the $3.3 billion in fees paid to a team of private lawyers hired to sue major tobacco firms." The case has not yet been heard and, not surprisingly, Morales continues to maintain that the 12-count indictment, including such charges as fraud and conspiracy, is falsely based (*Reuters* 03/07/03).

It is well to remember that the political power that comes with unlimited money protects all but the most blatant abusers. The instances of such abuse that make it to court or even to the press represent only a small part of the misuse to which smokers' money has been put. The money grab that was supposedly justified to garner public support as being intended to pay for the medical expenses of sick smokers has instead been used for everything from tobacco marketing (!) to golf courses (Bob Woodruff. "Smokescreen" *ABC News Good Morning America* 07/22/02).

Greed is a vice never satisfied. The more it is pandered to the greater it becomes. In the middle of 2001 the American Medical Association noted that the money being poured into Antismoking activities from just state monies alone amounted to **over 880 million dollars** a year! (*AMA Annual Tobacco Report 2001*) Despite this truly phenomenal amount, the background efforts of the Antismoking Crusades' Public Relations people produced a front-page bold banner headline article in USA Today just prior to the publication of that report boldly proclaiming that "**Anti-smoking Funds (are) Sparse.**" (*USA Today* 01/30/01)

Sparse like crocodiles' teeth!

There are many Idealists among Antismoking researchers, organizations, and even (perhaps) lawyers, but many fall under the heading of The Greedy as well. The greed is not only greed for money, but for recognition and influence. Those who lead the attack on the unpardonable vice of smoking and manage to lead it well can find fame and power as well as fortune! Professors who wrangle frequent appearances on TV and million-dollar research grants from Antismoking-designated funding are guaranteed steady positions of prestige and influence within the university and beyond. Politicians grabbing airtime for their efforts to "save the children" can parlay that coverage into clout for re-election or elevation to higher positions far more effectively than with millions in mere political campaign contributions.

The thirst of The Greedy is as unquenchable as their moral standards are nonexistent. If by some chance they eventually succeeded in eliminating smoking from the face of the earth there would be virtually no time lapse before they sank their fangs into Big Auto, Big Meat, Big Soda, or whatever supposedly idealistic cause was out there that would promise them Big Money and Big Power. Indeed, we're already seeing one of the founding fathers of the Antismoking Crusade, ASH's John Banzhaf, leading the way in fast food lawsuits by proclaiming that "fatty foods can have addiction-like effects" (Sally Satel. "Fast Food Addiction..." *American Enterprise Institute*).

The ante is being raised by speculating that cheese gives rise to "morphine-like" breakdown products during the digestion process. Our children are being addicted to cheeseburgers! Quick! Somebody DO something! According to *Ananova:*

> *Dr. Neal Barnard, president of the Physicians Committee on Responsible Medicine, says cheese is addictive because it contains small amounts of morphine from cows' liver (Ananova 06/06/03).*

Ahhh.... the power of cheese!

"The anti-smoking movement is just as judgmental and moralistic as other groups who would infringe on individual autonomy – only far less candid.

... (T)he same kinds of people who accuse tobacco companies of misleading the American public rely on quite a bit of dishonesty to advance their own agenda.

And moral turpitude, unlike third-hand smoke, really is noxious."

-- Evan Gahr, *Washington Times* Op-Ed, 9/10/01

Figure 5

~Summation~

All nine groups work in concert when it comes to employing various psychological tools and tricks in their campaign to rid the world of smoking. Large nationwide and worldwide conferences costing tens of millions of dollars bring representatives of the various Crusading groups and organizations together to plan future goals and activities.

A ten million dollar conference held in Chicago (*The 11th World Conference on Tobacco or Health.* August 6-11, 2000) brought together over 5,000 Crusaders from 173 countries to hear such things as the American Cancer Society report on monitoring tobacco activity in 196 countries. They then laid out plans for a global war against smoking to be coordinated by the World Health Organization and reach years into the future. The Director General of WHO, Dr. Gro Harlem Brundtland, called for *"high cigarette taxes bolstered by heavy-hitting anti-smoking ads, a total ban on smoking in public places..."* and went on to say *"**We know what works!**"* (*AMA Annual Tobacco Report* 2001; Melissa Schorr. *Associated Press* 08/08/00).

The Antismoking Crusade has grown from a few scattered extremists in the late 1960s to tens of thousands of dedicated (and often well-paid!) lobbyists and activists today. Many of these people are being paid out of either general tax money or money taken from smokers through the services of Big Tobacco in its MSA deal with the Attorney Generals.

In California alone the state spent 134.5 million dollars on Antismoking efforts in 2001. When it made plans to cut that to about $90 million one Crusading official declared that 1,000 jobs would disappear virtually overnight: that's an average of $40,000 per Antismoking job! Sadly, many of these people are also funded heavily by money that contributors to large non-profits believe is going to basic health care and needed research (Jon Dougherty. *WorldNetDaily.com* 06/19/02).

Of every dollar that is contributed to a group like the "American (name your favorite organ) Association" or the "National (name your favorite smoking-related illness) Society," it is likely that only a few cents or even less is going to actual research to cure disease. Depending upon the group in question, many times as much may be going straight to efforts that translate into the harassment and vilification of smokers.

Some smokers have taken to answering charitable appeals from these groups by returning notes saying "I'm a smoker. I've already contributed thousands of dollars to your efforts to vilify me through my extra taxes." Many more have simply stopped or redirected their giving in silence.

Even if you are not a smoker it might be wise to ask for a clear and specific breakdown of how your money will be spent before you write future checks: refuse to accept vague breakdowns into fuzzy categories that obscure how the money is really being used... you're writing the checks, you have a right to clear information. There are many small grassroots charities, local hospitals, and neighborhood enterprises that are likely to use your contributions far more effectively in tune with your intents than the big Antismoking conglomerates.

Despite the above situation, some Crusaders decry even the miniscule amount that mainstream health groups **do** spend on research to actually help smokers. One complained on a private Antismoking mailing list that the National Cancer Institute was "wasting" that fragment of their total budget that is spent on actual health research by researching the prevention of diseases among smokers! I'm sure this fellow would have felt far better if **all** of their money went to activist groups such as his own! (Reference withheld by request of source.)

The Greedy are evidently alive and well.

The next section, Antismoking Tools and Tricks, will look at how Antismoking efforts at thought manipulation have surpassed the normal bounds of even wartime propaganda in the attempt to create a "smoke-free world."   Some of the techniques used by these groups of Crusaders have moved into realms that in the past were only imaginable in science fiction horror novels from the 1950s: stories of dim futures filled with Big Brothers, omnipresent observation, and lack of freedoms... stories of the few controlling the thoughts of the many while staying secure within their own privileged status.

The Antismokers' Bag Of Tools and Tricks

We've looked at those who make up the membership of this so-called Antismoking Crusade and seen that they are both numerous and highly motivated. The success they've achieved over the last two decades in terms of gaining support and money, as well as in instituting widespread bans, has been phenomenal. Smoking, once a cheap and nearly universal practice everywhere outside of dynamite factories and oxygen tents, has been limited and taxed far beyond what anyone would have thought reasonable or even possible just 20 years ago.

To a great extent this has come about because many smokers themselves have been taken in by the misinformation that has been spread about secondary smoke. Such smokers have voluntarily accepted rules that would in the past have been completely unenforceable. The image of the "rude smoker" smoking in a no-smoking zone with callous disregard for the well-being of others is grossly exaggerated: unless a ban is blatantly unreasonable the overwhelming majority of smokers will usually abide by it.

The success of the Crusaders has also sprung from the step-by-step planning of their goals: they concentrated first on simply having a nonsmoking section on airplanes, then expanded their efforts to include banning smoking in hospital rooms, then hospital care Emergency waiting areas, then total bans on airplanes with short flights, then on ALL flights; and so on to the point where we're now seeing smoking bans in bars and parks, on public sidewalks and beaches, and even movement toward extending bans to private homes where minors reside or where the neighbors object. Since most states still legally allow teens to smoke with parental permission this could lead to some interesting family dynamics: picture dad shivering out on the porch with his pipe while 17 year-old Junior relaxes in front of the TV with a Marlboro (*US Newswire.* "EPA Administrator..." 10/15/01; also, from the ASH website: " *'There is no legal right to smoke, even in one's own apartment...'* says law professor John Banzhaf," ASH's founder and Executive Director).

This nibbling and gnawing at the edges of a shrinking freedom has been accepted whereas driving a stake through Lady Liberty's heart right at the beginning would never have been tolerated. When people deride the dire warnings of smokers' rights advocates by saying "Oh, that's just the old slippery slope argument." they ignore the fact that the slippery slope can be an accurate representation of the process of social change when that change is driven by the efforts of well-organized fanatics with a good long-term plan and massive funding.

How have the Antismokers achieved this? What tools have they used and what impacts have the use of those tools had upon larger society? The number of approaches and the overall complexity of the question again demand a categorical break-down for clarity:

1) **Language**
2) **Secondary Smoke**
3) **The Spectre of Death**
4) **Pregnancy**
5) **Saving The Children**
6) **Bans**
7) **Discrimination**
8) **Hate**
9) **The Media**
10) **Fallacious Argumentation**

The widespread use of identical techniques and language by Antismokers has developed over the years. In the 1970s and 80s small independent groups who found success by using a certain approach or tactic would have had that approach or tactic simply spread by newsletters and through word of mouth. Nowadays the Crusade is more fully coordinated as major players on the national and worldwide scene plan and publicize specific themes and avenues of attack for months or years into the future.

Three of the more powerful of these groups are the previously mentioned ASH (the major "radical" group), the ALA (American Lung Association, a nonprofit Crusading organization), and the CDC (Centers for Disease Control, a federal agency founded to fight infectious epidemics which has recently sought to expand its power to controlling peoples' voluntary behaviors). These large American groups extend their influence to other countries and to international organizations such as the WHO by the same type of political and financial blackmail that created the universal drinking age and tobacco purchase laws within the U.S. (See the Synar Amendment discussed in more detail later.)

Countries that want consideration from the International Monetary Fund or who want their airlines to have landing privileges within the United States must bow to our dictates "for their own good." The Russian carrier Aeroflot was one of the last holdouts against this pressure and actually "accused the United States of breaking international law by banning smoking on all flights entering or leaving the U.S." Of course the U.S. eventually prevailed since no world-class airline can survive while passing up the U.S. market ("Turkey Passes Tobacco Law...." *Reuters* 06/21/01; *AMA Annual Tobacco Report 2001*).

The advent of worldwide instantaneous computer communication and coordination between the larger bodies with their almost unlimited funding and the smaller grassroots groups with their vast amounts of manpower has brought the Crusade to a new level. Focusing on specific areas such as those detailed below, Antismokers have achieved incredible power in bringing to reality the widespread social engineering and consciously designed behavior modification of the entire world population.

1) Language

If thought corrupts language, language can also corrupt thought.

-- George Orwell

To start off at the most basic and arguably the most dangerous level let's look at the way our language is used and misused by Antismoking Crusaders:

There are two fundamental aspects to consider here: the simple use of propagandistic styles and tools to shape opinion and the far more insidious and dangerous redefinition of basic words and terms in an attempt to actually control the way people think. There is a third and more extended level as well which is covered in the final chapter of this section: the skillful use of techniques of fallacious argumentation.

The most elementary tool of propaganda is simply the careful choice of the terms one uses to describe oneself, one's opponent, or the activity being propagandized about. From their early beginnings the Crusaders have shown recognition of the importance of accenting the positive: just as Anti-Abortionists prefer to be called Pro-Life, so do Antismokers prefer to be called Smoke-Free or Clean-Air proponents. The term "smoking" seems almost unknown to some Antismokers: terms such as "polluting the air with toxic sludge" are substituted at every opportunity!

In a recent testament to the conscious use of language as propaganda, SmokeFree Educational Services created a web page giving detailed advice on words and phrases Antismokers should use and avoid (www.smokefreeair.org/ses/PositiveLanguage. pdf). The growing confidence of Crusaders is seen by their willingness to share such thinking publicly. In the past it would have been hard to find such material outside tightly controlled private mailing lists, although its use was evidenced by such things as the name change of "Group Against Smokers' Pollution" to the kinder and gentler "Group to Alleviate Smoking Pollution."

The excerpts in Figure 6 provide a good introduction to the sort of training that is spread among the various Antismoking groups over the web. Uniformity of language and terminology has helped create a friendlier image for the media to work with and has also served to magnify the size and power of the Antismoking Crusade in public perception. This is an area where Free-Choice advocates need to work harder: at the present time the media sees smokers' rights and Free-Choice groups as either small quirks or as hidden arms of a Big Tobacco Conspiracy.

The subtle and sometimes not so subtle twisting and shaping of words in polls and surveys has also proven a powerful tool for propaganda in this area. For example, a poll put out by a true Crusading organization will never ask "Should private businesses be forced by law under penalty of closure to evict those customers who smoke on their premises?" Instead the phrasing will always be more along the lines of "Should people have the right to safe, healthy and smoke-free air within public places?"

Certainly more people will answer yes to the latter question than to the former, even though both are really asking the same thing. People generally don't want to see big authorities forcing unreasonable rules and regulations onto private businesses or owners, but on the other hand they certainly are in favor of "safe and healthy air," particularly in "public places" (which, evidently, includes virtually all private business establishments that serve members of the public!)

Extreme penalties involving outright business closures or jail terms are always played down by those pushing for new laws and regulations, but those who defy the Antismoking edicts will eventually find such penalties springing upon them from unexpected dark corners. As noted later, California's "three strikes and you're out" felony guidelines could well bring life prison terms to those sneaking a smoke in an airplane restroom as this is now considered to be interfering with a flight.

If somebody asks you if you are a smoker, answer them the same way you would if they asked you if were a Nazi or a child abuser.

Q: Are you a Nazi?
A: I'm not a Nazi!
Q: Are you a smoker?
A: I'm not a smoker!

...I'm healthy, smokefree, pro-health, a health advocate, in favor of clean indoor air, and normal.

A smoker, on the other hand, is un-healthy, smoky, anti-health, anti-clean indoor air, and abnormal...

In a battle of pro-smoking vs. anti-smoking, we will always lose. In a battle of pro-health vs. anti-health, we will always win...

-- Positive Language @ smokefreeair.org

Figure 6

It is doubtful that such bans would have been passed if the voters or legislators originally envisioned such penalties being imposed. Do you think that even today taxpayers are generally aware that they are paying for prison inmates whose "good time" has been negated and are presently still in prison simply because they were caught smoking tobacco? (David Hench. "Tobacco becomes..." *Portland Press Herald* 02/03/02).

In the same vein, it is now becoming common for the mere possession of a single cigarette on school grounds to count as grounds for suspension or expulsion of otherwise exemplary students. Indeed, in one Massachusetts high school "If two or more people confirm that a student smells like smoke, that student will face suspension under the assumption that he or she has recently been smoking" (*Wall Street Journal* 07/03/01).

In the old days of 30-minute after-school detentions for those who were actually caught (gasp!) **smoking** in school restrooms such an extremist response would have raised an immediate outcry from concerned parents. The power of language that occurred when smoking was reclassified as a "drug activity" is painfully evident in this case.

However, the above uses and misuses of language are not uncommon in the political arena. We've all seen the political power achieved by changing "inheritance taxes" (inheritances being something we usually associate with the privileged few) to "death taxes," (death being something common to all of us) and the importance attached to changing the term "suicide bomber" to "homicide bomber."

While the idea certainly hasn't won widespread accept-ance yet, at least one professor testified at a Texas hearing that: "*Cigarettes are a weapon of mass destruction....*" If that terminology catches on, residents of tobacco producing states might want to move elsewhere before they are nuked (*Las Cruces Sun-News* 01/09/02). The humor of such a suggestion may already be lost on American Indian tribes who have nothing to cling to but paper treaties and a long history of governmental disrespect for such treaties. When Crusaders start to paint the

Red Man as the "drug pusher to our children" the situation faced by those on reservations may not be funny at all.

The power of word choice in surveys and polls is similarly crucial. No one should **ever** pay any attention to any poll or survey results unless they've first seen exactly what wording was used in the questions, what population pool was sampled, and the size of the sample queried. "Four out of five dentists recommend Dentyne for dental health!" becomes far less compelling if one knows that the sample was limited only to dentists who actually recommended **any** brand of chewing gum for dental health!

Crusader efforts to push for increased cigarette taxes in 2002 and 2003 were often predicated on polls supposedly showing enormous public support for those increases. Most people were unaware that poll questions played up fears about smoking "particularly among kids" in order to get those results. (Questionnaire Survey of Registered Pennsylvania Voters, April 20-24, 2002; Susquehanna Polling and Research, Inc.)

What is unique, frightening, and a real testament to the power of the Antismoking Crusaders is their success in changing the basic definitions of words themselves in order to mold public opinion and reduce smoking rates.

In politics, words are power. And the power to control language through controlling the definition of words confers the power to control thought and political decisions. Those over forty will remember that "smoke-free" was a term that simply did not exist before the 1970s. There were "no-smoking areas," usually in intensive care type hospital wards and around explosive materials, but the very concept of banning smoking was seen as pretty unusual and was something that was always phrased in the negative form.

The origination and propagation of the term "smoke-free" was an early but very important victory of the Crusade in controlling the words and thoughts of people around the issue of widespread smoking bans and is now repeated constantly as a catch phrase whenever an Antismoker is before TV cameras.

Signs saying "Smoke-Free" and "Thank You for Not Smoking" are just **so** much kinder and gentler than the cold "NO SMOKING!" signs of yore, especially when the new signs are decorated with pictures of flowers and romping children. The "Thank You..." sign was itself relatively unknown until 1971 when one of Ann Landers' many Antismoking sermons suggested to readers that such wording would be effective (Don Matchan. *We Mind If You Smoke*. Pyramid Press. 1977 p.100).

My first experience of a City Council hearing on a smoking ban was in early 2000 when I took a bus trip from Philadelphia to a hearing where a friend of mine was planning to testify in New York City. I was struck by how the Antismoking Lobbyists presented what seemed to be a veritable mountain of information and cogent argument supporting their side. Arrayed against the impressive presentations of those Crusaders, the self-serving pleas of bar and restaurant owners and the solitary voices of a few independent citizens sounded weak, whiny, and utterly unconvincing. When I decided to add some testimony of my own I felt almost helpless in using my few minutes in any way that could effectively counter the barrage from the other side.

It wasn't until I reviewed the testimonies later that I realized how much of the lobbyists' power lay simply in their careful misuse or distortion of dozens of ordinary English words and scientific terms. These misuses and distortions were repeated so many times by so many different testifiers that it actually became difficult to think about the issue in any sort of objective or even rational way.

After sitting through the several of these hearings I can't really blame legislators who vote for bans: they are railroaded straight down the cattle chute by highly skilled and coordinated linguistic and statistical manipulation. Several dozen hours of heavily lop-sided testimony make it hard for politicians to vote against what has become one of America's most powerful lobbies.

My review of these testimonies made me aware of some of the dangers arising from this sort of attempt at thought management. I use the term "thought management" because that is what it boils down to when a group consciously and successfully alters the meanings of words so that common thoughts and expressions using those words come to mean something new and different than normally intended.

As Orwell noted so well in his book *1984*, if one redefines peace to mean a "condition of war in which we all work together for the state" it becomes harder to agitate for or even think about a simple cessation of armed hostilities. If safe air is redefined to mean smoke-free air, then it becomes difficult to agitate for allowing smoking since such agitation would, by definition, become the promotion of unsafe conditions.

The rest of this chapter will examine the misuse and conscious distortion of a number of words and terms by the Antismoking Crusade in their attempts to govern our thoughts. Each one may seem minor in itself, but taken together their impact is intimidating.

Tobacco smoke is a chemical stew
of 5,000 "*toxic*" chemicals

Not even the massive 1979 Surgeon General's Report itself tried to claim 5,000 chemicals in tobacco smoke. The proper number is closer to 4,000 than to 5,000 and even the source for 4,000 could be criticized: it comes from an offhanded estimate in a tobacco industry journal article that dealt with the flavor of tobacco smoke! (Roberts, D.L. "Natural Tobacco Flavor" *Recent Advances in Tobacco Science* 14: 49-81, 1988) 4,000 is still an impressive number but the widespread use of the larger number is so typical of exaggerated Antismoking claims that it deserves to be specially noted.

Of course even 5,000 chemicals would be fairly meaningless in face of the fact that our ordinary dietary intake includes roughly 10,000 different chemicals, but most folks are not aware of that fact. Nor are they aware that some of the "deadly toxins" (such as isoprene, acetaldehyde, acetone, and acetonitrile) that come from the end of a cigarette are also found in the normally exhaled air of nonsmokers as a byproduct of standard body metabolism (*Science.* 258: 261-265, 1992; *9th Report On Carcinogens.* DHHS; Lawrence Taylor. *Chemical Evidence: The Forensic Expert*).

To be sure, there **are** many elements in tobacco smoke that would usually be considered toxic if one were exposed to reasonably measurable quantities. However, for the vast, vast majority of these compounds, an ordinary nonsmoker, even in a heavily smoke-filled bar, would be likely to ingest quantities measured only in picograms or even femtograms! (A femtogram is just one one-quadrillionth of a gram... a gram is about the weight of Abraham Lincoln's nose on a standard American penny.) In truth, only a few hundred of these chemicals seem to have even been measured at all (*1986 Report of the Surgeon General* p. 128). Presumably the thousands of others exist in such incredibly small quantities that even Superman's Microscopic Vision would be boggled!

It's also good to remember that scary sounding chemical names do NOT necessarily mean "poison." That healthy serving of cabbage on your plate provides a prime example as noted by respected science writer Michael Fumento:

> *An innocent looking leaf of cabbage, for example, contains 49 natural pesticides and metabolites, with huge, ominous-sounding names like 4-methylthiobutyl isothiocynanate and 3-indolylmethyl glucosinolate.* (Michael Fumento, *Science Under Siege*, p.62)

Remember **that** the next time you order sauerkraut! Appendix E lists a variety of chemicals commonly found in our foods and beverages and shows how they can be combined to make for a festive holiday meal.

As for toxicity, there has never been any official claim that all or even many of these compounds are toxic at all. The Surgeon General's exact wording was that **some** of those compounds are toxic without any reference to proportion or number.   The Surgeon General also carefully avoided the question of what quantity of any of these would actually **be** toxic. Such a question is normally considered by scientists to be fundamental to any such discussion but which, in the case of the infinitesimal quantities involved when speaking of secondary smoke, would clearly indicate all of them to be toxicologically harmless.

Remember: salt is a deadly toxin if you ingest even a few ounces at one time and manage to keep it down... your brain tissue will react like a garden slug that has had salt poured on it and you will die. Is it therefore accurate to call salt "toxic"? But with no salt at all in your diet you would also die. As seen in Figure 7 the EPA can be pretty choosy when it comes to defining some things as toxic or not toxic.   As mentioned later with respect to the definition of addiction it would seem that these designations sometimes depend more on politics than science.

To return to the case of our nonsmoker, and to take one particular element that is often pointed to in Antismoking publications, let's look at the toxic chemical "arsenic." Now we all know that arsenic is toxic, but we also all know that if we wanted to kill someone with arsenic we'd have to give them a certain amount to accomplish the task.   How much? I don't actually know the lethal dose of arsenic, but I **do** know that even the proposed new stricter standard of arsenic in drinking water of 10 ppb (parts per billion) allows for 10 nanograms (billionths of a gram) of arsenic to be present in one gram of "safe" drinking water.

Ten nanograms per gram equates to about 5,000 nanograms for a sixteen-ounce tumbler of water. Now, in 1999 a landmark analytical study was done by all four major tobacco companies under the coordination and according to the standards of the Massachusetts Department of Public Health. This study examined the total smoke output, both mainstream and sidestream, of 26 brands of U.S. cigarettes. Forty-four separate smoke constituents were measured. Measurements of total arsenic in the smoke output of their average brand style gave a value of 32 nanograms. In most well ventilated smoking situations our nonsmoking water drinker would inhale no more than about 1/1000th of this: an amount equal to about three hundredths of a single nanogram. See Appendix B for an explanation of why this exposure assumption is reasonable (The 1999 Massachusetts Benchmark Study. Final Report. 07/24/00).

Thus our nonsmoker would have to sit in a room with a smoker while that smoker smoked more than 165,000 cigarettes to get the same "dose" of arsenic that he or she would get from their government-approved watery beverage! Actually, under 20th century standards of 50 ppb for safe water the smoker would have to smoke 825,000 cigarettes. So is it correct to say that the nonsmoker is "threatened by toxicity" from ordinary levels of exposure on this basis? Of course not... unless we want to completely redefine the concept of threat so that we'd all flee in blind stumbling panic from a glass of water!

As discussed further in the chapter on Secondary Smoke and in Appendix B, very few, if any, of these "toxic" compounds would ever be present in quantities that would form even the lowest levels of threat to a nonsmoker if we use normal EPA and OSHA safety guidelines as standards. Indeed, when the issue of exposure to the much more complex chemical mixture produced after the World Trade Center's fiery collapse was in the news the EPA hastened to reassure people that the fumes billowing through the air of New York were not "toxic" (See Figure 7).

In reality of course the fumes from what was described as a "furnace of burning jet fuel, insulation and other synthetic materials" were far more toxic than anything that would ever come from the quiet burning of a few leaves wrapped in paper. That fact didn't stop Governor Pataki from seizing the opportunity for money though: in December 2001 the Governor moved to pay New York's costs from the terrorist attack by once again taxing the smokers an extra 39 cents a pack! This tax came on top of a 55-cent increase in 1999 to pay for a package of health care plans (which somehow didn't seem to have been covered by the 50 cent increase from the MSA's unlegislated tax that was supposedly covering those health care costs). (McKinley. "Pataki Is Said..." *The New York Times* 12/05/01).

Then, in 2002, the smoking citizens of New York City got clobbered with a triple whammy: Mayor Bloomberg succeeded in getting a 1700% increase (Yes, you **did** read that correctly: seventeen **HUNDRED** percent!) in the city's own cigarette tax, raising it from 8 cents to $1.50. At this rate the nonsmoking citizens of New York may soon be relieved of paying any taxes whatsoever due to the enforced generosity of smokers (Gordon Fairclough, *The Wall Street Journal* 02/20/02). On the bright side however, Mayor Bloomberg joined the governor of Connecticut in claiming publicly that cigarette taxes are "voluntary," so perhaps New Yorkers will take to simply laying $5 or so on the counter and walking out of convenience stores with a carton of ten packs in their arms (Eric M. Weiss. *Au Courant* 01/25/02).

NY -- A vast choking plume of smoke from the ... World Trade Center has engulfed much of lower Manhattan.... Federal health officials say the fumes...pose no serious hazard to the millions of people breathing them....

"The good news for the residents of New York is that the air, while smoky, is not dangerous," said (the) EPA ... "There are dangers of smoke from the fire, of course, but it is not something we would classify as toxic."

-- LA Times 09/15/01

Figure 7

The linguistic image of 5,000 different and dangerous ingredients in tobacco smoke is a striking one though, and not one the Crusaders are willing to give up easily. It's funny however that they never mention another piece of data about that nasty "stew"... close to 90% of the weight of tobacco smoke is composed of oxygen, nitrogen, carbon dioxide, and plain water (*1989 Report of the Surgeon General* p. 80). For those not scientifically inclined this mix is usually called "fresh air." Nor do they mention that ordinary city water itself would likely have several thousand of these chemicals present if the water were analyzed down to the femtogram level.

A final side note that is relevant to burning jet fuel, levels of toxicity, and fresh air may be of concern to those who go to or live near airports. According to an EPA study a 747 landing and taking off at an airport emits 31.55 pounds (14,300,000 milligrams) of carbon monoxide and 115 pounds (52,210,000 milligrams) of nitrogen oxide. According to the Surgeon General's Report of 1986 a single cigarette emits a total of about 40 milligrams of carbon monoxide and about 3 milligrams of nitrogen oxide ("Technical Data .... Commercial Aviation." 09/29/95; *1986 Report of the Surgeon General*. pgs. 129, 130, 136).

Doing a little simple arithmetic tells us that the average large jet takeoff spews the equivalent of over 357,000 cigarettes' worth of carbon monoxide and over 17,000,000 cigarettes' worth of nitrogen oxide into the nice fresh air that is being sucked into the pleasant smoke free airport lounge.

Of course a large airport might have 500 such takeoffs in a day, producing the carbon monoxide of over one hundred and sixty five million cigarettes and the nitrogen oxide of eight and a half **billion** cigarettes... and all that pollution is being directly sucked into the family-friendly smoke-free airline terminals without a second thought. Granted, the air may be run through some filters, but as Antismokers proclaim repeatedly and loudly at public hearings, filtration of air is not a solution, not even when talking about relatively innocent wisps of tobacco smoke!

As for anyone actually living near an airport... Well, they're in the situation of having almost ten times the entire population of U.S. smokers planted right next door to them all day, every day, smoking away like chimneys. Yet the EPA and FAA will rush to assure worried parents in those neighborhoods that it's perfectly safe for their kids to run outside and play!

Obviously there are many other elements aside from carbon monoxide and nitrogen oxides that could be referred to, and some of them (for example nicotine) might not be present at all in jet fuel. However it's equally fair to point out that there are probably a number of quite "toxic" things that **are** produced in one of those takeoffs that would never come out of your neighbor's cigarette. Personally, I'd take some wisps from a Camel over jet fuel exhaust any day of the week.

Don't take this information as an encouragement to light up next time you're at an airport however. Timothy Leary was supposedly quite willing to allow his last drug arrest to have been for smoking tobacco at Austin International airport, but the atmosphere is somewhat different today. As we'll see later, that aromatic Marlboro or Virginia Slim might just land you on the wrong end of a loaded M-16 held by a nervous National Guardsman!

Tobacco smoke is "*addictive*"

Before the 1980s the word addictive was generally reserved, by both the scientific community and the general public, for those compounds which, when ingested regularly over even a short period of time, were likely to create a condition of severe physical dependency and incapacitation. "Severe" was generally understood as meaning that withdrawal symptoms resulted in extreme or even life-threatening physical manifestations such as high fever, crawling on the floor, lethal convulsions, or potentially fatal shock reactions and that the drive to obtain the addicting substance would commonly drive addicts to burglary, criminal assault, even outright murder.

It's easy to see the way the lines of distinction in language and science were drawn when one examines the early Surgeon General's Reports and notes how careful they were to use the words of science properly:

> *The compulsion (to smoke) appears to be solely psychogenic since physical dependence does not develop to nicotine ... nor does tobacco, either during its use or following withdrawal, create psychotoxic effects which lead to antisocial behavior ... In contrast to drugs of addiction, withdrawal from tobacco never constitutes a threat to life. These facts indicate clearly the absence of physical dependence.* (1964 Report of the Surgeon General p. 352)

Note that this conclusion rests purely upon directly observable physical facts: not upon statistical manipulations, not upon the mushy and malleable opinions of experts, and certainly not upon the redefinition of common English words.

In the *1979 Report of the Surgeon General*, Dr. Luther Terry continued this line of thought in correctly observing that while smoking fulfilled a few of the requirements of "the addiction model," it by no means fulfilled enough of them to allow smoking to be classified as an addiction (pgs. 16-7 to 16-9). At that point the question of whether tobacco use represented an addiction was still a matter of science rather than one of politics. The decision to change this classification in the late 1980s by Surgeon General Koop and others under pressure from Antismoking Crusaders was clearly more a decision based on politics than a decision based on science.

Commonly cited justifications for the change, such as evidence of changes in hormones and brain chemistry upon nicotine ingestion, would apply almost equally as well to substances such as caffeine and chocolate, yet there was no call by Dr. Koop to label Coca-Cola or Hershey Bars as addictive drugs or to classify cans of Pepsi and chocolate milkshakes as "drug delivery devices." The grandfather of tobacco lawsuits, John Banzhaf of ASH, has now moved on to more lucrative pastures and declares that there is "growing evidence that fatty foods can have addiction-like effects" so perhaps someday we'll see a Happy Meal box equated to a syringe (Sally Satel, "Fast Food Addiction." *American Enterprise Institute* 2003).

Similarly, to claim that the change was based on secret tobacco company research is silly: the general scientific community had researched nicotine dependence widely and openly for many years, and in any event the "secret papers" of the tobacco companies that supposedly lend some support to this claim weren't revealed until almost ten years after Koop's declaration. Surgeon General Koop had far more compelling reasons than afforded by mere science for his redefinition of addiction.

Most importantly, by labeling smoking addictive, Crusaders were able to justify labeling smokers as "sick," justify the need to "prevent addiction in children," and justify their future efforts to bring tobacco under the control of a vastly expanded Food and Drug Administration. Ultimately -- as activist Antismokers know and have bragged about on the Internet -- the FDA would eventually be forced under its own rules to decree that cigarettes would be outright illegal since they could not meet the standard FDA drug certification of being "safe and effective."

Of course the FDA, seeing this potentially enormous growth in its regulatory powers and staff, has voiced no objection to such a change in definition: remember, the coin of The Greedy is not always measured in gold alone. When one realizes though that while busily working for this goal the FDA let the approval of an anthrax vaccine sit moldering on its shelves from 1996 through the time of this writing, one must shudder at the thought of how such an extra workload might be accommodated.

Oddly enough, addiction considerations are often thrown by the wayside when Antismokers push for bans on long-haul air flights since "smoking is just the individual's choice and the smoker can easily abstain." How many of those Crusaders would be willing to be locked up in a cabin with a few dozen heroin addicts who were being forced to skip a dozen of their fixes?

Educators, Crusaders, and even the World Health Organization itself have fallen into the trap of citing a piece of "research" that ranked the addictive powers of a number of substances and placed nicotine near the top of the list. Actually this particular paper by Henningfield and Benowitz was never meant by them to be presented as an actual research finding.

Their work was neither in fact research nor even a study as such, but rather an essay. It was largely the simple opinion of the two authors as to which substances were most dependency producing: an educated opinion, but still, simply an opinion. This opinion of two people has now been translated in the popular mind and media as having the substance of actual laboratory-produced scientific research and is constantly cited at smoking ban hearings by Crusaders as though it were reproducible scientific fact (Philip J. Hilts. "Is Nicotine Addictive?" *New York Times* 08/02/94).

An interesting sidelight to the addiction question was uncovered in the research noted in Figure 8. It would appear that genetically, part of what encourages a person to remain a nonsmoker even if they try smoking for a while is a gene that is actually defective. Those with healthy genes are better able to perceive and process the stimulus of nicotine as a pleasurable input and are both more likely to take up smoking as a regular activity and more likely to find it difficult to give up.

Heaven help us all when the genetic engineers start offering to "help" our children by breaking the various genes in their bodies that would let them enjoy alcohol, tobacco, marijuana, or perhaps even teenage sex or rock 'n roll! Heaven help us even more when government starts mandating such genetic "improvement" for the general social good or for the benefit of state coffers!

On the more immediate horizon, the seemingly innocent implantation of computer "locator chips" in children as part of an effort to combat kidnapping could quickly become more sinister as such chips are "improved" with programming or vaccines to regulate or prevent undesirable behaviors. Scientists are already busily at work on a version of an anti-nicotine vaccine for our children.   A brand named Nic-Vax has been tested on rats, and human trials of similar vaccines are already being carried out in Florida and in Britain. Imagine the success of future Prohibition movements aimed at all sorts of behaviors once we open the door to the first few wedges (Andy Coghlan. *New Scientist* 06/23/02; Boca Raton – *PRNewswire* 02/28/00).

Scientists say they have identified a gene that, *when defective*, helps protect some people from getting hooked on cigarettes.... (This gene) tells the body how to make an enzyme... that breaks down nicotine.

Defective forms of this gene lead to a defective version of the enzyme, impairing the body's ability to process nicotine.

<Emphasis added>
--Malcolm Ritter, *Associated Press*, NY 6/24/98

Figure 8

The fact that some Big Tobacco executives, covering their legal butts, have testified under oath: "under some definitions nicotine is addicting" has added to the folklore as Crusaders now repeatedly cite the tobacco companies themselves as having declared nicotine is addictive! Expanding the mythology was ABC's 1994 *Day One* report indicating that Big Tobacco was spiking smokes with extra nicotine to make them more addictive.

While perhaps 90% of adult Americans heard of that story and accepted it, very few are familiar with the fact that ABC quickly withdrew the claims, agreed to pay Philip Morris $16 million for legal costs, and even apologized for their "mistake" (Gene Borio. www.tobacco.org/History/Tobacco_History.html; Public Broadcasting Service *Frontline* 04/02/96).

As with the nullification of the lung cancer conclusions of the 1992 EPA Report by Judge Osteen in 1998 (detailed later), the initial news story was the one that got the coverage and has stuck in the collective psyche. The retractions, voidings, and apologies are unknown to most people, and such stories get little or no prime time play in the news media.

And while tobacco executives' Congressional testimonies under oath received wide coverage, a refusal to testify under similar oath by FDA Commissioner David Kessler and by Surgeon General C. Everett Koop got almost none... after all, they were the "good guys," so why should **they** have to take an oath?

We see no reason for the committee to suggest that our testimony about tobacco now requires that we be put under oath or treated akin to tobacco executives (New York Times. 03/05/98).

Such an outrageous refusal by two of the nation's leading Antismokers to be held to even a minimum standard of honesty should have made banner headlines all over the country... but of course it did not.

To return to the question of addiction, this particular distortion of language may have proved particularly dangerous in terms of the effect it has had on our children. Antismoking programs in schools commonly either equate the addictive powers of tobacco with those of heroin or even declare with full sincerity that tobacco is MORE addictive and dangerous! California's Proposition 99 tax on cigarettes is used to fund at least one active youth program that teaches kids, "Nicotine is the most addictive substance" (www.ymn.org/newstats/legacy.htm).

Finally, in describing an ad campaign running in 2002 fashion magazines the American Legacy Foundation's president has stated unequivocally that "nicotine is more addictive than heroin or cocaine" (Stuart Elliott. *TheStar.com* 06/06/02). This Foundation is currently funneling hundreds of millions of dollars to Antismoking efforts aimed at our children through television and school programs every day of the year. This is what our children are being taught.

We would like to think that most kids have the good sense to shrug off this sort of propaganda, but we need to realize that for those under 18 this information has been presented to them as absolute fact for virtually their entire conscious lives. They have no experiential yardstick of common sense to measure these claims against.

There are certainly a number of impressionable children out there who have either experimented with tobacco themselves or seen others do it without becoming irrevocably addicted. There are also many who have seen a relative or friend of the family quit smoking without extraordinary pain. And finally, there are the vast multitude of TV ads by Big Pharma's "medical nicotine cartel" that promise kids that they'll be able to stop smoking as easy as pie with the patch, the pill, or the pretty pink placebo.

At least some of them, guided by the sort of misinformation referenced above, must have then felt it would be comparatively safe to play around with inhalants or felt safe in snorting or smoking heroin "just at parties." What they don't realize is that not only is heroin in reality far more seriously addicting in a purely physical sense, but that occasional or even first time use of heroin or inhalants entails a serious risk of actual instant death due to its illegality lending a lack of control over dosage or contaminated content.

As Antismoking Crusaders seek to control smoking by extreme tax and price inflation, we may soon see the same sort of instant deaths arising from teenagers smoking homemade or adulterated pseudo-tobacco products as we've seen in the hard drug world. Unfortunately only those in their 80s or above are likely to have any first hand memory of the deaths and blindness caused by wood alcohol during Prohibition. If things continue on their present course we may find ourselves reliving that nightmare in the future, with our children being the victims.

The deadly use of both heroin and household inhalants among 6th to 12th graders in recent years has skyrocketed. The 1977 National Household Survey of Drug Abuse found that heroin use among 12 to 17 year-olds increased from less than one half of a single percent in 1991 to almost four percent in 1996! While Antismokers dominated the news with tales of teen smoking increasing by twenty percent, these figures show teen heroin use increasing by eight hundred percent. To repeat, just for anyone who didn't notice: teen heroin use increased by **EIGHT HUNDRED PERCENT!**

A 1999 survey by the Parents' Resource Institute for Drug Education showed that while only four percent of 10 year-olds had smoked cigarettes almost six and a half percent had used inhalants! Additionally, a recent report by the Caron Foundation, one of the oldest drug and alcohol treatment centers in America, found that more than **fifteen** percent of adolescents abuse inhalants. And unlike occasionally smoking cigarettes, occasional inhalant use translates far too often into the deaths of our children while they are still children (Cincinnati. *Business Wire.* 04/07/99; Wernersville, PA *BW HealthWire* 04/24/00).

Are these distressing numbers a direct result of the blurred thinking about drugs that Antismoking Crusaders have encouraged in our society? There's no way to really know, but it's a definite and worrisome possibility. As noted later in the chapter on The Media we do know for sure that spending on Antismoking advertising has **far** outstripped spending on advertising aimed at deterring our kids from hard drug or inhalant use. And a 2001 survey by the National Center on Addiction and Substance Abuse found that teens are now finding it easier to buy drugs than to buy cigarettes while a Canadian study found marijuana smoking in 7th to 12th graders to be at almost **double** the rate of tobacco smoking! (Greg Toppo. *Associated Press* 09/13/02; *Regina Leader-Post* 06/26/03).

Perhaps an even sadder aspect of all this is that the multi-million dollar school-based Antismoking programs using this theme that were supposed to have given us a Smoke Free Class of 2000 have instead brought in a Class of 2000 that actually smokes even more than most classes before them! Although there's been some drop off among teenaged boys from the peak levels in 1997 the idea that the class is "Smoke Free" is laughable.

For most of the years of recent Antismoking efforts smoking rates among teens did nothing but increase steadily. And for girls over the age of 16 the rate is **still** climbing, despite the programs, taxes, laws, stings, ads, and bans! Thus we have wound up with the worst of both worlds ("Report Shows Slight Decline..." *Reuters* 04/02/02).

One caveat should be noted with regard to the recently publicized surveys purporting to show such a drop off. Such surveys are rarely adequately corrected for the tendency of teens to lie about behaviors they are nervous about admitting or which they would feel the interviewer/surveyor would not approve of.

Given the very hard-hitting negative media campaigns on the topic over the last ten years it's not hard to realize that most teens would likely have such feelings while taking such a survey today and that those feelings are likely to have increased. Such feelings would of course translate directly into the lower smoking rate numbers that Crusading groups use to tout their effectiveness while vying for increased funding and higher taxes on smokers. The lower rate is then selectively credited to whatever goal the particular group is currently seeking: increased funding for themselves or higher taxes actually intended to reduce adult smoking.

Despite these negative side effects, Antismokers stick solidly to their push for the application of the term "addict" to smokers. The term's power in promoting the Crusade carries more weight with them than consideration of the kids who have died thinking that heroin or inhalant use was relatively benign. What power could the term have that would be worth such a price to them?   Let's take a look at some examples from the Internet for a clue:

One Antismoker urged in a forum on the Internet: "*Walk right up to the addict. GET RIGHT IN HIS/HER FACE. Refer to him/her as 'THE ADDICT' to stress his/her relationship to decent people.*" (Message ID#: <7iepqk$85q $1@nnrp1.deja.com) (Emphasis in original)

Another Crusader offered the opinion that: "*a smoker will do anything .to ensure that they be allowed to continue to engage in their addictive habit, much like a crack addict will sell his or her own baby to a local drug dealer for another fix.*" (MessageID:<19980115170500. MAA09074@ladder03.news.aol.com)

Consider how the term addict allows a full blown venting of hate that would be unimaginable if it were simply directed against someone engaging in a plain habit: "*Get a life JUNKIE, addict, YOU are a NICOTINE JUNKIE!! you cant go a day, or hours, without a FIX!!! YOU HUDDLE at the doors, outside in the SMOKING sections in a frenzy feeding your addiction, coming inside and going thru withdrawals after the FIX wears off, and being in a panic till the next fix!!!*" (Message-ID:<19980131110501. GAA19608@ladder02.news.aol) (Emphasis in original)

Finally, the simple designation of a smoker as an addict has skillfully rendered futile any attempts by smokers to defend their habit or claim they enjoy it. We all "know" that the reasoning of an addict about drugs cannot be trusted, and we all "know" that family, friends and society as a whole has the right to step in to save the hopelessly addicted from their own self-destruction.

An addict has no rights and, as noted earlier, may simply be relegated to the role of a patient who "needs treatment." Without such a label, smokers would constitute a far more dangerous potential adversary to the Antismoking Crusade.

Misusing the word "*children*"

American standards regarding the cutoff age for maturity have always been confusing. We have driving ages, drinking ages, big-city curfew ages, ages for consensual sex and for marriage, ages for the purchase of pornography, ages to be tried as an adult (which mutate depending on the State and the severity of the crime), and a whole stepladder of ages for viewing various popular films, playing computer games, or even listening to songs!

New York's Mayor Bloomberg poignantly exemplified this confusion in the tobacco area as he defended the $1.50 per pack tax increase on cigarettes against accusations that people would simply circumvent it by buying outside the city. He called up the "saving the children" argument by saying "Children don't drive, so they don't go to other states" (Michael Cooper. *New York Times* 07/01/02).

In a classic example of doublethink the good mayor conveniently overlooked the fact that the vast majority of underage sales are made to 16 and 17 year-olds... many of whom are certainly quite comfortable driving around with their new licenses and some of whom, in the real world, probably **will** die as they drive outside the city for cheaper smokes.

In 1984 (the real world... not the novel), driven by a very effective campaign to save the children that was created by Mothers Against Drunk Driving, the federal government clearly overstepped the intention of its Constitutional bounds. Under a Congressional appropriations directive the government refused to give billions of dollars in highway money to any states that did not fully comply with and enforce a universal drinking age standard set at 21 years of age. Undercover operations and secret police moved out of the hard crime and drug world into being an integral part of the normal life experience of legitimate bar and restaurant businesses (Porfiri, Daynard. WP #9: "An Analysis..." *Tobacco Control Resource Center*).

In one way this was a good and positive thing: thousands of young drinkers had been involved in car crashes related to driving across state lines to get liquor or get drunk. In another way however this set a very dangerous precedent: the use of federal purse strings to enforce a nationwide adherence to what most would consider a private moral standard has great potential for abuse in a country where the states have become increasingly dependent upon ballooning amounts of federal money over the past few decades.

The same technique was repeated in the 90s when the Federal Government threatened to withhold substance abuse and treatment funding from states that did not raise and strictly enforce the minimum age for tobacco purchase to 18. The "Synar Amendment," as this regulation was called, may reduce the number of teen smokers in some states while at the same time increasing the numbers of heroin addicts roaming the streets in other states that fail to meet purchase control goals (*Associated Press* -NY- 09-21-99).

Setting legal definitions for citizens' rights and behaviors that depend upon their ages is a tricky area, and there's no list of concrete guidelines. However, the use of the word "children" to describe individuals as old as twenty is clearly wrong when it is used solely to manipulate public opinion in favor of particular laws and further restrictions. Derek Yach, the head of WHO's Tobacco Free Initiative, campaigns tirelessly against Big Tobacco's marketing to "children" under 21, but in his own research on alcohol use he cites figures for "adults, 15 and up." Evidently a 15 year-old drinking straight whiskey is an adult while a 20 year-old smoking a cigarette is a child in this activist's eyes (Derek Yach. "Noncommunicable Diseases...." 06/29/01).

Joe Cherner, a high profile Crusader from New Jersey, has his own view on the question when he states to his newsletter subscribers that *"Like almost all smokers, they started smoking as very young children...."* Since the great majority of smokers start smoking between the ages of 15 and 21, it would be interesting to hear Mr. Cherner's definition of "very young children" (*Joe Cherner – Announce*. Newsletter 04/30/03).

The original study supporting the idea that "3,000 children a day" were becoming smokers had in fact set its query level at age 20: *"The 3000/day number was derived by dividing by 365 the estimated number of current smokers 20 years of age in the United States population in 1985."* Not only do Antismokers refer to 20 year-olds as children in referencing this study, but they also ignore the fact that the entire number was nothing more than a number derived from an estimate of another number to begin with! (Pierce J.P. et al. "Trends in cigarette smoking...." *JAMA* 261: 61-65 1989).

You would never know that this was the original research standard when driving down our highways and seeing the thousands of billboards picturing 6 year-olds as representing those 3,000 children a day. On the other hand, a poster showing a bunch of 18 and 19 year-old punks lounging around and smoking in an alley wouldn't have quite the same emotional impact as those cute and innocent little children, now would it?

This approach to smoking control makes liberal use of the claim that over 80% of smokers started smoking as teens. Of course, just as with Mayor Bloomberg's example above, it conveniently ignores another well-known fact: 80 to 90% of alcoholics started drinking in their teens. Thus, the massive hike on tobacco taxes to save the children should logically be followed by a similar hike in the price of a six-pack to $25 or so. The removal of beer ads and sponsorships from TV shows and pro-fessional sports would also logically follow... as would the demise of many of those shows and sports.

The movement to protect children in middle school or high school from smoking has now moved into protecting college age "children" who might be tempted to smoke on campuses where it is allowed! Antismokers again show their skills at doublethink by claiming that not only do 90% of smokers start smoking before age 18, but also that college students are a particularly vulnerable group of innocents being targeted for addiction by Big Tobacco. The battleground today is the college campus, and new statistics showing that most smokers start their habit in college will be created for the war.

Colleges refusing to go along with demands that their campuses ban all indoor smoking, even in private dormitory rooms, may be pressured with threats of losing millions of dollars in drug education and research funding as well as having to face the possibility of being pilloried before parents. Activist Antismokers threaten to expose them as "promoting smoking by their students" if they refuse to give in to such extremist bans.

This is not the first time in history that colleges have come under such attacks. All the way back in the early 1900s Carrie Nation would occasionally take breaks from her diatribes against alcohol and join Lucy Page Gaston in railing against such things as college smoking. Referring to Yale she said *"Parents ought to demand another faculty or refuse to patronize such a school."* and Harvard was favored with *"Parents should demand that the teachers... be free from... the use of tobacco."* (www. druglibrary.org/schaffer/history/e1900/cn/cn17.htm

Even though Carrie and Lucy had the beginnings of the power of a related Constitutional Amendment to buttress them, colleges for the most part resisted their tirades. Today unfortunately the ethical base of our universities is not as strong. As seen in Appendix H, some college personnel themselves are now leading smoking ban efforts.

Moving even beyond college age we've seen calls on the Internet for raising the minimum age for purchase to ages as high as 25! There's even a set of web pages seeking to restrict or ban cigarette advertising in printed media with more than a 15% readership under the age of 23 -- thus protecting those innocent little 22 year-olds from the sight of a picture of a tobacco product! Meanwhile we see Mike's Hard Lemonade and SKYY Blue (citrusey-sweet easy-to-drink alcoholic beverages clearly aimed at younger palates) advertised regularly on Buffy The Vampire Slayer... presumably to the exclusively adult over-21 fans of Sarah Michelle Geller.

Target Market, a "youth activist" Crusader group, claims that tobacco advertising in any publication with an under 21 readership of 15% or greater is "targeting youth." By this logic an advertising executive might commit millions of dollars to "targeting women" by taking out ads for feminine hygiene products in Playboy magazine, which boasts a female readership of up to 17%. Do you think he or she would last long in their job? (www.playboy.com/mediakit/print_demographics. html)

As we move into the early 2000's we are seeing Antismokers' efforts to expand the purchase age laws to include "children" up to the age of 21. Whereas they used to claim that the evil tobacco companies were trying to seduce grade school children with Joe Camel and high school children with Marlboro Team clothing and paraphernalia, we're now seeing increasing claims that Big Tobacco is playing upon the insecurities of innocent and immature children who happen for some reason to be at a university. The pervasive drinking and rampant drugs are getting little attention on some campuses compared to the "deadly threat" of tobacco smoke.

An interesting, though slightly off topic, contrast is provided by Canadian legislators who are pushing not only to decriminalize the purchase and use of marijuana, but to set the cutoff age for such legal purchase and use at sixteen years old (Darren Yourk. *Globe and Mail*. 09/04/02). The old joke about the "revenge of the hippies" in which they'd grow up to legalize pot while outlawing tobacco and booze isn't a joke anymore.

As discussed more thoroughly later, the concept of protecting or saving the children is a VERY powerful propaganda tool often used in times of full-blown war. By fuzzying the very definition of the word children, the Antismoking Crusade has increased the power of this psychologically manipulative tool enormously.

The meaning of "*risk*"

Antismokers quite reasonably ask "Why should nonsmokers have to risk their health purely for the convenience and comfort of the smoker?" and then go on to proclaim that contact with even undetectable amounts of secondhand smoke is a grave risk that demands immediate and extreme political action. What exactly is meant by the word risk when it is used in this way?

Normally when one speaks of a "risky" activity, one is referring to an activity that carries a much greater than normal chance of producing severe injury or death in the very near. Thus, driving with ones eyes closed or while drunk is indeed risky. Walking alone at night through a blighted, drug-infested urban area is certainly more risky than sitting on a suburban porch to stargaze. Using heroin, whether it's only once, or even if one has done it many times before, is risky because, due to its illegality, the user never knows its purity and strength and can easily overdose or be poisoned. Eating a Big Mac, though many millions have died from heart disease partially caused by a meat/fat/cholesterol-rich diet, would not generally be termed a "risky" activity in the English language.

Smoking itself is usually thought of as a risky activity, even though most of its effects lie far in the future, because studies have shown such large increases in danger for the contraction of serious diseases among smokers as they grow older and because these increases have been widely publicized and exaggerated. Some of these "smoking related" increases are a result not of smoking but of other disease causing conditions that simply correlate with smoking (e.g. alcohol consumption, the use of illegal drugs, and a lack of education and medical care) but it's pretty widely accepted that a lot of the increases are due purely to the effect smoking itself has upon the body.

The increased "risk" due to normal exposure to secondary smoke is **far** more questionable however. It exists, if at all, at such a low level that most epidemiologists would generally refuse to acknowledge it as worthy of even the slightest concern were it not such a useful tool in the war against smoking. While Antismokers are often fond of proclaiming that studies have proven that such a risk exists, the results of the studies themselves make a far stronger argument for the idea that any risk that might possibly exist is so small as to be beneath rational consideration.

Indeed, one Australian doctor a few years back went over the preliminary copy of a major government report on the risk from Environmental Tobacco Smoke (ETS) and sent an urgent cautionary memo to the rest of the panel that had produced it. He warned:

> *I am deeply concerned about the implications for the credibility of our whole report... a reasonable conclusion will be that the idea that there is ANY lung cancer caused by ETS in Australia will be seen as a huge joke...we had better get out a thesaurus and find a lot of words to express the words 'conservative estimate' in hundreds of different ways...we are looking down the barrel* (sic) *of a MAJOR public relations problem.* (Emphases in original) (Fax from Professor S. Chapman to A. Farrant et al. 06/08/96; Available for viewing at FORCES.org)

Generally accepted standards of epidemiology look for risk ratios of at least 2.0 or 3.0 before reaching important conclusions. The reason for these standards is not simply statistical uncertainty. In the field of epidemiology it is widely recognized that confounding correlating factors can have a very significant impact on results and that those factors are often not easily seen or understood.

In addition, motivational bias by researchers easily enters into both the gathering and interpretation of data and the overall design of studies that are not contained within a laboratory and subject to rigorous and reproducible measurement. When studies concern areas that might be controversial, where confounders are particularly difficult to correct for, or where researchers might have real reason for bias, adherence to such standards is particularly vital (See Figure 9).

Most secondary smoke studies however, if they show a positive relationship at all to diseases like lung cancer, average a risk ratio of far less than 2.0, and a quick check of the 130 study results listed in Appendix A shows that only four of the 130 would pass the 3.0 standard. **Not a single one** of those four actually reach full statistical significance!

The heavily criticized EPA meta-analysis claimed a risk of only 1.19 ... an increased risk of 19%: far less than the 100 to 200% increases thought to make good epidemiology (a risk ratio of 2.0 represents an increased risk of 100% over the baseline) and certainly far less than the sorts of increases that wide ranging and intrusive public policies should be based upon. This risk increase would mean that the absolute lifetime risk of lung cancer for a nonsmoking wife married to a smoker for thirty or forty years would increase by about a single tenth of one percent (i.e. 1.19 x the .4% lifetime risk of a non-exposed nonsmoker) even after such decades of constant daily exposure.

In a recent weird twist on this issue, the Crusaders working with Stanton Glantz have put out a paper claiming that the entire insistence on sticking to higher epidemiological standards is simply some sort of evil plot by the tobacco companies to discredit Antismoking research! Whether they'd consider all the sources cited in Figure 9 to be part of a Big Tobacco Conspiracy isn't clear (Yach et al. "Junking Science...." *Am. J. of Pub. Health* November 2001).

One of the largest case-control studies ever done on secondary smoke exposure and the later development of lung cancer was recently released by the World Health Organization after a British newspaper accused them of a cover-up. The study actually found no significant relationship between secondary smoke exposure and lung cancer, but the WHO nevertheless ballyhooed their finding of a **nonsignificant** 1.16 risk ratio into a boldfaced headlined press release proclaiming that "**Passive Smoke DOES Cause Lung Cancer!**" (Berlau. *Investor's Business Daily* 04/08/98).

"As a general rule ... we are looking for a relative risk of 3 or more before accepting a paper for publication."
– M. Angell, Editor, New England Journal of Medicine

"Small associations below 2.0 may be beyond the limits of reliable epidemiological inference."
– J. Peto, International Agency for Research on Cancer

"My basic rule is if the relative risk isn't at least 3 or 4, forget it."
-- Robert Temple, FDA director of drug evaluation

"Relative risks of less than 2 are considered small and are usually difficult to interpret. Such increases may be due to chance, statistical bias, or the effect of confounding factors..."
--National Cancer Institute

Figure 9

Somehow the WHO's press release failed to mention the only scientifically significant finding that the study *did* produce... namely that children of smokers were 22% **LESS** likely to come down with lung cancer as adults! (Bofetta et al. *Journal of the National Cancer Institute* pp.1440-1450, Vol. 90 1998). This sort of protective possibility was deliberately downplayed in the abstract with the comment "no association." Picture how the publicity would have been orchestrated if the only scientifically significant results of the study had shown the opposite effect!

It's clear that the news of an actual significant finding of a possible protective effect against future lung cancers among children exposed to smoke should have been far more news-worthy than the news of just another study showing insignificant findings about spousal and workplace exposure. As far as the media were concerned however, the finding about children was literally invisible: American news networks generally presented the WHO findings as strongly supporting a connection between secondary smoke and lung cancer and made not a single mention of the opposite and much stronger finding regarding children!

Is eating a Big Mac a "risk"? Certainly, if one's diet consisted purely of Big Macs every day of the week for 40 or 50 years, one would likely be courting a vastly higher risk of heart disease than if one subsisted on a gruel made of wheat and soy paste. But is it a risk to eat **one**? Certainly it's more risky than subsisting on gruel and raw fruit... but if you truly enjoy Big Macs and an occasional side order of fries would you be rational in constantly opting for the paste instead?

Is driving while sober a "risk"? It's certainly more risky to drive 25 miles to work each day than to drive 15 miles (with all else the same), but is such an increase in risk something that most people would or should take into account in their living and working life choices? How about the difference in risk between driving 25 miles and 24 miles? Should one seek to protect oneself by changing jobs if offered such a choice, or is worrying about such microscopic differences in risk a symptom of mental illness?

How about protecting one's children from the cancer risk of drinking whole milk?   An American Cancer Society study found that drinking one glass of whole milk each day resulted in a statistically significant relative risk of 1.62 for lung cancer. That's **more than triple** the excess risk the EPA claimed was due to lifelong daily exposure to secondary smoke. Should a parent be condemned for giving a glass of milk and a cookie to their child? (.62 and .19 are the actual claimed excesses in risk in the two studies.)   ("Milk Drinking, Other Beverage Habits, and Lung Cancer Risk." Curtis Mettlin, *International Journal of Cancer* 43.608-612, 1989)

What about parents who refuse to sell their houses and move away from power lines despite a 2001 British study that found literally a 100% increase in leukemia risk to children due to contact with their electromagnetic fields? British research commissioned by the National Radiological Protection Board (NRPB) found that such an increase was real but concluded that the excess risk was *"so low that it was unlikely to pose any real danger to British children"* (*Reuters*- LONDON, March 5, 2001).

While both the above statistical examples are far scarier than the statistics concerning secondary smoke they are rightly ignored because, in the case of the power lines, in absolute numbers, the increased risk is phenomenally low on a practical level while in the case of milk the nutritional benefits seem to substantially outweigh the miniscule and quite possibly non-existent risk. There is no massively funded Anti-Milk or Anti-PowerLine Crusade, and thus the numbers receive the attention and the concern that they likely deserve: very little. This may change if PETA's lawsuits ever bring money to the Anti-Milkers. See MilkSucks.com for a sample of the future.

Commonly, when arguing for smoking bans in bars and offices, Antismokers will emphasize the "risk" to nonsmokers of being exposed to tobacco smoke on the job. They do this both in the hope of pulling the power of OSHA regulations in on their side and also in the hope of combating the counter argument that the occasional and passing exposures of customers are simply too ridiculously small for any level of consideration.

Even if one were to accept the studies that have been done in this area as unbiased (a questionable assumption due to funding pressure to produce significant results and due to knowledge that highly placed Crusaders will not be very happy with researchers who produce unfavorable studies), one is faced with an increase in absolute risk that is truly minute. Indeed, when one looks at the magnitudes of risk involved, the studies done to date seem almost a testimony to the safety, rather than the risk, of ordinary contact with secondary smoke.

Don't forget: we're talking about a speculated absolute increase in risk of cancer of less than one in a thousand after decades of constant daily exposure, and with that figure only holding true after meeting the truly ridiculous preconditions laid out below in the discussion of the EPA report. If the subject was almost anything other than secondary tobacco smoke, OSHA and the EPA would never have involved themselves in such silliness.

Even such a neutral and detached body as ASHRAE (American Society of Heating, Refrigeration, and Air-conditioning Engineers) gets pressured: Richard Daynard, the lawyer who sued for $150,000,000 of Massachusetts' MSA money, brags on ASH's web site of how he's worked for 13 years to influence ASHRAE decisions by becoming a voting member and promoting zero-tolerance standards for tobacco smoke. The power of a few well-placed and highly vocal Antismokers has changed public policies for all of us (http://no-smoking.org/june99/06-24-99-5.html).

It is sad to see this perversion of OSHA intention and standards. Those who would like to see what real workplace risks are about and see the **real** value of the work that OSHA, the FDA and similar organizations can do should read Upton Sinclair's excellent novel *The Jungle*. Workers **should** be protected from invisible or excessive dangers on the job... protecting them from the pet peeves of activist groups seeking social engineering goals is **not** the task for which these administrative agencies were formed.

Can this situation be put back into some sort of rational balance? That's hard to say: even Oakley's heavily referenced

600-page book, *Slow Burn: The Great American Antismoking Scam (And Why It Will Fail!)* (Eyrie Press. 1999), made barely a ripple in the pond. Even the dissolution of the entire ETS/cancer link that formed the basis of workplace smoking bans, the EPA Report, met with a virtual stonewalling by the mass media.

The EPA analysis is the classic in this field and eventually resulted in smoking bans in hundreds of thousands of businesses throughout America in the 1990s. The fact that the study was thrown out in a federal district court in 1998 got very little press or public recognition and there was little support for reversing the bans once building managers realized they could save money by reducing fresh air circulation within smoking-banned offices.

It's important to note that although the judge in this case was from North Carolina he is actually known as being an "anti-tobacco" judge. He ruled against Big Tobacco in the important case that sought to put cigarettes under complete FDA control. While Antismokers quickly refer to Osteen's origins when discussing the EPA, they never mention the FDA ruling that contradicts their *Ad Hominem* attack (*New York Times*. 05/02/97).

Here are Judge Osteen's exact words:

> *In this case, EPA publicly committed to a conclusion before research had begun; excluded industry by violating the Act's procedural requirements; adjusted established procedure and scientific norms to validate the Agency's public conclusion, and aggressively utilized the Act's authority to disseminate findings to establish a de facto regulatory scheme intended to restrict Plaintiffs' products and to influence public opinion.* (Judge William Osteen. U.S. Federal District Court. 08/17/98)

{Note: Judge Osteen's decision has recently been set aside, not because it was wrong in substance, but because the EPA Report "*was advisory and not a final agency action.*" However, his detailed condemnation of the Report was neither questioned nor criticized and is still quite valid.} (Larry O'Dell. *AP* 12/11/02).

Five years ago, the networks treated the (EPA) declaration... as huge news. But this year, they downplayed a federal judge's ruling that the EPA had manipulated statistics in assessing the risks of passive smoke.

Back in 1993, the networks could hardly have been more aggressive. (Examples given of multiple news stories on all networks)

But when a federal judge ruled against the EPA ... second-hand smoke was suddenly deemed non-newsworthy. CNN ignored the story completely. NBC Nightly News gave the story just 21 seconds on July 19, ... CBS anchor Russ Mitchell began his 14-second report by saying, "The (EPA) is expected to appeal a ruling by a federal judge...." ABC's Carole Simpson led off her 17-second story by noting that "the (EPA) is standing by a report linking second-hand smoke to cancer."

- www.mrc.org/fmp/medianomics/1998/199808pg2.html

Figure 10

Intriguingly, a high court in Australia ruled in a very similar fashion in a case considering smoking in casinos. The court ruled that:

> *While ETS is annoying and of discomfort to non-smokers it has not been proved at the required standard, or at all, in this prosecution, that it a risk to the health of the employees at the casino.*

Among the evidence considered and rejected by the Court was the EPA Risk Assessment (Leland Modesitt Jr, Former Director of EPA's Office of Legislation. *Federal Focus.* November 1993).

Even if we were to accept the EPA meta-analysis as valid, we would be looking at an increased risk of lung cancer on the order of **less than one** extra case per thousand workers, assuming that those thousand workers all worked at least **30 or 40 years** around smokers in situations with antiquated ventilation systems **and** assuming that all medical science immediately grinds to a standstill with absolutely no further work being done on cancer prevention or the production of safer cigarettes **and** assuming that the original studies were all carried out without bias on the part of Antismoking researchers.

Such assumptions are ridiculous of course, but they are representative of the often-unstated background assumptions upon which Antismoking Crusaders base the fantastic statistical numbers they constantly masquerade as fact. That such misrepresentations bombard us daily through taxpayer paid press releases and advertisements in the media is nothing less than a crime.

So, is it proper English to refer to normal levels of secondary smoke exposure as a risk? While some extremists might argue the point, it's pretty clear that frightening restaurant customers or park goers by using the word "risk" to define their situation when confronted with occasional whiffs of smoke from a distance is enough of a perversion of language to simply be called an outright lie. Having read and examined the results of many of the studies involved I would even feel quite comfortable calling this term an outright lie when it is applied to full-time workers in most offices, bars, and restaurants.

Antismokers have consistently and deliberately refrained from mentioning the fact that the effects that **have** been claimed have only been found after decades of such daily and intense lifelong exposures and have also only been found as the result of statistical speculation, not as actual fact. Crusaders know that the fear of casual contact with others' smoke is a vital ingredient in winning public support for widespread smoking bans. Indeed, in the chapter that focuses on such bans you'll see an early and candid admission by them that the engendering of such fear is seen as vital to the goal of eventually eliminating smoking (See Figure 11).

Involuntary or "*Passive Smoking*"

A lie repeated often enough becomes the truth.

– Goebbels, Hitler's Minister of Propaganda

As with the term "smoke-free," the terms "passive smoking" or "involuntary smoking" were simply not part of the English language before the 1970s. The terms were not unknown however. According to Robert Proctor (op.cit. *The Nazi War On Cancer*), the phrase *Passivrauchen* (passive smoking) was created by Fritz Lickint, the author of a thousand page book entitled *Tobacco and the Organism* which was produced in association with the German AntiTobacco League in the 1930s. Fortunately, the concept never caught on in America until activist Crusaders resurrected and translated it in the 1970s.

Of course everyone has always realized that if you were in a room with a smoker that you would be inhaling some minute portion of the smoke in the air, just as one would be inhaling a minute portion of the chemicals put off by someone's perfume or invisible amounts of alcohol as it evaporated from someone's drink. But to generally describe such inhalation as "smoking" would have been considered laughable, particularly to anyone who was familiar with experiencing smoking firsthand! Indeed, the initial reaction of many smokers to these terms when they were first introduced **was** to simply laugh: it was unimaginable that such kookiness could ever catch on!

The power gained by convincing nonsmokers that they were being "forced to smoke" by smokers was so self-evident to Antismoking Crusaders that they simply constantly repeated the terms over, and over, and over again, until they began to be accepted. Today millions of people, many of whom have joined the ranks of The Innocents referred to earlier, would identify themselves as "involuntary smokers" whenever they are within an enclosed area with a smoker, no matter how large or well ventilated that area might be.

The lack of sense behind these terms can be seen when looking at two other similarly silly examples. First of all it's scientific fact as well as common knowledge that alcohol is a very volatile liquid: it evaporates into the air at roughly twice the rate of ordinary water. (That's why it's cooling when applied to a fevered patient's forehead!) Thus, if you are a teetotaler in a restaurant and people around you are drinking glasses of Chablis and Scotch, you yourself are being "forced" to inhale and ingest small quantities of alcohol vapor. The fact that such vapor has neither the visibility nor the aromatic qualities of tobacco smoke does not detract from the fact that such inhalation and absorption exists.   Would it then be proper to call such rest-aurant patrons "Passive Drinkers?"

Or, to take a somewhat less palatable thought to similar lengths: It's known that a large amount, perhaps as much as 80%, of the dust particles floating in the air of such public places as restaurants can consist of microscopic particulate skin cells that are sloughed off constantly from our bodies. These cell particles are constantly settling and are inevitably falling upon the fine dinner that you have in front of you. As you eat that dinner, you will indeed be eating the flesh of your fellow diners. Are you then an "Involuntary Cannibal?"

Both the above examples seem like so much nonsense, despite the fact that from a solidly scientific viewpoint their truth is indisputable. Actually, in the case of the "passive drinker," our teetotaler would routinely be exposed to airborne concentrations of carcinogenic alcohol up to 2,000 times as great as their exposure to the combination of all human carcinogens present in secondary smoke!

A shot of grain alcohol will evaporate in a little over a day in a warm room. That's 45 grams of human (Class A) carcinogen spewing into the air... almost a hundred thousand times the one-half of a single milligram present in the smoke from a cigarette (*1989 Report of the Surgeon General.* pps. 86-87). The chapter on Secondary Smoke will examine some of these figures in more detail.

However, despite the cold scientific facts, no one in their right mind would consider the teetotaler to be a drinker or the diner to be a cannibal. Granted, tobacco smoke is far more noticeable than alcohol fumes or microscopic skin cells, but the absolute quantitative differences are so small that linguistically speaking, "involuntary drinkers" and "involuntary cannibals" make roughly the same amount of sense as "involuntary smokers" in such public situations... namely, to any rational person, no sense at all.

The truly amazing thing is the extent to which this distortion of the English language has become accepted purely due to the conscious activity of a small and well-funded group who realized the power of language and forced their vision of proper behavior and attitudes upon the entire citizenry.

Dangerous Territory: Mutating Medical Conditions

In the words of a wise physician, it is part of the doctor's function to make it possible for his patients to go on doing the pleasant things that are bad for them.

-- Rene Dubos, microbiologist and Nobel Laureate

Doctors have long known that even dedicated smokers will often kick the habit quickly if confronted with a diagnosis of heart attack, cancer, or emphysema.   Many of them must have frequently mused in private: "If only some way could be found to convince the recalcitrant smokers to quit **before** they developed these conditions!"

Never ones to miss an opportunity in their quest for a smoke-free world the Antismoking Crusaders took on this daunting challenge in the later 1990s.   Spearheaded by the aforementioned Idealists in the medical community, an emphasis was put on taking the diagnostic criteria for the precursors of these conditions and then attaching the scary labels of the conditions themselves to those precursors. Thus, miraculously, millions of previously healthy smokers could be truthfully informed by their doctors that they had had heart attacks, were in the early stages of emphysema, or had "reversible" cancer in their oral/respiratory tracts.   Dr. Sidney Smith, a past Heart Association president, actually sees this sort of change in definition as a "positive thing," going on to note that "… it's hard to get patients to change" (Shari Roan. "Physicians Give Added Meaning…" *LA Times* 07/13/00).

Voila! Quit rates increased and perhaps many lives were extended (at least in theoretical duration if not always in actual quality). As with their support for the publicity surrounding the supposed danger of normal contact with secondary smoke, The Idealists saw sound science and good medical practice as secondary in importance to considering the potential number of lives extended. The end justified the means.

A lesson learned is a lesson to be repeated: we are now seeing the same strategies being employed in the war against fat. With a simple change of definition millions of people who would have been considered healthy in the year 1997 became "obese or overweight" in the year 1998. Just as taxes for social engineering are now being used with regard to cigarettes, so we are seeing such people as State Senator Deborah Ortiz (CA) seeking to implement taxes on soda in order to "*discourage consumption of those high-caloric beverages,*" and fight obesity! (consumer freedom_headlines@burst.sparklist.com04/17-18/02)

Why is such mutation of these medical terms a dangerous thing? Obviously the first casualty, in its purest sense, is truth. The public perception of and emotional reaction to these terms is largely based upon their historic meaning. The perceptions and reactions of individual patients are similarly based.

When someone was told they had a heart attack they knew it meant that part of their heart muscle had died, that they themselves had been close to dying, and that another such attack was likely to be imminent if they did not quickly mend their ways. When someone was told they had cancer, even in the early stages, they knew that they were skating closely with Death on a pond slanting toward an icy plunge. When someone was told they had emphysema or chronic obstructive pulmonary disease they knew that it usually meant that within a few short years they would be hooked up permanently to an oxygen bottle and would be lucky not to be dead within a few more years.

These understandings were important in ensuring that individuals who truly **were** at great risk of imminent death would recognize the necessity for rapid and drastic behavior changes. The average layperson depends on clear and under-standable communication with his or her health provider in order to be able to make correct and rational decisions about health care and lifestyle decisions.

To change the definitions without adequately informing and educating the public as to the nature of those changes was the same as simply propagating lies.   More than that, it was the equivalent of terrorizing people "for their own good" (at least as their "good" was seen by their doctors....) Inevitably, people will become aware of this duplicity: their faith in the medical profession and in the health advice given to them by their doctors will be tainted beyond recovery.

How many lives will be lost in the future because patients will no longer believe ANY of their doctors' diagnoses or will refuse to heed sound advice in situations of dire medical conditions where following such advice can be vital?   There are some individuals who quite seriously should never smoke: those with certain types of peripheral circulatory problems or with a congenitally based emphysema-related anomaly referred to as PIZZ. When such individuals are currently told by their doctors to quit smoking how many of them are now simply ignoring the advice with the attitude "Oh, that's what doctors always say." and then going on to suffer truly devastating medical results?

This is not fantasizing.   In July of 2002, researchers discovered precisely this phenomenon when they gave a subset of smoking subjects special counseling about a genetic defect that made them more likely to develop cancer.   Despite intensive efforts to communicate the special risk to these subjects the advice was almost universally ignored (McBride et al. *Cancer Epidemiology, Biomarkers and Prevention* 07/02).

How many will slough off more general advice about safe sex, proper use of medications, or the importance of improving one's diet or losing weight because of a general skepticism developed and encouraged by doctors' constant emphasis on advice to quit smoking?   It is impossible to say for sure, and it's even quite possible that more lives will be saved by these definition-deceptions than will be lost, but the one fact that we'll know for sure is that the truth and a patient's faith in their physician will have been undermined.

Playing with language as a tool for large-scale behavior modification is dangerous. When such play occurs in an area where decisions concerning imminent life and death are made, it goes beyond dangerous: it becomes outright criminal.

Language Conclusion

My discussion of the misuse and basic distortion of language by the Antismoking Crusade began with and ends with an emphasis on the danger of attempting to tinker with the thought processes of a citizenry by seeking to alter the definitions of words. Words are the units of our language and our thought: neither governments nor pressure groups have the right to seek to re-engineer their meanings in the pursuit of a "higher purpose."

In the past when people read George Orwell's *1984*, the ramifications of this idea sent chills up their spines. Today we are heading toward a society where such thought control by proxy will be accepted as the norm in engineering a better world and more perfect citizenry: as seen in Appendix J, Beyond Tobacco..., smoking is just the first of behavior changes envisioned by those who would force us into their visions of utopia.

2) Secondary Smoke

The great enemy of the truth is very often not the lie - deliberate, contrived, and dishonest - but the myth - persistent, persuasive, and unrealistic.

-- John F. Kennedy

Introduction

Secondary smoke is usually termed "second-hand smoke" by those seeking its elimination: the image of smoke already used and then being foisted off on others is distasteful and compelling. The fact that we are all breathing a good quantity of second hand air in public places is never thought of. A more neutral designation sometimes used is Environmental Tobacco Smoke (ETS). A third term, "secondary smoke," is less pejorative than the former term and more concise and widely understood than the latter and as such is used here.

The next few pages will digress from the concentration on the psychological aspects of the Crusade to take a brief but hard look at what secondary smoke actually is and what exposure to it means. The reason for this digression will be made clear afterwards when we examine how Antismokers have used the concept of secondary smoke to create unreasonable fears.

The Chemistry of Secondary Smoke

As noted earlier in the chapter on Language, about 90% of secondary smoke is composed of water and ordinary air with a slight excess of carbon dioxide. Another 4% is carbon monoxide, a gas that can act as a poison when in sufficient quantity by reducing the amount of oxygen your red blood cells can carry.

The last 6% contains the rest of the 4,000 or so chemicals supposedly to be found in smoke... but found, obviously, in very small quantities (*1989 Report of the Surgeon General* p. 80).

Most of these chemicals can only be found in quantities measured in nanograms, picograms and femtograms. Many cannot even be detected in these amounts: their presence is simply theorized rather than measured. To bring those quantities into a real world perspective, take a saltshaker and shake out a few grains of salt. A single grain of that salt will weigh in the ballpark of 100 **million** picograms! (Allen Blackman. *Chemistry Magazine* 10/08/01).

To refer back to our earlier example of arsenic, a nonsmoker would have to work with a smoker 8 hours a day, 5 days a week, 50 weeks a year, for well over a hundred years to be exposed to a quantity of arsenic equal to one grain of salt. While a lot of waitresses and bartenders may **feel** as if they've worked a hundred years at their jobs, there really aren't too many who actually have.

And, again as noted earlier, far from all 4,000 of those chemicals are normally labeled as toxic in the first place, with the 1989 Surgeon Generals' Report only noting that "some" are... without reference to how many or to what amounts would be considered toxic. One of the most basic principles of scientific toxicology is that "The Dose Makes The Poison."... a fact **always** ignored by Crusaders.

When speaking of secondary smoke many Antismokers will also refer to the "40 carcinogenic compounds" it supposedly contains. In reality only six of those have in fact been classified as "known human carcinogens" (*1989 Report of the Surgeon General*. pgs. 86-87). Most of the rest of the 40 compounds have shown insufficient evidence of being human carcinogens and many are commonly found in foods, coffee, and the general environment (*Science*, 258: 261-265 (1992). The exposure of nonsmokers to the six actual human carcinogens is usually so minuscule as to be almost imaginary in nature and is sometimes far less than other everyday environmental exposures.

Secondary smoke is the mix of all of the smoke that enters the air in a room where someone is smoking, both the smoke exhaled by the smoker **and** the smoke coming off the tip of the cigarette. You've heard the claim that secondary smoke is twice as bad as what the smoker gets? In a way this is true: if you held your nose a quarter inch above the burning end of a cigarette and inhaled a slow deep breath through your nostrils you'd be getting a concentration of smoke and its chemicals twice as great as what the smoker is pulling into his or her mouth.

In the real world no one does that. Even the most hardened of smokers would generally be reduced to paroxysms of coughing from such concentrated inhalation. The secondary smoke that a nonsmoker comes in contact with is usually an extremely diluted mixture of exhaled smoke and the smoke produced directly from the cigarette's tip.

Something that's usually forgotten in the rush of concern about the nonsmoker is that the smoker is **also** breathing all the secondary smoke produced, and, given the closer proximity to the source, the smoker is inhaling it in far greater quantities and concentrations than most nonsmokers ever would! If the concerns about the dangers of secondary smoke were really true it would make perfect sense for a smoker with a smoking guest to insist that the guest go outside to smoke even if they were both smoking at the same time. Indeed, smokers would want to rush outside themselves out of fear of their own secondary smoke!

The exact chemical composition of secondary smoke depends largely upon how many seconds it's been in the air. Just as happens in the case of most combustion products, the chemicals change and break down very quickly, and some elements will tend to settle toward the floor or deposit themselves on walls or curtains. In pursuit of some arguments Antismokers want to assume from the start that secondary smoke is carcinogenic: this is when they will claim that it's chemically very similar to mainstream smoke. However, when they want to argue that comparing secondary smoke exposure to "cigarette equivalents" is unfair (This method generally produces very low measures of exposure... sometimes as low as six cigarettes per year even for bartenders), they will claim that it's chemically very **different** than mainstream smoke and can't be compared in that way!

No, I am not kidding... this is an example of the type of doublethink that I call the "Catch 22" argument later on. It's very useful as an argumentation technique unless the opponent both notices it and has the time available to fully show how both sides of the street are being straddled by the shape-shifting opponent. The later chapter on Fallacious Argumentation looks at this verbal scamming tool in more detail.

In examining what risk there could be to a nonsmoker we need to develop and accept an estimate as to how much smoke a nonsmoker is likely to inhale when around one or more smokers. Rather than go into mathematical detail here, the supporting figures are presented in Appendix B. Those figures will show that, in most reasonably ventilated situations, whether a private home with one or two smokers, or a bar with dozens or hundreds of them, a nonsmoker will usually be exposed to the equivalent of about a thousandth of a cigarette or less per hour.

It could well be argued that anyone concerned at all about secondary smoke shouldn't be in such a Free-Choice bar or restaurant to begin with, since there are many venues that have already banned smoking on their own; but Crusading activists generally insist that even if 95 out of 100 businesses are "smoke-free" that smokers should not have the right to keep those last five places to themselves and their friends. This is not in any sense an exaggeration or misrepresentation: Antismokers call it "leveling the playing field" and it has served as the basis for many legislated universal bans.

The need for such leveling arises because, despite Crusaders' claims to the contrary, restaurants and bars that accommodate both smokers and nonsmokers almost invariably do better business than ones with total bans. Nonsmokers want an atmosphere that is comfortable, clean, and well ventilated: they are usually quite happy to accompany their smoking friends to establishments that meet those criteria while allowing those friends to smoke without being forced outside. The only exceptions to this rule occur when an establishment is truly one of the few in its geographic/economic niche that has such a ban: in that case there can often be enough of a specialty demand to make up for other losses.

To return to the chemistry of smoke, let us look at the 6 elements in tobacco smoke that IARC (The International Agency for Research on Cancer) classifies as Class A (Human) carcinogens. One of those is arsenic, which we looked at earlier. You'll remember that you'd have to sit in a room with a smoker smoking 165,000 cigarettes to be exposed to as much arsenic as you would get from a large glass of water.

What about the other five carcinogens though? Are nonsmokers likely to be exposed to enough of those to have them correctly perceived as threats? While most of them occur in even smaller quantities than arsenic (naphthylamine, aminobi-phenyl, vinyl chloride and chromium average only about fifteen nanograms apiece), let's look at the one with the largest quantity present so as to clearly make the case that is least favorable to our own argument. This is benzene: a human carcinogen that cigarettes produce in quantities not measured in picograms nor even in nanograms, but in micrograms, a unit that is one million times larger than a picogram, but still only one one-millionth of a single gram (*1989 Report of the Surgeon General.* p.87)

The average cigarette produces roughly 300 micrograms of benzene (*1986 Report of the Surgeon General.* p.130). If the estimates of smoke exposure for the average nonsmoker in Appendix B hold true, then such exposure would equal roughly three tenths of a microgram per hour of sharing a space with a reasonable number of smokers in a decently ventilated public indoor setting.

Benzene is normally found in fruits, fish, vegetables, nuts, dairy products, beverages, and eggs. The National Cancer Institute estimates that an individual may **safely** ingest up to 250 micrograms in their food per day, every single day of the year. Thus, the "safe" exposure to benzene from **one day** of a normal diet is roughly equal to the exposure experienced by a nonsmoker sharing an airspace with smokers for over 750 hours. Another way of looking at it would be to compare it to the normal work exposure of a waiter in a decently ventilated Free-Choice restaurant: the waiter would have to work there for **four months** to receive the equivalent benzene dosage ingested in one day of a "safe" diet.

In 1994, the Air Resources Board of California estimated that California vehicles emitted close to 50 million pounds (i.e. about 23 billion grams) of benzene per year into the atmosphere of California. At 300 micrograms per cigarette, it would take 70 trillion cigarettes to produce what California's vehicles produce in a single year. Try to imagine all the smokers of the entire world, with each and every one of them smoking well over two hundred cigarettes a day, and all crowded into California, and you'll have a rough comparison to California's normal vehicle emissions.

During the course of New York and Philadelphia City Council hearings on vastly enlarging existing smoking bans, Crusaders trotted out the claim that the recently enacted smoking bans in California had reduced the lung cancer rate there by 14%. The claim seemed impressive unless one realized several things. First of all, smoking related lung cancer generally has a time lag of between 20 and 40 years, while the total indoor bans in California were only in place about three years when the claims were being made. Secondly, California has led the country in the past thirty years in reducing vehicle emissions and correcting its air pollution problems. And thirdly, the age composition and immigration patterns for the state have changed enormously over the past few decades.

By picking one particular statistic however, and ignoring all the background variables, confounders, and other scientific factors, testifying Crusaders were able to mount a convincing and seemingly powerful argument to City Councilors in both cities. Of course they also helped their case by not mentioning that they got the figure from a study that ended two years **before** California's universal smoking ban was enacted! (*Master Plan For a Smoke-Free California*: www.dhs.cahwnet.gov/tobacco /documents/ TobaccoMasterPlan2003.pdf)

The other four human carcinogens in the smoke from a cigarette, all added together, equal less than a single microgram, thus contributing to an exposure for the average nonsmoker in a smoking environment of roughly one nanogram or one one-billionth of a gram per hour (*1986 Report of the Surgeon General* p. 130, *1989 Report of the Surgeon General* p. 87, and Appendix B). Such a level of contact would never be considered as a "risk" for any substance not associated with tobacco smoke.

It's not just carcinogens that Antismokers worry about though. There's now a push to put a label on packs that will warn folks that "*cigarettes contain formaldehyde, used in preserving corpses.*" Now isn't **that** a pleasant thought? Of course the Crusaders never want to mention the **amount** of formaldehyde produced (less than one third of a single thousandth of a gram) or the fact that cooking a healthy vegetarian dinner at a gas stove puts roughly 100 times this amount into the air for your family to breathe (Huber et al. "Smoke and Mirrors." *Regulation* 16:3:44. 1993).

The situation is the same for almost all the compounds in smoke that the Antismokers point their fingers at. Upon examining the amounts of the substances involved and checking the values of OSHA and EPA safe concentrations for them, you would find that you'd have to be locked up in a small un-ventilated bar with hundreds, thousands, or even millions of smokers before even approaching levels thought to be unsafe by actual government standards. Appendix B presents a number of examples in a well-formatted table. You'll note that in the real world significant concentrations of **any** of the supposedly dangerous elements in secondary smoke would never actually occur.

The Use of Secondary Smoke

Now that we have seen the infinitesimal quantities involved and seen also how the threat from such levels of exposure is likewise incredibly low, the question asserts itself: why has such an enormous amount of attention been focused on secondary smoke over the past 30 years? Why would government agencies, health organizations and doctors *lie* to us about something like this? What possible motivation could there be for creating, spreading, and perpetuating such a monstrous lie? The answer lies in the power of the tools and opportunities that the fear of secondary smoke makes available to the Crusaders.

In the past Antismokers had to rely on either the arguments of the Moralists, the power of taxation, or the cogency of the fear of one's own mortality to convince smokers to give up their nasty habit. Even after the Surgeon General's Report came out in 1964 and publicly concluded that cigarette smoking was a primary cause of lung cancer in America, the vast majority of smokers kept on smoking, and tens of millions more people started smoking. The threat to one's own health proved to be insufficient to bring about the radical behavior change needed to satisfy those responsible for the public health.

In the 1970s we saw the advent of the concept of secondary smoke as a threat to all rather than merely an annoyance to some. At first mainstream health organizations such as the American Cancer Society (ACS) and the American Lung Association were slow to jump on the bandwagon of the more radical Antismoking Crusaders leading the parade. In the mid 1970s the ACS (along with the Lung and Heart Associations) even refused to ban smoking in its own offices. The ACS claimed such a move was "too dictatorial." They may also have been influenced by the stark fact that as of that time there were **no** studies of any type indicating **any** level of threat to long-term health from the low levels of exposure that nonsmokers would normally experience (Don Matchan. *We Mind If You Smoke.* Pyramid Press. 1977 p.124).

But as the 1970s progressed we saw the acceptance by mainstream health organizations of the necessity for pushing the concept of secondary smoke as a danger. In 1975 Sir George Godber, British delegate to the World Health Organization, presented his blueprint for eliminating tobacco use worldwide by changing social attitudes. (See Figure 11).

> *"...it would be essential to foster an atmosphere where it was perceived that active smokers would injure those around them, especially their family and any infants or young children who would be exposed involuntarily to ETS."*
>
> -- Sir George Godber's plan, referring to the worldwide elimination of smoking. 1975 UN 3rd World Conference on Smoking and Health (Huber et al. *Consumers Research Magazine.* 04/92).

Figure 11

Sir Godber's proposal is one of the Antismoking Crusade's best-kept secrets: the ETS battle strategy was decided upon years before any of the epidemiological research supposedly linking second-ary smoke to long-term health consequences had been produced. This pre-setting of a desired conclusion regardless of what evidence may be found to support it is precisely one of the grounds that formed the basis for the judicial nullification of the EPA Report. But in the public mind, the myth has taken root. As Hitler's Minister of Propaganda knew all too well, *"A lie repeated often enough becomes the truth."*

Finally in the mid 1980's some epidemiological studies were conducted that supported, although weakly and with mixed results, the concept that intense exposure to secondary smoke in an enclosed home or work setting for periods of forty or more years could slightly increase one's absolute risk of developing lung cancer. Not a single study in the 1980s was able to produce a statistically significant result relating social contact such as would occur in restaurants or other enclosed public settings to cancer. None dealt with work exposures in situations with modern ventilation either. This latter is not really their fault: since they were using epidemiological data based largely on smoking habits in the homes and workplaces of the 1940s, 50s, and 60s, they realistically had no way to correct for this.

The EPA does not have this excuse. By the 1990s, when issuing a report that was specifically intended to impact widespread social and business behavior into the decades of the next century, such a factor should obviously have been recognized and taken into account. However, if they **had** tried to correct for the effects of improved ventilation technology, their desired conclusion as to the deadliness of secondary smoke would have been thrown out from the start. Not a very scientifically valid excuse, but a politically understandable one.

The motivation behind the secondary smoke scare is clear to any who look, but unfortunately most Americans have simply accepted media headlines as fact without realizing the existence of a hidden agenda. A table summarizing the results of studies from the early 1980s through the late 1990s is presented in Appendix A along with some analysis.

Note that while Crusaders often speak of the results of these studies as being "unanimous and unequivocal" in point of fact only about one in ten of them showed significant positive findings, and a good number even produced NEGATIVE findings (Negative findings indicate that exposure to tobacco smoke might have actually **reduced** the incidence of later lung cancer occurrence!)

Unfortunately for the Crusading cause, the idea that mere occasional social exposure to tobacco smoke in public places could be of significant long-term harm was initially **so** outrageous that it was difficult to get legal force behind smoking bans.   With the publication of the EPA Report however, Crusading groups realized that a powerful tool had been put at their disposal: the cry to protect the health of American workers.

Lawsuits and laws reducing or eliminating smoking in public settings began to be based on the purported health risk to workers exposed for eight hours a day, five days a week. Thus, suddenly, the power of the Occupational Safety and Health Administration was added to the arsenal of the Antismokers.

In addition to using the fear of the effects of secondary smoke on the health of workers to bring the power of OSHA to focus on smoking bans, one of the more extreme Antismoking groups, ASH, discovered a way to create yet another level of big government pressure.   In a press release reproduced on their web site they have proclaimed that *"...a cloud of tobacco smoke contamination constitutes as great a barrier to access* (to a public facility*) as flights of stairs present to a disabled person in a wheelchair"* ("The Americans with Disabilities Act As Applicable to Nonsmokers." www.setinc.com/ash/papers/ h211.htm).

With this pronouncement ASH tried to equate the image of wheelchair bound people trying to drag themselves and their chairs up flights of stairs with the plight of a nonsmoker trying to walk past a few smokers near a doorway on their way into a building. Such equation, if accepted, would bring the full legal power of the Americans with Disabilities Act into play and lay the groundwork for extensive smoking bans even outdoors!

As the Virginian-Pilot opined without basis in an editorial: *"Walking through a cloud of smoke – even briefly – when entering a building is hazardous to your health.... moving smokers away from public areas is a reasonable policy"* (*Virginian-Pilot* 12/06/2001). The truly astonishing thing is that Antismokers have actually had the political clout to push laws through City Councils on the basis of such phantasmagorical arguments!

As with OSHA and the EPA, the Antismoking Crusaders have weakened the real intent of the ADA with this abuse. We've already seen such incredible statements as that made by Julia Kendall of the Chemical Injury Litigation Project about the need for protection against "scents": *"No one should be wearing perfume to the theater. Why should we have brain damage because people are wearing toxic chemicals?"* (Quoted in Michael Fumento, "Sick of It All." *Reason* June 1996, p.26)

Eventually as more and more bizarre things are brought under the purview of these agencies we'll see their power weakened to the point where their real functions will be damaged. And then, sadly, we'll all be the losers for it. As mentioned earlier, we've already lived through the 1990s fiasco of the FDA concentrating so much energy on getting control over tobacco that it let an application for anthrax vaccine languish on its shelves until after anthrax was loosed on the public years later.

Conclusion

Let me include a final and somewhat amusing note on secondary smoke to bring our spirits back up. Antismokers have historically been partial to using scatological imagery to add impact to their descriptions of tobacco smoke in the air. Sometimes these are deliberately humorous, (as in "Do you mind if I smoke? No, do YOU mind if I fart?"), and sometimes unintentionally so, (as one Antismoker found when she reduced a TV hostess to laughter by comparing smoking to wandering around a restaurant placing warm buckets of manure on everyone's tables – [*"It's Your Call with Lynn Doyle"* 07/14/01 – Gabrielle LeVecque and Regina Carlson]), but one of the most common of such arguments concerns public swimming pools.

In this argument the Antismoker will state as fact that having a nonsmoking area in a restaurant is like having a non-pissing section in a swimming pool. This image has power unless you think about it for a minute or two, but the "naughtiness" of the image usually precludes the idea of such closer examination.

In reality of course the restaurant changes its air six times or more every hour. The pool water is lucky if it's changed twice in a **year**! The analogy is imperfect by a factor of about 15,000 air/water changes!! In addition, any decently designed non-smoking section will have an air current that will be toward, rather than from, the smoking section. Pissing somewhere down stream in a river (as almost every riverside American city does) would be a more appropriate analogy than pissing in a pool.

Let me make a final observation: if any adult out there seriously thinks they can dive into a public pool with a hundred screaming kids and NO piss... they probably also believe in the tooth fairy!

Those who would like a far more detailed look at the various studies that have been done on secondary smoke and the criticisms of claims that have been made about it will find a wealth of information at the FORCES web page on the subject at www.forces.org/evidence/ets-whop/index.htm. It is also worth looking at an essay by Dr. Elizabeth M. Whelan, the director of the American Council on Science and Health. Even though she is known to be strongly against smoking and Big Tobacco, and despite the fact that she generally approves of smoking bans, she feels strongly that the hype generated around secondary smoke has been more harmful than helpful ("Warning: Overstating the Case...." www.acsh.org/forum/ tobacco/index.html).

I'll end this chapter with a thought provoking news item:

> *Research by the National Cheng Kung University in Taiwan revealed that the level of an incense chemical believed to cause lung cancer was 40 times higher in a temple than in places where people smoked tobacco! ... churches that use it, notably the Catholic Church, said use was so minimal that any risk to congregations was inconsequential* (Alan Samson.*NewsMax*08/20/01).

Toxic smoke inconsequential? *Heretics!*

...the rejection of truth and the acceptance of unproven hypotheses to further one's concept of ethics or social justice is wrong too. Many studies involving secondhand smoke are not convincing, and answers about whether it causes lung cancer are far from established. Unfortunately, it has become customary to torture the data until they confess.

We need more science, less hyperbole and less enthusiasm for unproven points of view.

-- Dildar Ahmad MD, W. Keith Morgan, MD, Chest Diseases Unit; London Health Sciences Centre, *CMAJ* 1998;159:441-2

Figure 12

3) The Spectre of Death

Despite the fact that the initial proclamation targeting smoking as a cause of lung cancer and heart disease did not lead to the habit's disappearance, that proclamation did produce a sizeable drop of more than 20% in the American smoking rate.   The Crusaders have tried ever since to continue making progress by ramping up such fear with ever more dire pronouncements about the number of deaths due to smoking:

> *400,000 deaths per year* (CDC).   *20 million deaths since 1950* (Ed Shaw of the "Ruth and Ed Shaw Show").   *10 million more in the next 20 years* (*BBC online* <medical_ notes/newsid _473000/473673.stm>). *10 million EACH YEAR in decades to come* (Dr. H. Nakajima, Director-General of WHO, 1997). *ONE BILLION in the next century* (Robert Proctor, author of *The Nazi War on Smoking*, 2001; Emphases added)

The primary tool used to generate these horrific numbers that are so freely thrown around in the press is a computer program called SAMMEC (Smoking Attributable Morbidity, Mortality and Economic Costs). Of course what's never mentioned in any of these pronouncements of doom, as with the pronouncements about secondary smoke, is that they're based on a number of funny assumptions and theorized statistical projections rather than on actual known deaths.

First of all, we need to understand that all the various formulas and risk ratios used by SAMMEC are **assumed** to be correct. Some human being, sitting at a computer console somewhere has typed in something like "Smoker Lung Cancer

Death Rate = 15 Times Normal Lung Cancer Death Rate." If that assumption (or any of the other hundreds of assumptions that are made in deciding what figures to input) is wrong, then the total number produced by the program will be wrong.

Of course, to be fair, it should be noted that these numbers are not totally arbitrary. They represent estimates someone has made after examining the bulk of the studies that have been done and usually represent the best estimates available from researchers prominent in their fields. But still, they **are** estimates made by fallible human beings, and not necessarily accurate ones given all the sources of bias and error along the way to their ultimate derivation. An additional valid criticism of SAMMEC can be based on the fact that a good chunk of the supposed deaths come from conditions showing a relative risk of significantly less than 2.0, and as noted in Figure 9, such findings are usually treated with a serious degree of caution.

SAMMEC also generally, and incredibly, does not try to correct for such things as the correlation of smoking with drinking, economic status, diet, drug use or medical care. Thus a poor, fat, stoned out alcoholic couch potato who gets a heart attack and also happens to smoke will likely be counted as a "death due to smoking" despite the other factors involved. The structure and methods of SAMMEC have been criticized by others and many of those criticisms can be found at the forces.org website or at Steve Milloy's JunkScience.com website.

Secondly, when applied to long-term projections, SAMMEC's figures assume, as in the case mentioned earlier concerning secondary smoke, that ALL medical progress grinds to an immediate halt; and/or conversely, they assume as well that all poverty-related, parasitic and infectious diseases are cured while all smoking related diseases are still running rampant. Either assumption is obviously, to use a technical term, bananas.

Thirdly, the ages at which these deaths occur are usually glossed over. A US Senator gave a 1994 speech in which he proclaimed, "Tobacco is killing our children!" and was echoed in 2003 by ProtectMontanaKids.org that worded it as "Tobacco is killing our kids." Neither the Senator nor the Crusading group mention that most of those theoretical deaths will occur after the age of 70, with more than 15% of them even occurring after the age of 85! Most of us would be well pleased if we knew that our children were going to reach such ages. However, given the recent effort by Crusaders to redefine the term "middle age" to include 69 year-olds, their claim that almost half the deaths occur in middle age can claim to have at least some fragment of truth in it if one references the proper Newspeak Dictionary. (Levy & Marimont. "Lies, Damned Lies, and 400,000 Smoking Related Deaths." *Regulation* Vol.21 #4, 1998).

The Senator does not stand alone in this sort of usage. The Atlanta Journal Constitution had an article on 10/8/96 that noted, *"If current tobacco-use patterns persist, five million kids nationwide who are 17 or younger will die because of a smoking habit...."* This was followed in the same newspaper a few months later when the National Center for Tobacco-Free Kids took out a three quarter page ad that proclaimed in big black letters **"The Lives of Five Million Kids Are About to Go Up In Smoke"** (*Atlanta Journal Constitution* 12/18/96). Such claims deliberately blur and ignore the difference between a 15 year-old dying and an 85 year-old dying... a difference that is generally rather important to parents.

About the only statistic more outrageous than this that has made it to public print comes from a newspaper article claiming that *"In schools across our area, students have been telling their peers to stay off the stuff because it kills one in five Americans each year"* (http://fredericksburg.com/News/FLS/2001/062001/06222001/314710).

For the mathematically challenged that equates to over 50 million Americans a year meeting the grinning reaper. If these numbers were true America would be populated by nothing but rabbits within five years! The figures concerning proportions of smoker deaths due to smoking have risen from claims in the 1970s that one smoker in five dies from their habit to claims in the new millennium that one in every two dies from smoking! At this rate we're likely to see claims in the near future that there are more smoking related deaths than there are smokers (Given the possibilities of statistical double counting techniques this is actually not out of the question).

Some of the fantastic figures used in ad campaigns concerning secondary smoke are just as specious. Not only are they almost always based on the squirrelly EPA figures for lung cancer, but they often include tens of thousands of extra hypothesized deaths due to heart disease. The connection between heart disease and secondary smoke was so tenuous that not even the EPA tried to include such figures in its original report!

But the fear of death is indeed a powerful motivator, and the bigger the numbers and the scarier the threats the more powerful that fear becomes. Thus, despite the very shaky grounds that many of these numbers are based on, Antismoking Crusaders continue to brandish them at every conceivable opportunity: just listen to the next few news reports you hear about smoking and see how often they appear simply as side editorial commentary on whatever story or study is being covered! They have become truisms: part of the basic superstitious mythos of our supposedly modern and scientifically objective society, made all the more holy by being framed in the structures of mathematics and statistics.

4) Pregnancy

Just as we instinctively react protectively to a threat to a child, so too do we react to a threat to an expectant mother. The mere suggestion that casual contact with secondary tobacco smoke might harm a pregnancy is enough to instantly garner masses of support for wide-ranging bans despite the fact that there's literally no evidence at all that such harm exists. The lack of evidence has not slowed down the Antismokers who see the special emotional vulnerability of a mother-to-be.

The studies that have been done on smoking and pregnancy have generally focused on the effects on a baby of the smoking habit of a mother herself and are often confused with those examining secondary smoke exposure either prenatally or after birth. This confusion often seems at least partly deliberate: the evidence for the chances of some degree of harm from maternal pre-natal smoking itself is far more substantial than any evidence concerning secondary smoke exposure by an expectant mother. It is also partly circumstantial: it's hard to find substantial numbers of cases where women are exposed to smoke while pregnant but not after giving birth.

Evidence of such deliberate confusion-mongering can be seen in the presentation of a 1998 study that examined the effects of maternal smoking on infants' likelihood of developing wheezing sounds during post birth instances of viral infection. The study was explicitly designed to avoid confusion of maternal smoking with exposure to secondary smoke. This fact doesn't stop the Crusaders at the American Lung Association however: their headline on the study reads: "Tobacco Smoke Exposure Can Harm Babies' Lungs Two Months Before Birth." News reporters focusing on the headline and simply skimming the abstract were all too ready to report that casual contact with tobacco smoke during pregnancy was threatening babies throughout the world! (http://www.lungusa.org/press/tobacco/asnbabies.html)

Of course there is a side benefit to the Antismoking Crusade from their focus on smoke exposure during pregnancy: mothers themselves are prime candidates for quitting smoking. If the mother can be made to believe that even wisps of smoke from a cigarette across the room are harmful to a fetus then it will be far easier to convince her that it is absolutely vital that she stop her own smoking. The pressure to quit out of guilt intensifies as doctors, family, and even strangers on the street feel justified in harassing the mother-to-be about "smoking while in that condition." The harm produced by the stress of such interactions has not been studied, but it would seem reasonable to assume that such stress could produce more real harm to a fetus than low levels of maternal smoking.

Given the strength of the fears that have been stirred up around the issue, it is quite likely that there have been extreme cases of psychological and emotional abuse of women by Antismoking partners who feel that the smoking mother is recklessly endangering their unborn child. Unfortunately it's also quite possible that there have even been cases of physical abuse resulting in both maternal and fetal death on these grounds.

One case that was documented in the media concerned the mayor of London. According to press accounts he "manhandled" his pregnant girlfriend at a public event when he caught her smoking and his abuse was extreme enough to spark a brawl (*Associated Press* 06/23/02). A more extreme example is examined later in the chapter on Hate: in that case the pregnant woman was **shot** by an angry Antismoker in a parking lot!

While heavy smoking during a pregnancy is certainly something that a woman should do her best to avoid, light levels of smoking seem to be of significantly less concern. Alcohol use, poverty, poor diet, or simply not getting good prenatal care can all be more serious factors than light tobacco use. For women who find it relatively easy to give up smoking during a pregnancy it's probably a good idea to do so: there are indications that maternal smoking increases the chances of preterm births, low-birth-weight babies and several rare but more serious conditions. For those to whom quitting poses more difficulty the option of cutting down to lower levels of smoking should be considered.

Using a mother's fear for the welfare of her gestating child in order to secretly manipulate her behavior for generalized social goals is nothing short of despicable, but it's been done by the Antismoking Crusaders ever since the successful poster campaign of the 70s entitled "Don't Start a Life Under a Cloud." The secondary smoke spin is the only thing new about today's efforts.

One particularly horrendous example of misusing such parental love was highlighted in a TV production a few years back that featured a mother and father in a living room with their two profoundly retarded children. Some doctor had told them --

and they fully believed and repeated such to the TV crew -- that it was unquestionably their smoking that had destroyed their children's chances for normal lives. The lifelong guilt inspired by such misinformation, particularly if such guilt is being inspired more frequently in our society as time goes on, is appalling to even imagine.

Expectant mothers should strive to lead the healthiest lives possible during their pregnancies: eating right, exercising moderately, getting proper pre-natal care, avoiding or cutting back on alcohol, tobacco and perhaps even caffeine and chocolate. These choices however should not be dictated by the state or by manipulative special interest groups. Using a woman's pregnant condition as an opening to browbeat her over the choices she has made, or using it to win unjustified public sympathy for the support of bans purporting to "protect the mother and her baby," is a low point for even the most strident Antismokers.

5) Saving The Children

Protecting innocent and defenseless children is an almost universal aspect of the basic human psychobiological system. The knowledge of the extreme emotional reaction experienced by the average person when confronted with any threats to the safety and well being of children has been used by war propagandists since time immemorial (See Figure 13).

Whom is Cruella Deville mean to? Not just dogs, but "puppies." How did Hitler rev up the Germans? By picturing evil Jews corrupting Aryan children and then drinking their blood in secret ceremonies. How did George Bush Sr. capture the energies of the American people and direct them against Saddam Hussein? By playing on an image of Iraqi soldiers grabbing incubators and dumping premature babies onto cold linoleum floors.

Protecting our children is such a primal human instinct that the use of it in any political argument should be immediately suspect. Unfortunately, the blatant obviousness of this propaganda ploy is usually not enough to deter its use: the raw power of the imagery is far too useful to manipulators.

Adolph Hitler said in Mein Kampf: "*The state must declare the child to be the most precious treasure of the people.*"

As Rabbi Daniel Lapin has noted, Hitler believed "*that as long as the government is perceived as working for the benefit of the children, the people will happily endure almost any curtailment of liberty and almost any deprivation.... In the name of the children, incursions into the private lives of American citizens have been made that (the) Nazis would have gazed at with open mouthed admiration.*"

www.towardtradition.org/pubs/hitlerletter.htm

Figure 13

Antismoking Crusaders have never been shy about playing the "save the children" card but the use of this stratagem has increased notably in recent years as the power of their other arguments has started to fade with repetition and familiarity. It has become a common phenomenon for children to be dragged to City Council hearings by parent activists to testify that they are being choked to death by the fumes of evil smokers in public places. Mothers even bring toddlers to hearings primarily concerning smoking in bars and actually dress them up in little gas masks to show the urgent need for fast implementation of universal bans.

Children and Cigarette Litter

Taking this to an even more absurd extreme, Antismokers will produce tearfully emoting grandmotherly types seeking bans on open-air smoking by conjuring up verbal images of piles of dead children on beaches and in sandboxes who have had the mis-fortune of ingesting carelessly discarded cigarette butts (op. cit. "*It's Your Call With Lynn Doyle*"). A quick check of Poison Control Center and CDC stats puts the lie to this particular scary image.

For the record: I have been able to find absolutely **no** news or reports of incidents of children dying on beaches or in playground sandboxes or anywhere else in public from eating carelessly discarded cigarette butts, though there are tens of thousands of incidents of children drowning at beaches or dying at home from ingesting household cleaners and medications, or even simply by choking on hot dogs. Ingestion of tobacco products by children occurs 98% of the time in the child's own home, not in public places, and usually results in nothing more than an upset tummy and a frantic mom. If there have ever been any number of serious cases of child endangerment from ingestion of publicly discarded tobacco products it somehow seems to have avoided the eyes and ears of the news media and Antismoking advocates (CDC's MMWR of 2/14/97).

The hypocrisy of the recent emphasis on the necessity of smoking bans as a means of controlling child-endangering litter is evident when one looks at who shows up at public debates and hearings on the issue. Representatives of those actually involved in sanitation are virtually invisible compared to the presence and activity of Crusaders from Antismoking organizations, and the figures presented on cigarette litter are distorted in ways that make a relatively small problem seem earth shaking in its urgency.

Numbers are played with in ways that would make a third grader blush: one article in Seventeen magazine posited that lining up 12,000 one-inch cigarette butts would create a line, not 1/5th of a mile long, but 146 miles long -- off by a factor of about 1,000 times. Other figures in that same article examined the weight of those butts that the NY Sanitation Department had to clean up from Times Square and arrived at a scary figure that would have required each butt to weigh roughly **three pounds!** (Café Column. *Seventeen*. 5/22/96). Talk about treating truth lightly!

Entering the realm of the outright silly, the Crusader speaking on the Lynn Doyle show referenced earlier claimed that one of the reasons her group was pushing for open air beach bans was because of the fire hazard. Note: this was in reference **not** to boardwalks, but to the smoking on the sand, next to the ocean. On the sand. Next to the ocean. Fire hazard?!?

The entire issue of world environmentalism is called into play on the web pages of www.cigarettelitter.org as a theoretical threat to the world's marine life is claimed. However, if one uses the figures on those pages and computes world water volume vs. number of smokers it becomes clear that it would take all the smokers of the world littering at will over tens of thousands of years to even form the beginnings of a general problem. Of course such computation is never done by the Crusaders making the argument since it would undermine the entire issue of a real environmental threat.

Any kind of litter, including cigarette litter, is unsightly, inconsiderate, and a form of environmental pollution. The solution to smokers who litter should be sought in a combination of better provision of receptacles when smokers are forced outdoors and stricter enforcement of littering laws on everyone. Whipping up fears of poisoned toddlers and oceanic fires to justify outdoor smoking bans is a cheap and nasty tactic.

In any event such bans are an unreasonable response to a litter problem caused by a small minority of smokers. Using such logic it would be reasonable to ban fast food outlets from cities since take-out wrappings generate so much trash. As is the case with so much of the activity and well-funded media splash created by Crusading organizations, the purported goal of reducing litter is usually nothing more than a cover for the real goal, eliminating smoking.

Secondary Smoke and Asthma

Referring to another aspect of the threat of smoking to children, there have in fact been some studies that may explain the mysterious rise in asthma cases that we've seen over the last few decades as smoking in the home drastically decreased. Smoking around children in today's homes is far less common than it was twenty or thirty years ago. Yet, adult and childhood asthma cases have increased from approximately 6.7 million in 1980 to 17.3 million in 1998, according to the Centers for Disease Control and Prevention. This finding was backed up by a 20-year intergenerational study in the British Medical Journal that found asthma rates doubling between 1976 and 1996 while smoking rates were halved ("...Baffling Surge in Asthma." *New York Times* 10/18/99; Upton et al. "Intergenerational..." *BMJ* 08/00).

Indeed, according to the most recent studies on urine cotinine levels in children it would appear that these asthma rates have doubled while childhood exposure to secondary smoke has been cut by 75%. How can this be explained? (www.cdc.gov/exposure repor4t; CDC 2001 National Report On Human Exposure To Environmental Chemicals).

One possible explanation for these surprising findings is offered by the results of a recent, well-designed and very large study (about 10,000 cases) conducted in Sweden and reported in a journal devoted to allergic and asthmatic problems. The study indicated that children exposed to moderate levels of tobacco smoke in the home while growing up were appreciably **less** likely to develop atopic/allergic disorders and this finding actually showed strong and consistent levels of statistical significance!

To quote from the Abstract:

> *In a multivariate analysis, children of mothers who smoked at least 15 cigarettes a day tended to have lower odds for suffering from allergic rhino-conjunctivitis, allergic asthma, atopic eczema and food allergy..., (ORs 0.6-0.7). Children of fathers who had smoked at least 15 cigarettes a day had a similar tendency (ORs 0.7-0.9).* (Clin Exp Allergy 2001 Jun;31(6):908-14).

Whether such exposures have an actual causal effect in relation to reduced levels of allergy and asthma needs further research, but the Swedish study does clearly indicate the possibility of a protective effect, perhaps similar to that which may exist for lung cancer and childhood exposure to smoke (See Appendix A), perhaps through a mechanism involving early challenges to the immune system or perhaps just due to a build-up of tolerance to normal environmental impurities.

Again though, one shouldn't jump to conclusions of causality on the basis of epidemiology unless the case is both strong and consistent across a large number of studies. In this area there are indeed other studies showing conflicting effects, and even this study itself might be explained by such a simple confounder as smoking homes often having better ventilation! ORs of 0.8 don't meet the epidemiological standards previously set forth any better than the EPA results, although at least here the results **did** meet normal statistical significance standards.

Children as Political Pawns

The power of using children for political ends is seen in a more active way when Crusaders give them free t-shirts for attending rallies, offer them prizes for creating posters designed to make smokers seem dirty or stupid, or even offer them scholarships for their dedication to vilifying smoking and smokers.   In a particularly egregious form of child abuse Antismoking activists will even use the children as tools of pressure against their own parents as they are encouraged to confront mom and dad with the question "Why are you killing us with your smoke?" Frightening an impressionable child by telling them that their smoking parents are killing them or telling them their parents are going to die soon and leave them as orphans is nothing short of contemptible ("NJ Youth Mobilize...." *PRNewswire* 04/20/ 02; "Youth Against Tobacco." *PRNewswire* 01/05/95).

During the conflict in Afghanistan, President Bush appealed to American children to mail dollar bills to the White House that would go to Afghan children.   Just a month after the attack on the World Trade Center, one Antismoking opportunist had a brilliant idea that he urged others on his private mailing list to emulate.   This Crusader took it upon himself to lobby schools for permission to meet with their children, provide the kids with letter templates that they could send to the President, and even gave each kid a dollar to put in with the letter.

What was the catch you may ask? Simply that the letter the kids were to write was the following:

> *Dear Mr. President, This is a dollar to help the kids in Afghanistan. Thank you for protecting us against the terrorists. Would you please also do everything you can to protect us from the tobacco industry. Please make them stop selling this deadly addictive drug.* (www.geocities.com/ madmaxmcgarrity/anticrap19.htm)

Adding insult to injury, it's a pretty safe bet that this particular patriotic huckster was using money taken from smokers through the MSA as his funding source for those nice little dollars!

Stealing our Children

Finally, the scary image of children gasping for the breath of life is played upon in a more organized and even uglier way by groups like Action on Smoking and Health: their web pages offer legal advice (or as close to it as they can legally get away with) and supposedly lawyer referrals as well for divorced parents locked in custody battles. Of course the bulk of such advice and referrals are only made available to the nonsmoking parent after he or she agrees to fork over the $25 membership fee, but evidently that's what being "non-profit" is all about.

The idea of throwing this issue into the midst of the emotional turmoil that already exists in a child custody dispute in order to advance a political agenda is simply disgusting. This is in even worse taste than the earlier mentioned offer by Crusading groups to teach lawyers "How to Win Giant Settlements From The Tobacco Companies!"

The next arena in which the Antismoking Crusade will attempt to assert its power will be in private homes with healthy families. Using the "threat to the children" as their rallying cry they will move from simple interference in custody disputes to actual intervention into private family life itself. Parents who smoke in a home where 17- or even 20-year-old "children" live will be formally labeled as child abusers.

A hidden motivation is at work in this area too: Michele Bloch of the American Medical Women's Association made the point: "... *in addition to putting youth as our top priority, we (should) not tie our hands from working on reducing adult smoking through penalties, etc.,* **when the time comes**" (Jacob Sullum. *Reason Magazine* 10/97; Emphasis added).

As unlikely as it may now seem, we will probably find that one of the banner headline areas of the new millennium, trumpeted by the EPA, ASH, and the various Crusader nonprofit groups, will revolve around the "abuse" of children who live with parents who smoke and the importance of having the government do something about this "problem." While it's right for government to step in to save children who are being beaten or starved, or even children suffering significant psychological abuse, does it make any sense to formally label a third of all families as being "child abuse situations" and then seek to take their children away if they don't "correct their behavior"?

Such a scenario is not simply fantasy. Antismokers on the Internet are now using such terminology, and movement toward formalizing the idea is growing within Crusading organizations. The "rescuing" of children from smoking parents has so far been largely confined to custody cases, but the activists have well functioning nuclear families in their sights too. The quotes in Figure 14 may not be mainstream at the moment, but the frequency with which these sorts of views have been publicly expressed on the Net and by public figures has increased at a frightening rate over the last few years.

While writing this book I have found life overtaking art: In April of 2002 Bryan Robinson of ABC News reported on a judge's ruling (see Figure 14) that, despite the fact that there were no health effects, asthma, or allergy involved, a mother would lose all visitation rights with her son if she did not agree to stop smoking at all times in her home and car! According to one of the lawyers in the case the father can even require her to give urine and air samples to prove that she hasn't been smoking!

In September of 2002 things proceeded even a step further. A family court judge hearing a case that had nothing to do with smoking at all ruled that the estranged parents involved would not be allowed to smoke in the presence of their child, despite the fact that the child had no health problems nor expectation of developing such. This case can now be used as a precedent for any Antismoking judge anywhere in the country at any time during a family court hearing on any subject.

From Yahoo:
Darwinna: *"you should be locked up. Smoking around children is child abuse, pure and simple"*

seeking.geo: *"I want smoking in the presence of a minor child to be a CRIMINAL charge...most child abusers are smokers ... smoking Is the worst form of child abuse."*

From officials:
J. Garbarino, director of Cornell's Family Life Development Center: *"Let's call it what it is: Parental smoking is child abuse,"*

ASH Press Release: *"Law Is Finally Beginning to Crack Down on... Child Abuse... 15 States Will Take Away Custody... to Protect Kids"*

NY Judge Julian: *"... the best interests of (the child) dictate that he shall not reside in, or visit, or occupy any residence or motor vehicle of the parties in which smoking of any type occurs at any time..."*

Figure 14

The ruling, filled with extremist claims and language, reads more like a cut and paste of literature from the ASH or GASP websites than an actual legal document, but legal document it is! It now appears that any family seeking recourse to the family law system may suddenly find itself at the mercy of judicial whims with regard to their heretofore-private lives (Paul Singer. "Judge Orders Estranged Parents..." *Associated Press* 09/12/02; Case No. 97-PR-755 in the Court of Common Pleas, JD, Lake County, OH 08/27/02).

The Swedish asthma study mentioned above didn't get much in the way of press coverage, but given what I've noted earlier this should not be too surprising. If these results are replicated in future studies though, perhaps those parents who **don't** smoke will be brought up on charges of child abuse! Now wouldn't **that** be a pretty kettle of smoked herring!

We have already seen instances where drug education programs in schools have demanded that children identify parents who are "tobacco addicts." Those who think that the Crusaders will never implement laws and programs to "save" such children should look back a few years in history and consider how likely it seemed that police would be diverted to enforce smoking bans in Los Angeles bars while drug gangs still roamed the streets unchecked!

... And Children *are* the Victims

A final sad note as to the effects that the Antismokers' emphasis on children has had comes from a news story where a "good" teenager was discovered in possession of an unlit cigarette on school grounds. Her three day suspension from a Wausau, WI school and the trauma of her parents finding out that she was one of those dirty, addicted smokers led to her suicide by hanging a few hours later (*AP* 11/09/99). While simplistically pinning responsibility for this death totally on Antismokers would be ridiculous, the attack of the Crusade on teen self-esteem in their advertising imagery is self-evident (Figure 15).

Antismoking programs aimed at teens that encourage the shunning or isolation of smokers, or that encourage smokers to see themselves as inherently being losers, failures, and undesirables need to pay more attention to the negative effects such education may have on those kids. To this date there have been no studies of what impact the Antismoking Crusade has had upon teen depression and suicide rates...who would fund them? The tobacco companies don't want to publicly admit that teens smoke in the first place and certainly wouldn't fund any study that might seem to condone such smoking, and the Crusaders are certainly not going to support research that might hurt their cause. Who are the real losers? Our teenage sons and daughters.

The camera zooms in on a teenage girl in a robe, puffing a cigarette in a bathroom before she starts brushing her perfect teeth. But instead of toothpaste residue falling into the sink, it's wiggling maggots.

She recoils as her mirrored face turns green and clumps of her hair fall out. Within seconds, the beautiful girl is rotting flesh.

(Arizona's award-winning Antismoking campaign)

Walter Berry. *Associated Press* 05/24/01

Figure 15

6) Smoking Bans

Prohibition ... makes a crime out of things that are not crimes ... A prohibition law strikes a blow at the very principles upon which our government was founded.

-- Abraham Lincoln (December 1840)

Introduction

Smoking bans in and of themselves are not the fundamental end goals of hard-core Crusaders. The ultimate desire is to see the end of smoking as a human activity altogether. Smoking bans themselves are simply seen as a very powerful weapon in the war to achieve that goal.

In the past Antismokers have generally denied that their push for smoking bans had any motivation other than a concern for clean air and the health of nonsmokers. As they've grown more powerful however, they have started to admit to the hidden agenda behind these bans.

Sir George's concept of frightening nonsmokers into supporting smoking bans (Figure 11) was important because the simple banning of smoking in multiple situations changes the status of smoking as a normal and accepted activity. When out in public a smoker must now think carefully before lighting up and determine whether smoking is actually allowed in whatever location that smoker is currently in. Indeed, as the bans grow in number and size, smokers now find that they must greatly curtail their habit or risk not just a fine, but sometimes even a jail sentence when confronted about breaking the rules.

This formerly understated motivation for smoking bans is now being admitted more publicly as Crusaders have sensed a wider acceptance among Americans of the idea that smoking is undesirable enough to justify social engineering tactics. Chris Tholkes, a project director for the American Lung Association has put it this way: *"We're changing social norms.... Having more smoke-free places pushes people into quitting..."* (Phelps & Rybak. *Minnesota Star Tribune* 11/19/01). Reuters put it the following way: *"This concept of denormalization is best instituted by laws and local regulations making smoking inaccessible in public places..."* (*ReutersHealth.com*/wellconnected/doc41.html).

Denormalization... the very term should frighten any citizen when it is applied to deliberate government policy affecting people's private behaviors and decisions. For groups to covertly use government funding in a planned campaign to ostracize and denormalize a population subgroup is made only scarier by the fact that it no longer needs to be done covertly. Ten years ago such open admission of their motivation would have outright killed the public support Crusaders needed to institute widespread bans in workplaces and public gatherings. Today it seems to simply be accepted with an attitude of "Ho Hum. It doesn't really matter... smoking's bad anyway."

Oddly enough, as mentioned earlier, the same Antismokers who trumpet the belief that tobacco smoking is an uncontrollable addiction will simultaneously contend that smokers should have no real difficulty in abstaining from smoking during 10-hour air flights and 20-hour layovers in smoke-banned airports. However, as most smokers know, refraining from smoking when one is accustomed to it is at least somewhat annoying, and for some, actually quite uncomfortable.

Many smokers will feel the urge to smoke strongly enough that they will go outside such no-smoking zones even if it means standing outdoors in weather that is decidedly far less than pleasant. Some will even risk the sometimes-extreme consequences of smoking in a restroom while aboard a train or a plane. The smoker who finds him or her self constantly being forced to put up with such bans may simply decide to give up smoking altogether: no surprise at all to the Antismokers quoted above!

On a less direct front the bans serve another purpose: by forcing smokers to leave the main areas of a business or public place in order to go "somewhere else" to smoke, the Crusaders have partially succeeded in their goal of labeling smoking as an abnormal activity: something that cannot be done in the usual places where "normal" people congregate. It is a short jump from labeling an activity abnormal to labeling it undesirable, and an even shorter jump to labeling it dirty, perverted, or outright criminal. And once the activity is so labeled it is an even shorter jump to attach the labels to those practicing such activity and bring into play severe societal penalties that would otherwise never have been acceptable.

Airline Bans

Indeed, someone flying into California who is caught attempting to use the old ashtray in the plane's restroom may wind up being charged with a felony for interfering with a flight. Picture what may happen if the offender happened to have two other minor felonies on his or her record from years past. Under California's inflexible "three strikes and you're out" rule it's quite conceivable that we'll someday see smokers receiving life prison terms for practicing an activity that was universally common on hundreds of thousands of safely and peacefully completed air flights. Of course that was before Congress and the FAA intervened in the 1980s under pressure and lawsuits from Crusading groups like Action on Smoking and Health.

Actually, just as I was writing the draft for this chapter in the wake of the World Trade Center disaster, a plane was escorted back to a Los Angeles airport by F-16s after a man was discovered smoking in the bathroom.   He was dragged off the plane by an armed SWAT team upon arrival with the excuse given that he had said anti-American things after being found with his tobacco product!

The alternate report that he was simply repeatedly making the plea "I am an AMERICAN!" got short shrift in the

general media... after all, he **was** a smoker.   One witness said
that officers *"put an automatic rifle to the back of the guy's
head, I thought he might get killed for smoking while being an
Arab."* Subsequent news reports indicated that if convicted of
the charges against him he could get up to ten years in prison. As
of this writing I have been unable to determine his current status
(*Associated Press* NY 09/28/01 and 12/05/01).

Can you imagine the uproar if such results had been
envisioned when the initial bans were being put into place? One
of the standard steps in the Antismoker game plans for bans has
always been to ease new restrictions into being with low levels of
penalties while knowing that eventually those penalties will have
to be increased far beyond what would have initially been
acceptable.

The argument that such severity is justified in terms of
aviation fire safety seems to be an outright lie: If airline pilots are
to be believed there may well have been more problems with
airline fires started by sneaked and improperly extinguished
smokes **after** the bans went into effect than there were before.
According to a pilot writing in the Air Safety Forum of airborne.
org's web pages :

> *The present no-smoking regulations on board
> aircraft are welcomed by many. However, these
> smoking restrictions have resulted in concealed
> smoking by passengers, and in some cases even
> crewmembers, **increasing** risks of an in-flight
> fire.* (www.airborne.org/flying/forum_fly3.htm;
> Emphasis added.)

During the first decade or so of airplane smoking bans it was
difficult to get statistics on how much air rage was resulting from
them.   Statistics that were released seemed to hide the number
of incidents caused by resentment of these bans under the
heading of "alcohol related" since incidents that caused notice

were often caused by passengers who had had a couple of drinks. As noted in more detail later it was in the airlines' economic interest to minimize reports of resistance to such bans in order to maximize their public acceptance and avoid calls for their repeal.

Today it's a little different. As air rage has increased and public concern about it has escalated, more detailed information about its causes has come out. The International Federation of Airline Pilots' Associations itself has even spoken in favor of getting rid of these total bans, citing unreasonable universal bans as a major cause of air rage. To quote from a Sunday Times article by Roger Makings, *"According to statistics in Germany, during a period in 1997 and 1998 of the 1,252 cases of sky rage, 566 were attributed to the ban on smoking and 389 on alcohol."* (*Sunday Times* 07/15/01).

Adding into the equation is the excess risk entailed by extra landings and takeoffs (the most dangerous part of a flight) after smoking-ban inspired altercations. It's clear that this particular type of ban has proven to be exceedingly dangerous in its consequences. There is clearly **no** reason why airlines should be prohibited from designating certain flights as allowing smoking if they wished to do so. Rather than bail out failing airlines with taxpayer money, such a rational approach might lure smokers back to shorter haul flights, reduce extra landings and takeoffs, lessen the risk of fires arising from clandestine smoking, and also reduce the hostile confrontations inspired by resentment of smokers at the lack of reasonable accommodations.

Fast Food Bans and Consequences

Sadly, another negative side effect of the bans has been to discourage teens from hanging out at the fast food restaurants that used to be their most popular gathering spots. In the mid 90s, using the persuasive power of the EPA report, several state Attorney Generals, led by the now indicted Texas Attorney General Dan Morales, threatened a massive lawsuit against

McDonald's unless the fast-food chain banned smoking. Faced with the overwhelming legal and monetary resources of the combined states (and aware that more states would probably join in later) McDonald's agreed to a total smoking ban throughout its company-owned stores while claiming it had planned a smoking ban anyway. Burger King followed quickly thereafter. Only the Wendy's chain showed some fortitude and stood up to these threats of bully tactics, but has since been subjected to letter writing and boycott campaigns led by Crusading groups.

The reality is that better than a quarter of the mid- and older teen population smokes. Therefore groups of teens, most of which will include some smokers, will move to locations far less well lit and without any adult supervision for their informal recreation. This movement into the back lots of strip malls, vacant commercial and industrial properties, under old bridges and in dark parks has probably contributed to the incredible rise in hard drug and inhalant use among teens; increases, as noted earlier, of up to several hundred percent over the last decade.

This change in hangout locales has also exposed teens to predators who would never dare approach or befriend them in the brightly lit and adult-supervised confines of a Burger King or McDonald's. When it concerns those who prey upon our children any rules or regulations that help separate them from the mainstream adult world are seen as a godsend by predators and should be perceived as a nightmare by concerned parents.

There's been at least one documented case of a high-profile Crusader, Mayor Muller of Friendship Heights, MD, who was arrested and pled guilty to sexually abusing a 14-year-old boy in the restroom of Washington's National Cathedral. Mayor Muller had led a fight to ban all public smoking in Friendship Heights in order to protect the children from bad example and whiffs of smoke from smokers on the streets.

During the months just prior to his arrest Mayor Muller had become the canonized poster boy of the nationwide Crusading organizations for his efforts in the battle to save the children by banning public smoking and getting teen smokers off the streets. One of his supporters in the fight even stated that the ban *"would reduce teen-age smoking by giving children fewer places to smoke."*   Restrooms would evidently not have been covered (John Stossel. 12/14/00; *Associated Press* 03/23/01).

The increase in enforcement of age purchase laws has added to this particular problem as finding an "older friend" becomes quite desirable to a smoking teen for cigarette purchases. Of course there's been no study of the results of what these bans and laws have done in the way of increasing such dangers to our children and no tally of what harms may have resulted: those controlling the millions of dollars in Antismoking research efforts would never fund such an inquiry.

In addition, fast food establishments had some ulterior motives for going along with the ban aside from the lawsuit. By banning smoking they solved two other problems: first of all, the groups of teens and senior citizens who would hang out for hours over cigarettes and cups of barely sipped beverages were a pain to store managers (though few of them would ever admit it in public... particularly with regard to the seniors!). Such custommers couldn't be asked to leave without causing other potential problems for the store, but meanwhile they took up lots of space for little in the way of profit.

The teens and senior smokers also served to discourage the more lucrative family and children's birthday party trade that would ensure a future generation of customers hooked on "Big Meat." And just as the teens found other far less healthy hangouts, so did many seniors as they escaped summer heat and winter cold in the local taverns instead. The true social cost of the fast food bans is unknowable, but surely significant.

Bans and Air Quality

Fast food magnates realized that there was not only the extra expense of cleaning up after smokers, but the extra money required to pay for the higher air exchange rates needed to keep visible smoke from hanging in the air and discouraging potential diners.   There's no available data on how much lower the infusion of fresh air into these establishments is now than it was before, but it seems to be enough so that many people have commented unfavorably on the increase in odor of stale French fries and grease. Perhaps Wendy's should fund a study as to how the freshness of the air in its dining areas compares to that of its smoking-banned competitors!

Whether the lower air exchange rates have produced an increase in airborne disease transmission is also unknown, but with the increased incidence of such airborne diseases as tuberculosis and increased concern about bioterrorism in America it could definitely develop into a serious problem: perhaps someday we'll see smoking restaurants recommended as generally having truly healthier air! Even without disease concerns, the odor of grease in the air of some of these venues indicates that significant levels of heterocyclic amines and other cooking related chemicals may be high enough to pose a real health hazard. Unfortunately that hazard seems to be ignored by the big chains and Antismokers in favor of politics, profit and political correctness (*Reuters Health* NY 07/03/00).

Without the marker of tobacco smoke the customer cannot easily determine whether a healthy level of fresh air is being circulated, and government inspections do not adequately address this issue at all. It's ironic, but the true air quality in restaurants and airplanes may well have gone **down** since smoking bans appeared. It's notable that the first instances of "sick building syndrome" appeared in concert with the spread of such bans and that the first time Consumers Union Reports devoted a cover story to the problem of "What's Happened To Airplane Air?" was several years after total airline smoking bans went into effect (*Consumer Reports* August 1994).

Indeed, a 1989 D.O.T study found that the putative risks from secondary smoke on smoking flights were about 1/1000th (yes... one one-thousandth!) of the risks due to increased cosmic radiation exposure on ordinary high altitude flights. Passengers are routinely assured that flying is safe, and yet the risk from cosmic radiation while flying is 1,000 times greater than the risks from the secondary smoke they are advised to be afraid of.

The same study also found that by some measures the air on smoking flights was actually healthier than the air on non-smoking ones! One measurement in particular that might be of concern nowadays was that nonsmoking flights had nine CFU/m^3 (nine "colony forming units" of fungi per cubic meter) as opposed to only five or six CFU/m^3 on smoking flights! (Report to Congress: Airline Cabin Air Quality. U.S. D.O.T. 1989)

Such problems may now be even worse as airplanes take advantage of the absence of smoking and refresh the air of planes only 20% as often as they did back when smoking was allowed! This reduction in fresh air is not a vindictive act in any sense, merely a normal response to an opportunity for financial savings: fresh air at high altitudes costs money... and without smoke in the air the health risks are effectively invisible (Boucher, quoting James Repace. *Rendez-Vous 64* 04/26/00).

The increased health risks of epidemic diseases spreading in the confined and now heavily recirculated air of our planes will never be apparent until a disaster occurs... and by then it will be too late. The worldwide spread of an airborne infectious disease may someday be laid at the doorstep of the Great American Antismoking Crusade. An airborne Ebola, antibiotic resistant pneumonia, or bio-terror horror could be the final legacy of those trying to save us from ourselves.

Ban Motives

One has to wonder why the thousand fold greater risk of cosmic radiation was ignored while smoking was focused on. Evidently the Anti-Cosmic-Rays Lobby isn't as strong as the Antismoking Lobby. It's also quite possible that the lobbyists from the airline industry itself may also have had something to do with this: increased radiation shielding would cost money in both materials and extra fuel. Banning smoking actually **saved** the airlines as much as $100 million a year, since they could depend more on simply using recycled air in the planes (Conner. "Airlines saved millions..." *Reuters Security News* 09/22/97).

Planes built since the 1980s have been designed with a smoking ban in mind, using 50% or more recycled air instead of the previous system of 100% outside air, in their air systems. The last 20 years have seen increasing complaints about contaminations of cabin air by such things as hydraulic fluids with over 1,000 such incidents reported in the Federal Aviation Administration's Service Difficulty Reports database. A number of these incidents resulted in crews having to don oxygen masks or make unscheduled landings: one incident even involved the captain and co-pilot becoming "dizzy and groggy" as the plane approached its landing (Byron Acohido. *USA TODAY* 05/09/2002).

The motivation for these bans extends further than any claim to a need for clean air. Antismokers have always been adamantly against any attempts at creating reasonable ventilation systems that would allow smokers and nonsmokers to co-exist happily in the same, shared space. One activist in particular, the same Richard Daynard who is suing to get $150,000,000 from the MSA money pot, has worked for over a dozen years to get the American Society of Heating, Refrigeration, and Air-conditioning Engineers (ASHRAE) to change its 1989 language that indicated that indoor smoking could be handled with normal levels of ventilation (http://no-smoking.org/june99/06-24-99-5.html).

A very important part of the unstated reasoning behind smoking bans is to make smoking as uncomfortable, unpleasant, and unattractive as possible. Well-ventilated situations where smokers and nonsmokers can happily co-exist would defeat the effectiveness of smoking bans as a tool of social engineering. Remember the recommendations from Sir George Godber's conference in 1975: for the Antismoking movement to succeed it would be essential to create an atmosphere and belief that secondhand smoke would hurt the infants, children and all people around smokers. Without that fear, and the ostracization it would bring, smokers would continue to insist on their right to enjoy their habit socially and the goal of official denormalization could never occur.

Bans: Other Approaches

Action on Smoking and Health has pressured the Occupational Safety and Health Administration for years in the hope of getting Permissible Exposure Limits changed so as to make indoor ventilation and air-cleaning solutions virtually impossible. So far OSHA has resisted this pressure to bring such politics into its scientific determination of safe chemical exposure levels for workers.

Indeed, as 2001 drew to a close, OSHA issued a news release indicating that it was withdrawing from its efforts to regulate workplace smoking partly because significant parts of its proposal had been called into question during the comments period. Another factor seems to have been ASH's willingness to drop its lawsuit against OSHA rather than have OSHA create a standard that would have allowed for "acceptable" levels of tobacco smoke in public places. According to an article in the LA Times, Antismokers simultaneously tried to blame George Bush for being in the pocket of the tobacco industry while quietly congratulating themselves on avoiding the possibility that OSHA might actually issue meaningful standards that would specifically allow for indoor smoking (http://www.tobacco.org/Documents/011213osha.html; Stanton Glantz. Newsletter 12/16/01; Lisa Girion. *Los Angeles Times* 12/19/2001).

Shortly after the OSHA announcement, the American Society of Refrigeration, Heating and Air-conditioning Engineers (ASHRAE) dealt another blow to the efforts of Crusaders to denormalize smoking and remove it from public view. Richard Daynard's quest drew to a bitter end as he failed in persuading ASHRAE to declare any level of tobacco smoke above zero to be "unsafe."

Instead, ASHRAE proceeded along its more traditional route, declaring it would set air quality standards based on odor and comfort, probably along its traditional lines of 30 to 80 cubic feet per minute of fresh air per smoking occupant. As of early 2003 this standard is still accepted although there are continuing pressures on ASHRAE to change its position (*ASHRAE Press Release* 07/03/02).

Despite the negative decisions from both OSHA and ASHRAE some Antismokers still seek universal bans on the basis of arguments as strange as that made by Steve Allen and Bill Adler when they declared that smokers **want** total bans and that such bans do a favor for smokers because *"smokers don't like being asked not to smoke when they light up; nonsmokers' rights laws eliminate that problem"* (Allen, Steve & Adler, Bill. *The Passionate Nonsmoker's Bill Of Rights.* p.111 William Morrow & Co. 1989).

That statement would almost be funny if it weren't meant to be taken so seriously. I've actually seen this argument used by Antismokers at City Council hearings and, to my astonishment, watched as dozens of heads nodded up and down in wise agreement at such an observation! I'm not in any way exaggerating when I say that there are times at these hearings when a neutral observer might almost feel as though they've been transported down the rabbit hole and were watching Alice conversing with the Cheshire Cat.

As far as truly satisfying the more extreme members of the Antismoking Crusade, the uselessness of any sorts of social bans short of total Prohibition is shown in the quotes in Figure 16, reprinted from a National Post article looking at citizens' reactions to how well the "successful" large scale ban on indoor restaurant smoking in Toronto is fairing. The comments show the lie to any plan that states, "All we're looking for is a partial ban." Compromise is **never** a long-term solution for a true fanatic. Antismokers will **always** use any sort of partial ban as merely a temporary steppingstone toward a total ban. Whatever venues are not covered under a partial ban will simply be referred to as "loopholes" when Crusaders come back a year or three later seeking a blanket prohibition.

"There are lots of tables inside but who wants to eat inside when it's so beautiful outside?... but it's like sitting in an ashtray."

"But a lot of restaurants open the windows and the smoke just comes wafting through,"

"This is perfect weather for patios and the smokers are ruining it,"

"Often, when you go inside the air conditioning is uncomfortable and then there is complete smoke outside.

-- Susanne Hiller. The National Post 08/15/01

Figure 16

Two examples of what may stand as the most ridiculous bans (aside from those forcing urban smokers out to the middle of the street to smoke) are the total bans on open-air smoking in sports stadiums built with money from specially imposed earmarked cigarette taxes and the ones banning smoking in cars where a minor is present. There's clearly no reason why sections of the open-air stadiums could not be marked off as smoking sections, and cases such as the ban at Cleveland's Jacobs Field, the construction of which was financed by a 4.5 cents per pack tax, are particularly obnoxious (*TIME*, 04/11/94).

One of the ludicrous side-effects of these open-air stadium bans comes in the form of smoking being allowed in the closed concourses that everyone uses on the way to restrooms, concessions, or exits. Instead of smoke disappearing innocently into the open air from a smokers' section of the stadium, everyone gets a concentrated dose indoors!

The car-smoking ban gives rise to such ridiculous situations as one where 17 year-olds smoking in a car driven by their parents would be fine; but if the parent lit up too they'd be fair game for the highway smoke cops! It's important to remember here that most states have refused to criminalize the actual act of underage smoking (thus avoiding labeling a third of teens as criminals) and focus instead on purchase regulations. A teen whose parents buy his or her cigarettes usually has little to fear unless they're in Florida or a handful of other similarly repressive states (In Texas a 10 year-old was strip searched at school because a security guard "suspected" he had cigarettes – none were found.) ("Parents Sue School..." *AP* 12/16/00).

In Florida those teens might be judged fit to be sentenced and perhaps even executed as adults for more serious crimes, though they might not be allowed a smoke with their last meal... after all it would be bad for their health. This is actually true for some on death row: see the last meal menus at http://tdcj.state. tx.us/ stat/finalmeals.htm. Fairness is not a favored word in the Antismokers' lexicon, not even for condemned juveniles.

And speaking of fairness, the process by which smoking bans are made into law sometimes seems to lack a bit of fairness. New York's billionaire Mayor, Mike Bloomberg, pushed very strongly for a total indoor ban that would include even bars. When some on the City Council had the temerity to oppose the idea they were met with a very unexpected big stick: According to an article in the *Brooklyn Skyline* a councilman has accused the mayor of threatening any Free-Choice supporters with a million dollar campaign contribution to their upcoming opponents. No mere City Councilperson can stand against that sort of threat, so the fact that the New York ban was swiftly voted in should come as no surprise (*Brooklyn Skyline* 02/17/03).

Dangers of Bans

Finally, one of the cruelest instances of such widespread government-mandated bans takes place in facilities that care for some of those who are most powerless in our society: those suffering from mental and emotional illnesses.

Many psychiatric facilities are now forced to ban smoking except in very limited outdoor areas and allow smoking only at times that are under the total control and discretion of nonmedical staff personnel.   Given the role of smoking as a self-medication for depression, the limiting of smoking to two or three very short break periods per day probably produces far more damage to patients than any amount of secondhand smoke in the world, particularly when those break periods are arbitrarily taken away on a staffer's whim.

Staffers at such facilities are often pleased with such rules because they provide a built-in punishment and reward system that is both efficient and effective: if a patient misbehaves they will simply be denied their smoke break! Once again we are faced with a situation where the damage from such rules really should be properly studied, but also faced with the reality that no one is likely to fund such studies. Sadly, even if funding were available it's likely that many researchers would be reluctant to perform such studies for fear of being labeled as tools of Big Tobacco.

It is not known how many patients put off checking into care facilities when they otherwise should and would have done so, but it's likely that more than a few depression-caused suicides would have been prevented if patients knew they'd be allowed to smoke after checking themselves in. Perhaps the ultimate tool for fighting such smoking bans will arrive someday in the form that's been so popular with the Crusaders: Lawsuits over fires, injuries and deaths caused by ban-created situations may someday form a potent incentive for their repeal!

Remember that sometimes when fires are labeled as "smoking-related" they may well have been caused by hidden smoking, marijuana smoking, and/or the improper and hasty disposal of forbidden butts. Remember also that the vast majority of such fires also involve alcohol: which factor receives the blame depends on which group is grinding an axe. Deaths from accidents due to drinking and driving are **always** blamed on drinking. Deaths from fires due to drinking and smoking are **always** blamed on smoking.

Aside from fire risk, encouraging people to sneak smokes in the face of unreasonable bans can have other unintended but dire consequences. The year 2001 saw a number of universities capitulate to pressure for smoking bans. In the fall of that year there was a report from the University of Arkansas about a student who fell to his death while smoking on a ledge of a dorm with a stringent smoking ban. The article stated that smoking on the ledges was "not unheard of," indicating that the University met it with some tolerance (Jeff Niese. *The Morning News.* NWAOnline.net 10/24/01). As seen in Appendix H, college officials pushing for such bans show little interest or responsibility in examining either their drawbacks or possible alternatives to complete bans.

Hopefully the parents of the above mentioned student will not accept the glib blame for the death as being "due to smoking" and will sue for every penny they can get. The college obviously knew that the ban was being ignored in ways that might prove dangerous to the students, but they ignored that danger in pursuit of whatever funding or political security they gained by the ban's implementation.

Relatives of students or senior citizens injured in dormitory or senior care center fires in situations where no safe indoor smoking accommodations were provided should consider the issue of liability carefully. These bans **do** result in clear and present harm and should be overturned before they produce more deaths or injuries. Suing for less real and tangible injuries such as the trauma and risk of diverted airline flights or increased drug use among teens may be harder, but once the lawyers scent money in it who knows what the future might hold?

7) Discrimination

Social groups create deviants by making the rules whose infraction constitutes deviance, and by applying those rules to particular people and labeling them as outsiders.

— Howard Becker. "Outsiders...." *Free Press* 1963.

While discrimination is more of a practical matter than a psychological tool, it is valued by Antismokers as a means of adding an extra element of fear or cost to the practice of smoking. It also reinforces the earlier-mentioned notion that smokers are somehow abnormal and unworthy of the usual rights and privileges of a "normal" nonsmoking person, thereby contributing to the overall goal of denormalization.

Aside from a recent but disturbingly increasing trend toward housing discrimination, discrimination against smokers exists in two main arenas: jobs and medical care. Usually Crusaders will attempt to justify such discrimination by claiming that smokers are deficient in various ways that make them less fit for those jobs and care. However, the telltale indicator that we're dealing with true discrimination here is that fitness is not the actual test: smoking status is.

Job Discrimination

While it may be true that **on the average** heavy smokers would be less fit to carry unconscious victims down four flights of stairs in a burning building, or less likely **on the average** to survive a grueling surgery, it's also true that a person's smoking status is just one of many factors that determine such things. In actual fact of course there are millions of smokers who are more "fit" than millions of nonsmokers for virtually any job or medical procedure. Smoking may be a factor, it may even be an important factor, in determining one's fitness, but it should never be used as a litmus test for something as vital to fundamental rights as being considered for a job or an operation. The theoretical behavior modification benefit of forcing some smokers to quit is clearly not worth the human cost in this area.

While firings of police and firefighters provide one of the most highly publicized examples of job discrimination based on smoking status they do not stand alone. Turner Broadcasting Systems, Seattle's Providence Hospital, Kimball Physics, Goodman Manufacturing, North Miami, St. Cloud, Oklahoma City and many other local governments and private companies, often at the behest of activist Crusaders in internal power positions, have attempted to make it clear that they will not hire smokers or have placed extreme restrictions on employees smoking even off-site at company functions. Some employers will actually fire anyone who has filled out a job application as "nonsmoking" only to be discovered smoking at a celebration or family gathering at some future date ("First Massachusetts Firefighter Fired..." *Associated Press* 10/31/02; John Makeig. "Fuming Woman Fired..." *Houston Chronicle* 10/22/96; "Fired Cop..." *Associated Press* 06/23/03).

Smokers facing instances of such discrimination usually experience shocked disbelief. A common theme in the letters received by groups like FORCES and smokersclub.com is "How can they DO this in America??? Isn't this against the law?" The answer, sadly, is no, it is perfectly legal: smokers are not a "protected group" in many states and Antismoking organizations have campaigned vigorously against laws that would define them as such.

Stephen King fans may remember the short story "Quitters Inc." in which the hapless protagonist was faced with dire reprisals from a Mafioso Quit Smoking Clinic if he relapsed. The reality of losing one's job and then perhaps one's house and one's family because you lit up a cigar to celebrate your brother's new baby boy is a possibility smokers actually have to consider in today's weird new Antismoking world. In Mayor Bloomberg's New York, workers who have the misfortune to get their pictures taken while on a smoke break may find themselves fired even if their break was legal and within time limits! (Editorial. *NY Post* 10/24/02). In Massachusetts photographic evidence isn't even required: in mid 2003 a 7-year veteran of the police force in that state was fired after an **anonymous letter** claimed he was spotted smoking tobacco at a party while off duty (*The Herald News*. 06/23/03).

Antismoking employers will sometimes try to justify such discrimination on the grounds of expense, pointing out that health insurance costs for the company may go down if they hire only nonsmokers. If such is indeed the case in a particular instance it's difficult to see why the company cannot simply pass the extra cost along to the smoking employee.

Of course if a company wanted to honestly get into this type of cost differentiation for its benefit programs it would have to cut smoking employees' contributions to retirement and pension funds. Certainly the same information used to justify the extra health payments would be reflected in the opposite direction when smoking employees retired and presumably died earlier than the nonsmokers. In practice, the absence of this reverse type of computation shows the inherent nastiness and pecuniary motivation behind such calculation and discrimination. Nevertheless, most Antismokers loudly insist on one side of the pie while ignoring the fact that real fairness would dictate the other side must be eaten as well.

At one point several years ago there was some discussion as to whether Federal Acquisition Regulations that forbid contracting to any organization that discriminates in employment for non-work-related reasons might protect smoking employees, but somehow this problem seems to have been solved by the Antismokers. In any event, job discrimination on the basis of normally legal activities seems to be alive and well in America as smokers may have the notable distinction of being the only group in modern America who are commonly told that they "Need Not Apply" for an increasing number of jobs. Note: these prohibitions are not simply rules prohibiting smoking ON the job... but prohibitions against the hiring of smokers altogether!

Most of us are aware that most decent jobs require a certain level of education. In Brazil nowadays it can be hard for a smoker to even get that education in order to apply for a job. Brazil's Centro Universitario da Cidade has begun giving notice to applicants that it will no longer accept applications from students "who cannot control their addiction." While a spokesman for the country's Lawyers' Association has expressed doubts about the legality of such a move, at the present time it seems to be the de-facto situation for smoking Brazilians (*Ananova* 08/08/02).

Medical Discrimination

Medical discrimination is even more disturbing than job discrimination. It has become increasingly common in recent years for doctors and surgeons to insist that patients give up smoking if they wish to receive the benefit of certain types of medical care and procedures. Such doctors are probably largely drawn from the ranks of The Idealists, with their motivation being the feeling that those demands ultimately result in more patients quitting and therefore supposedly living longer lives.

Sometimes such medical discrimination can seem almost innocent: a doctor is rightly concerned about a patient's health, and, as part of good medical practice, should instruct that patient about the effect lifestyle choices can have on health. It's only when the doctor oversteps the bounds of such education and advice into the territory of threatening the patient with the withholding of care that the situation becomes actually scary, and anyone who has experienced the helplessness that comes with hospitalization or acute illness will know that scary can quickly become truly terrifying.

Most people know that at some point they will be entrusting their doctor with their lives. Most people do not want to do or say anything that will alienate this person in whom they must trust. When a doctor makes clear that he or she "won't care about you unless you care about yourself" by giving up smoking, the patient is in a bind. If they simply refuse to cooperate they're literally placing their lives at risk.

The only practical alternative for most smoking patients is to claim that they are trying to quit and perhaps even to accept the doctor's pressure to take prescription drugs to help them in their non-existent efforts. And while most doctors are above such shenanigans there is certainly a subset that greatly enjoys the extra rewards they get from the pharmaceutical companies when they've shown special diligence in writing multiple pre-scriptions for various forms of "Nicotine Replacement Therapy" and pricey antidepressants.

As I write this, I can only hope that my own doctor, if he reads this book, will be fair-minded enough not to discharge me as a patient. Fortunately, I've been blessed with a pretty wonderful doctor and such an occurrence would be extremely unlikely. He is the polar opposite of the subset just discussed. Still, it's a sad state of affairs that such a concern should even come to mind as a possibility. If my doctor were an ardent Antismoker someone such as myself could be risking his or her life simply writing by writing a book like this: not unknown in world political reality (just ask Salmon Rushdie!), but sad to see in today's America.

It's in the world of surgery where we move from the simply "scary" into the realm of the macabre and terrifying. We must start off by acknowledging that in practice there may be situations where a person's smoking status can honestly be an important component of a medical decision for surgery, not so much because of the status itself, but because of conditions thought to be aggravated by smoking.

For example, a particularly risky and prolonged operation designed primarily to improve a patient's general quality of life might not be the right choice if the patient's respiratory health or peripheral vascular circulation is particularly poor. If the patient is a heavy smoker the doctor might recommend that they quit smoking in the hope that their respiratory or circulatory system will rebound to a point where such surgery is less risky. There's nothing particularly wrong, at least from the standpoint of medical ethics, with such an approach to optional surgery.

However, if the patient's respiratory or vascular health improves **without** quitting smoking, to continue to withhold the surgery should be clearly unethical. Imagine a less contentious area of concern: suppose such surgery were being withheld on the basis of a patient's high blood pressure and the surgeon said "Lose 50 pounds to bring that pressure down or I won't operate." Now if, instead of losing 50 pounds, the patient embarked on a reduced-sodium diet combined with an exercise program that lowered their blood pressure, would it be ethical for the surgeon to continue withholding surgery on the grounds that the patient really **should** lose 50 pounds anyhow? Of course not: so why is such reasoning not applied equally to the question of smoking and surgery?

I believe that the most dangerous and alarming examples of this type of medical discrimination lie not in the area of optional surgeries but in the area of necessary surgeries and organ transplants. If two otherwise similar people are listed as needing a new heart and one of them smokes, should the smoker be disqualified or moved lower on the list simply because of their practice? The Antismoker argument holds that the value of the new heart would be greater for the nonsmoker because the nonsmoker will live longer and supposedly places more value on his or her life.

This is not paranoid fantasy. There has already been a case in Australia where a 56 year-old man died after being denied an organ transplant because he refused to take the doctor's advice to quit smoking (Rortvedt. *Beyond California* 03/13/01). Austin physician Lou Irving questioned smoker transplants because "*It is consuming resources for someone who is contributing to their own demise*" (Tanya Taylor. *heraldsun.com.au* 02/08/01). Dr. Joel Cooper, a lung transplant surgeon from

Washington University, who has successfully transplanted a number of lungs, has made quite clear that he wants only those who have quit smoking to participate in his procedures (http://wupa.wustl.edu/record/archive/1995/08-17-95/6595.html).

But what if we're talking about a 50-year-old nonsmoker who has advanced arteriosclerosis, failing kidneys, and a bad liver versus a 20-year-old otherwise healthy smoker whose heart was damaged in a car crash? In this case the smoker would have the longer life expectancy.

Should smokers still be excluded simply because of their past sins or their reluctance to sign a paper committing themselves to behave in a societally approved manner for the rest of their lives? Certainly in such a situation most people would simply lie in the interest of self-preservation, but what if the evil motive of monetary gain should rear its head afterwards as such a lie comes to the surface?

Should self-interested insurance companies or cash-strapped hospitals be empowered to watch over the postoperative smoker and garnishee their future wages or take back an organ if they should ever be caught with a cigar or cigarette? The job of Repo Man might take on a sinister new meaning in the future.

Postoperative outcomes and life expectancies depend upon a multitude of factors. Heart transplant candidates who eat vegetarian diets and exercise would usually be better bets for long-term success than meat and potatoes couch potatoes. Would it be correct for the medical community and society at large to attempt to force dietary and lifestyle changes on people through the threat of withholding the promise of life? Obviously the ethical answer is no... but the sad reality is that in practice smokers are running into such threats with increasing frequency and this seems to be a tendency that will expand into the future if it's not addressed soon.

A related, though less direct, form of medical discrimination occurs when smokers delay seeking medical advice because of concerns about general interactions with medical personnel. A 60-year-old lifelong smoker who is also a regular alcohol user and who develops a persistent cough and hoarseness should definitely consult a doctor. That combination of history and symptoms is strongly indicative of forms of throat cancer that can be successfully treated if caught early enough.

> ... surgeons at Melbourne's top hospitals... are denying smokers elective treatment... lung and heart transplants, lung reduction surgery, artery by-passes and coronary artery grafts.
>
> ...respiratory physician Associate Professor Greg Snell said reasons for the ban were medical and moral... *'It is within our mandate to ration services and smoking is one way to define the patient population.'*
>
> -- "Surgery ban on smokers." Taylor. op.cit.

Figure 17

Unfortunately, many such individuals will delay a necessary doctor's visit simply because they know they'll be lectured and berated about their health habits and because they feel they won't be helped unless they agree, either honestly or dishonestly, to radically change those habits. Thus, what might well have been treatable disease becomes an early death... not because of outright discrimination but because of fears of discrimination and mistreatment.

Another unfortunate side effect of this medical discrimination has been the recent flurry of discussion and activity around the concept of smokers boycotting blood and organ donor programs. Many smokers seem to feel that if such programs discriminate against them on the receiving side there's no reason why they should participate in the giving side. Losing a quarter or a third of potential donors and blood givers is a high price to pay for this sort of discrimination.

As surprising as it might seem to the general public, many smokers seem to be both fully aware of and quite angry about this situation. If a full-blown boycott was to develop and a backlash was then created by radical Antismokers to deny **all** blood and organ supplies to smokers we'd have a real societal crisis on our hands.

As smokers become increasingly angry about unfair taxation and generalized discrimination at all levels of their lives the possibility of such spontaneous or organized actions and the unfortunate outcomes that would result becomes greater. At such a point, all of us, smokers and nonsmokers alike, would be the losers.

8) Hate

Discrimination, separation, fear, and hate go hand-in-hand during any serious propaganda campaign against a despised subgroup, and the Antismoking Crusade is no exception in its use of these. Whenever challenged on this point Antismokers will loudly proclaim that they promote hate, not of the smoker, but of the smoke itself. However, a look at the rhetoric and imagery that is tossed around so blithely by those active in the movement slices through this veneer of civility.

Part of the problem of course is that it's the nature of the human mind to simplify things. A hated object or activity, when connected to or performed consistently only by one segment of the population, invariably transfers its stigma over to that segment. The leaders of the Antismoking Crusade are astute enough to realize this, but they've made very little, if any, real effort to combat it: the emotional object confusion is far too useful a tool in their war on smoking.

One set of web pages calling itself *The Crime Prevention Group Homepage* stands out in particular for its sheer fanaticism in demonizing smokers. (http://medicolegal.tripod.com/tcpg.htm) The author posits that smoking is the root cause of virtually all of humanity's modern ills, responsible for everything from about 90% of its violent crime, to its high divorce rate, alcoholism, AIDS, homelessness... and even more.

Its outlook on crime and violence can be illustrated well with a single quote taken from the page on "Divorce":

> *In this **typical murder by smoker case**, this cigar smoker murdered his wives, 1932-1935, using hammer blows, snake bite, drowning, to collect accidental death insurance policies.* (Emphasis in original).

Incredibly, this Crusader goes so far as to blame the entire Holocaust on childhood smoking by Adolph Hitler!

While no one is suggesting that smokers are about to be rounded up and hauled off to crematoria, the intensity of the language used by some Crusaders against smokers is not far from that which was used against the Jews in the early days of Nazism. Remember, discrimination, ghettoization, and the building of hate came long before the ovens. And part of what buttressed that building of hate was the "findings" of Nazi scientists that purported to show the inferiority and depravity of the "lower races."

Hate, by its very nature, tends to be irrational in its roots and expression; but when those who hate feel that they have objective and scientific basis for their feelings, the extremes to which it will grow are hard to predict.

The top half of Figure 18 is an image that was sent to one of the largest smokers' rights activist groups in the world: FORCES International. The image seems to have been down-loaded from a neo-Nazi site, altered, and then sent as an attached file to one of the FORCES mailboxes with the address and other sender identification electronically scrubbed out. The message attached to the image referred to smokers as being subhuman and an infestation... language quite similar to that of previously cited British Health Minister Sir George Godber when he compared smoking in the home to an infestation of head lice (www.forces.org/hate/;www.library.uscsf.edu/tobacco/batco/59 00/5991).

The bottom half of the image is one of a series on a set of web pages put together by artist Josh Bakehorn. While Mr. Bake-horn may not care for smoking, the image seems to convey something more than simple distaste. His cartooning abilities are certainly superior to my own, and he was friendly and polite in his emails as I was asking permission to use his work, but I can't say that I appreciate his artistic sentiment. The text, a bit blurry in the figure, says "Quit Smoking Once and for all, you filthy, squalid, smelly, rotting Dung Pile!" (http://josh. bakehorn.net/squalor.html)

If these images stood alone they could be seen as an anomaly, the disturbed thinking of individuals in no way representative of a larger group. But all one has to do is look around the World Wide Web and within Internet newsgroups such as alt.smokers, and the rhetoric and venom of hate against smokers is easy and plain to see. The verbal poison comes not just from one or two perverted extremists, but from many Antismokers who are careless enough to speak aloud what is in their hearts.

Even schoolchildren are enlisted in this game of hate when they are encouraged with glitzy prizes and colorful T-Shirts to create posters picturing how nasty smokers are. The fine distinction between the act of smoking and the one who engages in the act are often lost on younger minds: pictures and verbiage that would have done justice to Goebbels have been produced by the thousands in classrooms around the country.

While the most extreme images are rarely released, the sorts of things that **are** released **and** applauded (See Figure 15 from earlier) give clear testament to what is produced. Do we really want our tax money used to teach our children this sort of hate? Should smokers really be forced to pay a surcharge on every pack of cigarettes in order to underwrite and reward such expressions of hatred against themselves?

On September 21, 2002, an older Florida teenager, after years of exposure to that state's exemplary hate campaign against smokers (Florida is the home of both Truth.com and the Center For Tobacco Free Kids) attacked and beat a 13 year-old to death because he (wrongly) **suspected** that this 13 year-old had given a cigarette to his younger brother. While this was reported on in the Orlando Sentinel, not a single mention of it seemed to make its way to CNN, Fox, or any other national news outlet. It was a hate crime, a particularly outrageous hate crime whose roots were watered by the forced contributions of smoking taxpayers, but it was deemed un-newsworthy by the media that has come to fear trampling on the toes of a powerful lobby. We have entered some frightening times in this country (*Orlando Sentinel* 09/21/02).

Figure 18

After most of this chapter was written and not long after the beating described above, there was another Florida news story that received little attention outside local newspapers. This time it was a pregnant woman walking in a parking lot who angered an Antismoker by her refusal to put out her cigarette, but on this occasion the Crusader was armed with a gun. The woman was shot in the shoulder and the shooter got away. The saddest thing about this story was the fact that some people reacted in print on the Internet by saying "she shouldn't have been smoking" (*The Times-Picayune*, 10/05/02).

Before ending this discussion of Hate as a weapon in, and a byproduct of, the War On Smoking, I will confess to some embarrassment at having "played the Hitler card" in my argument. Usually when references to Hitler are made in a political argument it's for the purpose of tugging deeper emotional chords at the expense of rationality. As discussed later in the chapter on Fallacious Argumentation it's a form of Argument Ad Hominem: attempting to discredit your opponent's position by discrediting their character or associating them with someone so discredited already.

However, the growing degree of hate I have seen expressed over the last few years on the Internet and in personal observations leaves me with little other recourse in the way of appropriate analogy. The factual matter of Hitler's own Antismoking campaign and the part it played in encouraging Aryans to hate those who were different is undeniable. Today's campaign to eliminate from public consciousness the fact that many of our own heroes, including such World War II figures as Roosevelt and Churchill, were smokers is also undeniable. Crusaders even succeeded in having Roosevelt's ever-present trademark cigarette holder stricken from the statue honoring his battles for freedom against an Antismoking regime. The airbrushing out of Britney Spears' balcony smoking from publicity photos seems inconsequential by comparison.

Recent decisions to remove cigarettes from historical figures portrayed on stamps and in newspapers are eerily reminiscent of Hitler's decision to airbrush Stalin's cigarette from photos of the two leaders appearing together. Jazz musician Robert Johnson, artist Jackson Pollock and Hollywood legend James Dean have all had offending tobacco products surgically removed from their postal stamp pictures! (Reason Editor Charles Freund. http://www.reason.com/0108/cr.cf.ifs. html; Christopher Hitchens. "We Know Best." *Vanity Fair* 05/ 2001).

The act of political editing that I believe most astonished me occurred in 2002 when the heroic stewardess who kept an airplane from being blown out of the sky by jumping on (and being bitten by!) the "shoe bomber" dared to light a cigarette upon her exit from the airport ambulance. The news networks almost universally consigned most of the 45-second scene of her joyful return to freedom to the trash bin. What should have been a celebration of this brave woman returning to solid ground and normalcy was sharply edited and cut to about 10 seconds just as she made the mistake of reaching into her pocketbook for what must have been a very long awaited smoke.

The entire scene DID make it unedited to MSNBC and it was only on this network that the public saw her gallant spirit as she lit up and joked with ambulance attendants after her ordeal. Stills from the scene are available on the web page of Darlene Brennan, founder of FORCES Maine (www.geocities.com/ shelioness/HerosDoSmoke.html).

The heroine, Christina Jones, despite saving hundreds of innocent lives at clear risk to herself, was evidently not welcome on camera if she didn't behave according to the dictates of political correctness. On the bright side at least Ms. Jones did not suffer any extended consequences for her ill-considered behavior: a Philadelphia cop who made a quick move to save an elderly wheelchair patient from a serious fall was not so lucky.

As officer Thompson was saving the senior citizen from a bad tumble at the icy scene of a winter fire, a camera caught him smoking and his Good Samaritan efforts earned him a rebuke and resulted in a city ban on public smoking by cops in uniform.

The fact that he had been on break and simply leaped in to help someone was unimportant. The police chief noted that the cop's smoking was *"potentially dangerous to not only the officer, but to the public as well."* A fanatic-pleasing dictum that cops on breaks who wanted to smoke should hide away from the public was quickly given to the news (Gibbons & Boyer. *Philadelphia Inquirer* 10/28/01).

A few weeks later when someone realized that perhaps it might be better to have smoking cops on breaks still out watching for rapes and muggings, the quick suspension of the order didn't merit much coverage. Many Philadelphians probably still believe that it is now illegal for cops to smoke while in uniform and have their respect for law lessened every time they see one doing so.

Finally, as will be pointed out in the next section, the ubiquitous association in the mass media of smokers with those designated as hate objects cannot be denied. From movie villains to comic strip bad guys, smoking is often specifically portrayed as the habit of those we are meant to emote against.

Hate is never something to be taken lightly and can be ignored only at the risk of the freedoms of us all. The hate that has been aimed against smokers may seem small in the larger scheme of things and it may seem mild compared to the hate against some other minorities in history, but it is there, and with the aid of our tax dollars it is growing. The time to stop such hate, the **only** time to stop it, is when those first seemingly innocent bricks are being laid in its foundation. Pooh-poohing the early stages of hate is a mistake other minorities have made to their lasting regret.

Smokers may be members of a minority group by their own choice, but the same could be argued about the choice of religion, sexual activity, or political party. While doing research for this book I was surprised at how many people were unfamiliar with the following quote by Protestant minister Martin Neimoller, reflecting upon Germany's fall to the Nazis:

In Germany they came first for the Communists, and I didn't speak up because I wasn't a Communist. Then they came for the Jews, and I didn't speak up because I wasn't a Jew. Then they came for the trade unionists, and I didn't speak up because I wasn't a trade unionist. Then they came for Catholics, and I didn't speak up because I was a Protestant. Then they came for me, and by that time no one was left to speak up.

Discrimination and hate, against **any** minority, should never be an accepted part of any democratic society.

9) The Media

To compel a man to furnish contributions of money for the propagation of opinions he disbelieves, is sinful and tyrannical.

– Thomas Jefferson, 1777

Advertising

More dollars are now spent on Antismoking advertising than on Antialcohol, Antidrug, and drunk-driving advertising all added together. Although it's hard to pin down exact monetary figures for the huge Antismoking campaigns of groups like ASH, the ALA and the ACS, and all the little campaigns funded by taxes in individual states, there is one group that it's easy to get a figure from: the American Legacy Foundation (ALF) is funded by the per pack surcharge levied on smokers and spends

more than 350 million dollars a year on Antismoking advertising and activities. By contrast, the total federal expenditures
on Antidrug advertising are less than half that... about $150
million per year (*Associated Press* 2/11/00).

Remember, that $350 million represents the
expenditure of just **one** Antismoking group seeking to
influence the way we think. The larger spending of the states
and nonprofit groups in this area is often hidden within
budgetary fog such as "health education" or "fundraising costs."
It is difficult to derive and prove any exact total, but it's likely
that such a total would be measured annually in thousands of
millions of dollars rather than mere hundreds of millions. As
noted earlier, the AMA itself provided the figure of 880 million
dollars a year as simply representing the official expenditures of
individual state governments on tobacco control.

So what is this massive investment in advertising
actually being spent on? Some of it targets tobacco companies
(Not too much of it... the cozy Master Settlement deal worked
out between the state Attorney Generals and Big Tobacco sets
strict limits on such ads); some of it focuses on the health
effects of smoking and the greatly exaggerated effects of secondary smoke; and some of it targets smokers in an attempt to
make smoking seem less attractive. Of course no limits were
set on attacking smokers in the Master Settlement Agreement:
the states and Crusading groups wanted their billions, the
tobacco companies wanted to be off the hook... and smokers,
the **only** ones whose money was actually up for grabs, weren't
even granted a seat at the table.

To put this monetary amount into perspective, it's
worth noting that the ALF's Antismoking advertising campaign
is just a small part of a much wider effort that blends into the
fundraising and education budgets of many other Crusading
groups and that the total expenditure for these efforts dwarfs
even fairly recent appropriations by Congress for defense
against biological weapons attacks. Given the incredible reality
of what's already being spent on Antismoking efforts, it's
almost unbelievable that just one month after the World Trade

Center disaster a Crusader report to Congress recommended that they *"triple the federal excise tax on tobacco to fund anti-smoking efforts"* (Todd Zwillich. *Reuters Health* Washington 10/11/01). Someone needs to tell these fanatics that anthrax is a good deal deadlier than secondary smoke.

In addition to its advertising power, the Antismoking Crusade seems to have also won an important victory in exerting a strong influence over both news reporting and general media content. This latter concept is particularly troubling to any who remember "Communist control of the press" in the old Soviet Union or to any who have read George Orwell's *1984*.

In a sense, advertising itself is fairly innocent in that most people KNOW that a company or advocacy group is manipulating them when they see or hear an ad. The manipulation may be successful nonetheless, particularly if it is aimed at a younger and less sophisticated audience or manages to display itself as coming from a news source or a community service or "non-profit" organization, but it's honest in that it usually represents itself clearly as a paid attempt to influence one's thoughts and decisions.

Few people, however, make the automatic leap to the realization that a good bit of the power and money that keeps workers, lawyers, and high-salaried CEOs employed at Crusading organizations flows directly from the perceived impact of and contributions raised by such advertising: it is not as altruistic as it appears at first glance. Indeed, when some funding cuts for New Jersey's Antismoking efforts were being considered recently, Paul Wallner of the Medical Society of New Jersey said *"Everything stops. There is no money."* despite the fact that NJ BREATHES (a local Crusading group) was still slated to get $14 million for its activities in 2002 (Ralph Siegel. *Associated Press* 01/08/02).

When fourteen million dollars is referred to as "no money" there is clearly something very, very wrong.

And while people will immediately realize that an employee of Phillip Morris or RJ Reynolds has a clear conflict of interest when making an announcement regarding something like nicotine addiction, very few make the same sort of connection when hearing similar announcements by "health researchers" who get a good bit of their money from the makers of Nicotrol, Nicoban, or whatever quitting panacea is currently raking in millions. Recent advertisements for Nicotrol don't even seem to mention quitting smoking as a prerequisite for using their product: their ads simply show a chewed on pencil and a pretty woman saying something along the lines of "My pencils used to look like this... Now I take Nicotrol!"

An earlier come-on for one of these so-called "Nicotine Replacement Therapy" products used to place their product name next to the slogan: "The Power To Calm, The Power To Comfort." That campaign seemed to disappear a few months after some Free-Choice Internet smoking activists began signing their posts and e-mails with the postscript: "Smoking: The Power To Calm, The Power To Comfort."

Some Antismoking advertising is even more troubling. Targeting a company seems like fair game, although the tobacco companies specifically wrangled provisions in the MSA to protect themselves; and targeting health effects of smoking is fine, although the distortion of facts in some of the ads is pretty extreme; but targeting smokers, making them appear stupid, ugly, sick, impotent, or just plain nasty, should not be socially or legally acceptable. Advertising inspiring hate, dislike, avoidance or segregation of a minority group should NEVER be acceptable, particularly if the minority is as helpless to change its status as Antismokers claim "addicted smokers" to be.

An example of a particularly odious piece of Crusader advertising aimed at teens is a takeoff on the Marlboro cowboy, but shows him with a "limp" cigarette in his mouth. Amazingly the tobacco companies have chosen to pretty much ignore their trademark rights when it comes to stuff such as this, and unfortunately smokers themselves don't seem to have standing when it comes to suing for group defamation.

It is true that some studies have indicated that smoking is correlated with an increased incidence of impotence among middle-aged men, however part of this correlation is due to associations with other factors (drug use, drinking, diet and so forth.) Even ignoring such confounders and the possibility of bias, the studies point only to an increase in absolute incidence of impotence of less than two percent in middle aged or older men   The statistical significance actually disappeared technically when confounders **were** accounted for as the 95% confidence interval included 1.0 in its range (Mannino DM et al. *Am J Epidemiol* 1994 Dec 1;140(11):1003-8).

Such a possible increase certainly does not justify picturing the "average smoker" as being impotent. And telling teenagers that smoking will make **them** impotent is the sort of outright lie that spurs them to ignore some of the sounder warnings they get about hard drugs and alcohol. Once again Don Oakley has made a very pertinent observation on this matter in *Slow Burn* (See Figure 19).

"The Baby Boom was a myth? All those cigarette-smoking GIs who came home from World War II merely *seemed* to be fecund? All those millions of babies were found under cabbage patches?"

-- Don Oakley, *Slow Burn* (Eyrie Press 1999 p.455)

Figure 19

Advertising aimed at the body or breath odor of smokers is similarly obnoxious. Body and breath odor are affected by a multitude of factors in each individual. To single out smokers as being particularly nasty in this regard is not much different than singling out Chili Eaters (in California this could be seen as a particularly offensive slur against Mexican Americans), Meat Eaters (ask some vegetarians about the body odor of carcass chompers sometime), or outdoor laborers who sweat in the sun all day.

      "Kissing a smoker is like licking an ashtray" actually sounds sort of cute as an effective Antismoking ad for young people until you see children taking it to heart and refusing to kiss parents or grandparents because of the image that's been planted in their minds. Mothers picking up their children at school may never learn why their sons and daughters start shying away from their embraces. And, as might be expected, a favorite approach of Crusader ad campaigns is to once again play the "saving the children" card: While examining the 2002 meta-analysis conducted by IARC, the Vancouver Sun noted that:

> *The Canadian government's anti-smoking ad campaign slogan is "*Tobacco. We can live without it.*" The ads feature smoke rings in the shape of targets over children to raise awareness of the effects of second-hand smoke* (Vancouver Sun, 06/20/02).

Comic Strips And Television

Far more dangerous and insidious than Antismoking advertising is Antismoking control of the content of the media we depend on for news and entertainment. As far back as the late 1970s radical Antismoking groups began pressuring the writers of cartoon strips such as *Brenda Starr* and *Dick Tracy* to include story lines of characters quitting. Even *Broom Hilda*, the ugly, obnoxious cigar-smoking witch, was forced to give up cigars because at heart she was supposed to be lovable and a lovable smoker was verboten.

As recently as early 2001 the strip *Rex Morgan MD* devoted months to a storyline involving an evil pipe-smoking grandfather who was killing his grandson with asthma attacks. A comic strip of course has no need to address the reality of the drastic **increase** in childhood asthma cases that has paralleled the drastic **decrease** in smoking around children (Mike Cooper, *Reuters* 05/02/96; http://www.cdc.gov/ exposure report).

Comic strips are only a minor example. Take a look at daytime soap operas over the last 20 years or so and see how many "good" or even "neutral" characters were allowed to smoke. With the exception of a few storylines in which a smoker would quickly succumb to a heart attack or cancer, such characters were virtually non-existent. With astoundingly few exceptions the only smokers on soap operas are drug addicts, wife beaters, serial killers, child molesters, terminal alcoholics, pyromaniacs, or, strangely, gay. All three of the major networks have admitted to pressuring producers of individual series to cut down on the smoking even in the few and far between instances where it is still allowed (Ellen Gray. "Unlike Cable...." *Knight Ridder* 06/16/99).

Made-for-TV movies have fallen in line with Antismoker pressures as well. Several years ago I happened upon *Amber Waves* in which I noticed Dennis Weaver prominently smoking as he drove his tractor in the opening scenes. As I was watching it with a friend I commented on how unusual this seemed and joked "Watch! He'll get lung cancer later in the movie!" Surely enough, the affliction of lung cancer on Weaver's character was one of the basic plot elements of the movie as it proceeded, and we watched as it ripped him away from his life and family. Not unexpectedly, virtually none of the other "good" characters of Middle America were allowed to smoke in this film.

Two more recent entries worthy of mention for their oddity include *Citizen Ruth* in which virtually the only smoker was a pregnant drug abuser who also liked to huff paint thinner and airplane glue, and another (whose name escapes me) where the evil space aliens all hung out and chain-smoked in a diner. Of course, the nice Earthlings didn't smoke, and one poor Earthling waitress in particular was always escaping out the back door to catch a breath of air!

Regular watchers of TV dramas and sitcoms may have also noticed how special episodes are sometimes devoted to Antismoking or Antidrug social themes. If you thought this was just happenstance, think again. According to Daniel Forbes, writing in Salon:

> *Under the sway of the office of President Clinton's drug czar, Gen. Barry R. McCaffrey, some of America's most popular shows -- including "ER," "Beverly Hills 90210," ... and "7th Heaven" -- have filled their episodes with anti-drug pitches to cash in on a complex government advertising subsidy* (Daniel Forbes. *A Salon Special Report.* Salon.com, 01/13/00).

One particular episode of *7th Heaven* featured an evil twin smoking after his smoking father passed away from lung cancer, while one of the regular teen characters started smoking, influencing two toddlers to emulate him by pretending to smoke with crayons as another teen regular kept loudly proclaiming all smokers' stupidity and another younger teen quit a newly acquired habit to prove that **he** wasn't stupid. To top it all off, yet another smoking character was thrown into the mix to rudely blow smoke in a nonsmoker's face at an outdoor café while the home she was house-sitting simultaneously burned down from one of her cigarettes... after which she simply lit up another smoke and stalked off with a comment about the place being insured and nonsmokers being uptight! (No, I am **not** making this up.)

Incredibly, TV networks even accepted having government officials review and alter scripts dealing with drugs to fit specified guidelines and received for this the equivalent of over ten million dollars a year in releases from PSA obligations that they could then sell to commercial sponsors. The idea of the government using our tax money to practice this sort of cultural indoctrination through our supposedly independent entertainment media should be deeply shocking to any American (Forbes. *op.cit.*).

While specially themed Antismoking episodes of 7th *Heaven, The Cosby Show, Full House, Roseanne, Happy Days*, and the rest of the sitcom circuit might be semi-tolerable since it's usually clear the shows' plots have been altered to impart a social message, the more subtle nuances inserted to make smoking or other politically incorrect behaviors seem socially undesirable in the course of normal programming smacks disturbingly of Big Brotherish thought control.

In *Buffy the Vampire Slayer,* Buffy's hometown of Sunnydale not only consists of the statistically unlikely population of 99.9% nonsmokers (except for one nasty alcoholic vampire named Spike) but her high school and college scenes are frequently decorated with background Antismoking posters. The sponsorship of this show by child-targeting sweet alcohol products was discussed earlier but shouldn't be forgotten: *Buffy* is not the only family time show where such things appear.

The Larger Screen

Movies made for theatrical release have shown some degree of independence from Crusader control, although the incredible vision of a smoke-free World War II given to us in *Pearl Harbor* and *Saving Private Ryan* was so absurd that it was singled out by Variety's Film Critic, Todd McCarthy, as "disgusting" (*Reuters* 03/15/02). Even in films where smoking activity more accurately reflects reality, it's notable how many times instances of smoking are coupled with disparaging comments and coughs, or simply how often the smokers are cast as "bad" characters.

Imagine the reaction if the film *Waterworld* had all the good guys being white and all the disgusting bad guys being black? (For those unfamiliar with *Waterworld*: the villains were **all** smokers, and formally labeled as such!) Or, for fans of Tom Clancy, note how his normally smoking hero and friends were totally smoke-free throughout pending nuclear disaster in the *Sum of All Fears*, while the half dozen Neo-Nazi nuclear terrorists smoked up a storm from the title screen to the closing credits.

While the aforementioned Stanton Glantz has come out repeatedly with statements and studies purporting to show that there's too much smoking in movies, a close examination of actual smoking incidence in films doesn't support his contentions. When one considers the fact that there are usually a half dozen or so major characters who get significant amounts of screen time in a film and given that about a quarter of the population smokes, one would expect by virtue of pure statistics that well over 90% of the movies would feature at least one fairly prominent smoker if they simply reflected reality. Statistics could be jiggled, and assumptions could be reset, but in reality there's no way that smoking is as over-represented in the movies as Glantz and his associates would have the public believe in their publicity-seeking press releases.

Unfortunately, millions of dollars in grant money given to Glantz and his fellow Smoke-Free-Films Crusaders can go a long way in creating a popular perception even when there's little to back it up. And if a popular actor or actress under 40 dares to light up in the public eye they're immediately castigated for being a bad role model and thereby killing innocent children.

Some of the bias and propaganda that exists in the area of smoking in films can be seen from just two characterizations that have been made by Antismokers: Winona Ryder has been accused of smoking like a chimney in Heathers and Margot Kidder's character of Lois Lane was held up as an example of chain-smoking in Superman II. In both cases the actresses in question smoked for perhaps a minute or so throughout the duration of the films (Randall. "Targeting of Women...." University of Dayton 1998).

Ms. Ryder has actually become the target of an organized Crusader pressure campaign. She lamented in one interview *"I'm sick of this 'Winona smokes' thing."*   This followed a *60 Minutes* segment with past Surgeon General Joseph Califano where he claimed:

> *Winona Ryder has probably done more damage to young girls and encouraged more young girls to smoke than any other actress in America, I think, because she does smoke all the time in every single movie that she makes.*

Mr. Califano somehow seems to have missed such movies as *1969, Age of Innocence, Alien Resurrection, Beetlejuice, Boys, The Crucible, Dracula, Edward Scissorhands, Little Women, Square Dance*, and others where she played nonsmoking characters.

After an activist in her hometown gathered 100 signatures on a letter telling her that her movies were having a deadly effect on teens, Winona commended the activist for her efforts to *"do a good thing,"* but went on to say, *"It's up to individuals to decide whether to smoke."*   Unfortunately, such individual choice has never been an item in the Crusading agenda and it's likely that Ms. Ryder has continued to be bombarded with organized avalanches of mail from school-children pleading with her to stop murdering innocent kids (Elizabeth Johns. *E! Online* 04/11/97).

In addition to such high-level pressures, movie producers are now beginning to feel a push from a new direction. Radical Antismoking groups have realized that political jawboning was not producing sufficient results and are now resorting to what in practical terms will amount to outright censorship. They are pushing for legislation dictating that entrance to movies should be age-rated based upon smoking content.

Unless a film meets a certain pre-mandated standard of being either totally smoke-free or portraying smoking in a correctly evil, distasteful, or other governmentally approved appropriate way it may find its circulation limited to those above 17 or 21 years of age. Americans for Nonsmokers Rights, flush with multi-million dollar grants, is now working to promote smoking film age restrictions and has proclaimed, *"It is time for the entertainment industry to accept responsibility for its actions and stop serving the interests of tobacco companies."*

Antismokers know full well that movie producers cannot afford the type of hit in their pocketbook that artistic independence might dictate in this regard, particularly since it's likely to be followed up by undercover Crusader "sting teams" seeking strict enforcement of movie age standards at theater multiplexes! The resulting fall-off in teen movie attendance would be catastrophic to the industry (*Reuters* 12/13/01).

This is not just a fiction in some screenwriter's night-mare: the United Kingdom is actually set to introduce such a law (*Daily Record and Sunday Mail* 02/09/01). In the United States, the *2001 Master Plan For a Smoke-Free California* actually calls for targeting movies where there is even a scene that **implies** tobacco use! Can anything like this actually trump the power of Hollywood though? Never underestimate the power of "The Children."

In 2003, a single New York Antismoking youth group named "Reality Check" orchestrated the writing and mailing of almost a quarter of a million letters to the MPAA, the Director's Guild, and stars. And that's just one group, in one state. No industry can stand for long against that level of organized threat (*PRNewswire.* NY 05/24/03).

Theatrical movies shown on TV are not exempt either: anyone who watched the Star Chamber style proceedings of Representative Henry Waxman vs. television network executives a few years ago will remember how he grilled them about showing movies with "pro-smoking content" and will know that the hand of Big Brother is not far from the tiller in today's America.

A less important, but still significant, sign of Crusader control of movie content has to do with product placement. Product placement, while almost universal for every other product shown in films, is now legally strictly off-limits for today's "kinder and gentler" tobacco companies; and given the degree of control over and surveillance of Big Tobacco's operations nowadays, it's highly doubtful that there's any significant amount of illegal placement going on. Nevertheless, movies that dare to show a recognizable tobacco brand name run the risk of pointed insinuations that they are taking illegitimate money. At least one director seems to have taken a slap shot at Antismokers by having his characters ostentatiously smoke "Victory" cigarettes... the only brand allowed in Orwell's *1984*! (Stephen Naysmith. "Spacek's Smoking...." *Sunday Herald.* UK 03/10/02)

Ironically, movies with characters drinking brand-name scotch, engaging in reckless high speed brand-name car chases, shooting with brand-name guns, and all sorts of sexual content (usually without brand-names, unless Trojans are mentioned) will still be available to younger children. We'll be able to rest easy though in knowing that they'll have to go out and look at real life to realize that some people actually smoke brand-name cigarettes while engaging in these other more acceptable behaviors.

Glantz' Smoke-Free Movies campaign actually provides a good example of how Crusaders alter reality to suit their own needs. Not content with boxes of documents stolen from private offices or the 33 million pages of "secret documents" taken from the tobacco companies through state litigation, Stanton Glantz seems to simply make up his own documents when there are no suitable ones buried in that mass. To promote his contention that the tobacco companies are still secretly pushing their products through film, Glantz proclaimed that the Brown and Williamson files contained a 1992 letter speaking of payments by cigarette manufacturers to ensure that central characters in films would be smokers (Naysmith, *op. cit.*).

There is no such document from 1992. The document speaking of product placement by Brown and Williamson is in fact from ten years earlier, 1982, when it was fully accepted, open, and legal for tobacco companies to do product placement just as beer, automobile, soft drink, and clothing companies do. Of course if he **was** called on this claim, Glantz might simply say it was just an innocent mistake. The likelihood of making a mistake of that magnitude about a point so central to his argument and in an area where he has vested so much time and research is laughably small however. A generous jury **might** grant the possibility that the internal drives of a true-believing fanatic could make him honestly believe in such an altered reality in his own mind, but I doubt that Smoke-Free Movies would want a psychiatrist to advance such testimony about its founder.

The Written Word

Written works of fiction are the one bastion of the media that we would expect to be relatively immune to such pressures. The freedom of the written word has always been more sacrosanct in America than that of the broadcast and entertainment media, but even fiction writers can find themselves under attack by Crusaders if they don't insert the proper Antismoker messages in their writings.

All the way back in 1991 Patricia Cornwell, author of *Body Of Evidence* (Scribner 1991), stated during a Nightwatch interview that her publisher had criticized her for having smoking characters and giving the appearance of "lobbying for the tobacco industry" because it would "offend a lot of people who are anti-smokers out there." To mollify the publisher and maintain her livelihood she proceeded to have her characters start quitting or at least start badmouthing their nasty habit in good politically correct format (*Nightwatch*. 03/11/91).

If such pressures were being felt by authors targeted by letter-writing campaigns by the much smaller Antismoking groups of the 80s, the problem must be exponentially larger now.

While I have no evidence to back this up, I wouldn't be surprised if the same sort of thing has happened even to Tom Clancy: one of his major tough-guy protagonists was a dedicated smoker who has recently retreated to being a closet smoker bumming Virginia Slims Menthol Lights from his secretary and hiding his relapses from the public and his wife.

In addition to pressuring current writers to conform in the creation of a politically correct fictional world for us to emulate, Antismokers are even creating an Orwellian revisionism for fiction writers of the past. While many of us are aware of how postage stamps and even some newspapers are air-brushing out offending cigarettes from images of famous people, very few are aware that even Mark Twain is sometimes having his work castigated in ways that would make him spin so fast in his grave that it should be airborne.

In Twain's classic *Tom Sawyer*, one of the bonding experiences that takes place between Tom Sawyer and his friends when they're hiding out on the island and playing at being pirates is when they all try to smoke a pipe just like Huck Finn. Of course they all turn green and lose their cookies, but Twain had them later go on to try it again and decide they liked it. Granted, that's not a message we'd ideally want our kids to get, but the idea of cutting it out of Twain's writing, particularly given Twain's attitude about do-gooders trying to censor things and control people, is outright infuriating. Ten years from now TV commentators may find themselves having to refer to "smokers" as the "S" word.

Rewriting fiction and history in order to conform to a current idea of political correctness is something we abhorred 40 or 50 years ago when we saw it being done in the old Soviet Union. The idea that we now embrace such revisionism because "it's for a good cause" **should** be abhorrent to any good American of today. Sadly, it seems to simply be accepted without so much as a second thought.

It may indeed be that, despite our pretensions of dedication to free speech and thought, we are simply "sheeple" waiting and ripe to be plucked when someday our leaders manage to completely circumvent the safeguards of our Constitution. In the presidential election of 2000 many who might normally have voted for Al Gore out of their political sympathies withheld those votes for fear of what a highly intelligent and motivated proselytizer of political correctness could do with the modern power of the White House, the media, and the Internet at his disposal. However, millions more cast their votes for him without giving even a single thought to this danger.

News, History, Reality

The attempt to create a fantasy world in our writings and films in which smoking does not exist among normal and good people may sound Orwellian, but when the efforts of the Crusaders extend into the worlds of current news and past history the frightening aspect of this effort expands to potentially nightmarish proportions in its implications for the future in other areas.

   According to a personal contact within a major TV news organization, there is actually a directive that has been put out to field reporters and cameramen to "avoid depictions of smoking as a normal or acceptable part of human activity." This directive went out in the early 1990s, almost a decade before Antismokers publicly admitted their "Denormalization Strategy."

   Thus, we can have the ridiculous situation of a cameraman in a foxhole insisting that a soldier extinguish his smoke just before filming that soldier being blown to bloody bits. While cigarettes still make occasional appearances in footage from live fire zones (Operation Iraqi Freedom contained a surprising number of examples, including one priceless still shot of a GI relaxing with a smoke on Saddam's couch in Saddam's bombed out palace!) and large-scale tragedies, one has to wonder just how much smoke-free-editing, either on the part of the cameraperson/reporter or on the part of the editor at the home desk, is taking place.

> # "Who controls the past, controls the future.
>
> # Who controls the present, controls the past."
>
> --Big Brother's Slogan. George Orwell's *1984*

Figure 20

In conversations with one New York City police officer shortly after the World Trade Center disaster I was struck by the amazing contrast between her descriptions of emergency personnel recuperating and smoking during off-site breaks and the total absence of images of any of these personnel smoking on news broadcasts. The amount of care that must have gone into editing out this horrendous activity from those scenes must have been monumental.

Such snippety editing may not seem too important, but the problem extends far beyond this. The leaders of China, many of whom are in their 70s and 80s and are heavy smokers, have been pressured about their public smoking and in 1997 over a hundred of them signed a pledge not to smoke in public places where their images might be projected. The fact that smokers might actually live to that age and still be active and healthy does not jibe well with the manufactured reality the Crusaders are attempting to convey to world audiences. Tiananmen Square can be tolerated. Public smoking cannot (Ross Hammond. *Addicted To Profit* 2000).

Note that when Prince Harry of England was taking up smoking the news outlets concentrated on concerns for his health while virtually no mention was made of the centenarian Queen Mother whose smoking had long been a scandal among British Crusaders. Similarly, when the Queen Mother died at the age of 101, not a word was said in the media about her smoking habit although frequent mentions were made of the fact that her daughter Margaret had died at a younger age of a "smoking-related disease."

Perhaps not too surprisingly, American media portrayal of public smoking by prominent government figures has made one minor comeback in the year 2003. Saddam Hussein's foreign minister, Tariq Assiz, can be seen lighting up in photos embellishing newspaper stories while the Iraqi dictator himself is often shown on TV news with a cigar in hand (See, e.g. CNN, 02/17/03 4:26 EST; FOX 02/25/03 4:29 EST to cite but two of dozens of instances).

One fairly invisible form of adjusting the news lies simply in the choice of what stories should get media attention. As Don Oakley pointed out in *Slow Burn,* the Media Research Center reviewed news shows on CBS, NBC, ABC, and CNN in 1995 – 1996. They found that: "***Tobacco as a risk problem is overemphasized.*** *Tobacco and smoking were the subject of 413 news stories, compared to 136 stories for obesity/fatty foods, 94 for auto safety, and 58 for alcohol*" (Timothy Lamer. "Addicted to Tobacco Stories..." *MRC Report No. 8* 10/07/96 -- Emphasis in original as noted by Oakley).

A less subtle form of laundering the news comes in the form of adding editorial material to news stories. Thus, it's not uncommon to see news stories about a specific piece of smoking or secondary smoke research that simply throws in a paragraph near the end that speaks of the "400,000 smoking-related deaths" or some similar truism. A TV news spot on Drew Carey's recent heart attack showed the actor brandishing a cigarette despite the fact that the actor does **not** smoke: The photo was taken as he was simply participating in a protest against extremist smoking bans and used a cigarette as an obvious prop!

Complaints to the network about this drew absolutely nothing in the way of a response, and no sort of apology, on or off the air, was offered (Audrey Silk, NYCclash.com).

In addition most news stories dealing with any sort of benefit from smoking such as reduced levels of Alzheimer's and Parkinson's, or lowered levels of obesity, will almost religiously add a commentary about how such benefits don't come anywhere near balancing the harms. The story of the millions of Americans who have self-medicated mild depression with the multiple tiny rewards they get from smoking throughout the day and who then go on to enter more severe and heavily medicated depression after being forced to quit smoking is one that is totally invisible in the media.

The fact that the pharmaceutical industry benefits to the tune of tens of billions of dollars with their promotion of stop-smoking aids and prescription anti-depressants couldn't have anything to do with this... could it? Consider the power the tobacco companies used to have over the media and consider how much power today's pharmaceutical advertisers must have... perhaps not as much as Philip Morris in the heyday of dancing cigarette packs, but still considerable.

Big Pharma beats Big Tobacco in the contemporary money race with billions to spare. While tobacco companies spent about 8 billion dollars promoting their products in 1999, pharmaceutical companies spent 14 billion dollars promoting theirs! (*FTC Report 2001*; Stolberg & Gerth. *New York Times* 11/16/00).

To be fair, in both cases most of the spending dealt with samples, promotions, and distribution rather than advertising, but the power of pharmaceutical ad spending should not be ignored, nor should the fact that its prominence on TV is creating a generation of youth who believe that all of life's problems can be solved by a little purple pill.

A common news slant on fires in facilities where smoking has been banned is to blame the fires purely on the smoking while never mentioning the fact that they might never have occurred had smoking **not** been banned and ashtrays and such things were allowed or provided. Generally the fact that a smoking ban was in place is not even mentioned, leaving the viewer or listener to think that such a ban would have prevented the fire!

In addition, there has never yet been an attempt by the media or the government to quantify the number of deaths caused by teenagers sneaking smokes in unsafe manners because of laws or propaganda-inspired parental and school restrictions. Only occasionally do we hear of the more catastrophic instances. One of particular note was the massive Colorado wildfire of 2002 that was sparked by students sneaking smokes behind a school where smoking had been banned: even then, the smoking was the focus, not the ban (P. Solomon Banda. *Associated Press* 04/26/02).

The pressure to hide smoking can be intense: some schools now treat possession of tobacco products as being exactly the same level of offense as carrying a deadly weapon! An infraction that used to merit a half hour detention for actually **using** tobacco products can now result in the outright expulsion and total ruination of an entire educational career for the mere **possession** of such (Alisha Hipwell. "New State Law...." *Pittsburgh Post Gazette* 04/04/01).

A particularly sad incident in this vein occurred recently not among teens, but among older folks. In 2000 there was a fire at a Philadelphia senior citizens center in which two residents died. From the content of news stories later it seemed that a quickly and improperly disposed of cigarette seems to have started the fire. Of the dozens of stories aired and printed concerning this fire, I saw only one that mentioned that a smoking ban had been put in place before the fire.

While specific details were not released, it seemed likely that the delay in calling for aid during the early and controllable period of the fire may have been due to the fear of the seniors involved that they would be thrown out alone into the street for violating the no-smoking rule. When you're 80 years old and without other resources such delay and confusion even in a burgeoning emergency would be almost unavoidable.

Finally, the news media can have a huge impact on our collective mind by simply NOT reporting the news, or reporting it very selectively. Thus, a news story about a Winnipeg woman who almost died from frostbite and hypothermia after getting locked out of a hospital at night when she went out for a smoke doesn't get much coverage. Nor does a tale about patients at a senior center who, although over 80 years old and wheelchair bound, sometimes wind up in snowdrifts while negotiating their way to the single outdoor trailer where they are allowed to smoke. The minimal coverage of the earlier cited case of the hate murder of a Florida teen is perhaps the most extreme example in this area (Linda Slobodian. *Calgary Herald* 02/17/01; Cary Castagna. *Seven Oaks* 12/20/00).

Reporters who don't fall in line with politically correct policy on smoking can run into rough times. Sidney Zion, a popular columnist at the *New York Post*, made the mistake of trying to submit a column blasting the local "Nico-Nazis" after his editor had told him to stay away from the subject. He was fired the following workday (Valerie Block. *Crain's New York Business* 10/03/01). Bill Maher was one of the staunchest defenders of smokers' rights on network TV for years... a fact that may have laid some of the groundwork for his ultimate dismissal after some profoundly politically incorrect remarks about the 9/11 disaster.

And as noted earlier, the story of the original EPA report linking secondary smoke to lung cancer received thousands of lines of print in the news and hours of coverage in various forms on television. When Judge Osteen threw out that section of the report it merited no more than a few dozen lines and virtually no network coverage. The EPA/Osteen example is probably the clearest case to date of how the smoking debate has been defined by the power of the media in engineering its portrayal to the general public.

10) Fallacious Argumentation

One of the most startling differences between a cat and a lie is that a cat has only nine lives.

– Mark Twain

This chapter began with a look at how individual words and concepts have been altered in the course of the Antismoking Crusade, and then went on to note how such alteration makes it difficult to engage in rational argument on the real issues when confronting Crusaders in public debate.

There is another misuse of language that Antismokers commonly engage in, and while it is not as dangerously manipulative of basic thought as fiddling with the meanings of words, it is fully as difficult to confront if one is not expecting it and aware of it. This misuse is simply the employment of techniques of fallacious argumentation. Such slippery tactics have been among the basic tools of propaganda ever since Plato was erecting straw men for Socrates to demolish.

I've picked out about a dozen examples and their variations below. No one is immune to falling into the traps of either using or being taken in by fallacious argumentation but if you are aware of the danger you are much less likely to get hurt. Earlier in this book I pointed out two examples where I might have been accused of Slippery Slope or Ad Hominem argumentation. In both cases I felt the realities at the bases of the arguments justified the approaches I was taking and explained why. I have yet to see an Antismoking Crusader recognize his or her own use of such arguments or of any of the other ones presented below.

When listening to a debate or reading an argument about scientific fact it's always helpful to strip away extra verbiage and side statements not central to the point. This helps to expose only the most basic and essential information upon which such arguments are based. Only then can one hope to get beyond the slippery words and the various language tricks that are so often used by skilled lawyers and professionals.

Argument Ad Hominem

In an argument Ad Hominem, unscrupulous debaters, when seeing that their opponent's facts are too strong to actually argue against, will instead seek to attack the character of the opponent. The rationale is that after the opponent has been painted as being a scoundrel of some sort or another, no one will bother to actually listen to whatever he or she was trying to say.

When it comes to the issue of smoking, the most common use of this form of argumentation appears when Antismokers try to dismiss the arguments of anyone who disagrees with their point by claiming that the opponent is a "tobacco company mouthpiece," or a "front for Big Tobacco." Of course no one in their right minds with any awareness of Big Tobacco's historical record will believe anything that they say, so if an Antismoker can succeed in painting an opponent as merely parroting Big Tobacco's line then he or she can almost guarantee that the opponent's message will go unheard.

It's amazing how effective this technique can be, even when the claim is patently ridiculous. In recent hearings in municipalities around the country it was common to see local bar and restaurant associations painted as being shills or fronts for Big Tobacco, thus rendering their pleas for the freedom to run their own businesses almost useless.

Even ordinary waiters and waitresses have their char- acters and testimonies attacked in this way. When Philadelphia's City Council held a hearing aiming to ban smoking in bar/restaurants one long-term waitress reacted furiously when such an accusation was made in response to her testimony. She proclaimed loudly to the Council Chamber "I am **NOT** a paid mouthpiece for **ANYBODY!**" and received a round of overwhelming applause (Philadelphia City Council Hearing, 05/31/00).

It's pretty obvious to anyone who thinks a bit about it that the financial clout of Big Tobacco in relation to the day to day concerns of anyone in the business of selling food and liquor is going to be far less important than the bottom line of engendering customer satisfaction and repeat business. But the power of the Ad Hominem argument is strong enough that many never make that leap of thought: they simply nod their heads in agreement with the idea that bar owners and workers are simply part of "The Tobacco Cartel."

Even Honeywell Manufacturing has been targeted as a tobacco "ally" by the Minnesota Smoke-Free Coalition because it makes air-cleaning systems that might give all patrons cleaner and more comfortable air in establishments where smoking was allowed. A properly sized and maintained air-cleaning system could quite easily produce a Free-Choice bar with air that is not only cleaner than the air in an average smoking-banned bar, but even cleaner than the air outside! (Phelps & Rybak. *Minnesota Star Tribune* 11/18/01).

This technique has also been used successfully against scientists and researchers. If a particular scientist dares to publish material contrary to the universal message that "Smoking is Evil" then he or she is likely to be labeled as an "industry supporter" and have future work or opinion discounted as tainted. A single slip may be overlooked, particularly if a study is so clearly well designed that it's impossible to attack, but repeated performances of this nature are not likely to be well looked upon. Researchers are implicitly expected to adhere to the "Glantz Standard" as outlined earlier in Figure 2.

In conjunction with the natural desire of researchers to develop findings that will increase their likelihood of receiving future grants, this fear of taint has probably influenced the design and reporting of many of the supposedly pure and scientific studies on the effects of secondary smoke. In writing this book I have gotten no funding support of any kind, nor would I have accepted it if offered since the source would almost surely have been from tobacco companies and would have rendered any attempt to reach and truly communicate with a wide audience totally useless.

In the future if a tobacco company decided it was in its interest to reprint anything I have written here and gave standard payment for such a privilege, my acceptance of such an offer would immediately open me for branding by Antismokers as simply being "A Tool of Big Tobacco." This is exactly what happened to Jacob Sullum, the author of *For Your Own Good*: when he wrote an op-ed piece critical of the Crusade, one of the big tobacco companies wanted to reprint it and gave him $5,000 for the rights. Ever since then, anything he writes on the subject is discounted ridiculed by Antismoking groups because of his "longstanding economic relationship with the industry."

In reality I could probably make the most money from this book simply by selling it to a well-heeled group like Florida's TRUTH.com or the American Legacy Foundation and then letting them bury it six feet under. Fortunately I'm a bit too much of a bullheaded Irishman to go for that sort of thing: bad for my pocketbook, but good for my soul. However, if Big Tobacco wants to buy and distribute a few thousand copies of this book as a regular customer, or if TRUTH.com wants to buy and distribute a few thousand at their next "Smoking Control" convention (not likely!), more power to them: the more people who see this information and discuss it, the better!

Despite my efforts to avoid providing any real grounds for claims of "contamination," Crusaders will probably still try Ad Hominem dismissals of the arguments and information presented in this book. Shortly before starting the actual writing of *Dissecting Antismokers' Brains* I wrote a letter to a small town newspaper I'd come across on the Internet that had published a rather extremist article (See Figure 21). This letter was noticed by the Americans for Nonsmokers Rights Foundation (ANRF). ANRF is a spin-off group of ANR, a group founded by Glantz.

Near the end of 1999 the *Los Angeles Daily News* exposed a program of the ANR designed to identify and discredit any critics of the Crusade by attempting to link them to the tobacco industry. The exposure created an upswell of public feeling against these unknown government-funded groups that were keeping track of the lawful activities of ordinary citizens and using those records to influence important decisions made by political figures (Terri Hardy. *Los Angeles Daily News* 12/06/99).

ANRF has inherited and continued the so-called "Enemies List" documentation on Free-Choice advocates and has published a public consumption version of that list on a web site titled "The Tobacco Industry Tracking Database." My letter to the Free Lance-Star was summarized in typical surveillance report language with that summary properly entered and indexed in that database. Thus, in the future when I testify at a Council hearing or publish an article or book critical of the Crusade, detractors can attack my veracity simply by noting that I appear in the "The Tobacco Industry Tracking Database" (See Figure 22).

The fact that I appear there simply by virtue of having expressed an opinion as a private citizen in a letter to a newspaper will appear unimportant next to the fact that I've appeared on a list with such an official-sounding and damning name. My plight will be similar to that of union activists in the 1950s who had had the misfortune of attending a socialist meeting in college or once signing a petition condemning fascism in 1930's Spain.

Being painted as having a tobacco industry connection today is almost as damning as being accused of communist leanings in the 1950s or child molesting in the 1990s: the accusation does the damage, and later corrections and retractions can never fully repair it. As Senator McCarthy knew all too well, the intimidating power of simply waving a list of names in the air can be enormous.

Finally, if the modern equivalent of red-baiting falls flat, Crusaders can attack this book simply on the grounds of credentials. I am not a doctor. I do not even have a Ph.D. or a collection of published articles in scholarly journals. My only response to this is to point to the evidence, arguments, and facts I have presented while urging the reader to evaluate the information on its own merit.

Cathy Dyson mentions that "... students have been telling their peers to stay off the stuff because it kills one in five Americans each year." Since only about 3 million Americans die each year from all causes, I somehow doubt that 50 million Americans are dying each year from smoking. But this is exactly the kind of "funny statistic"... antismokers preach as gospel.

... 400,000 yearly deaths from smoking comes from a computer program called SAMMEC ... change some of those formulas and, presto, the number of smoking deaths could be cut in half!

3,000 deaths a year from secondary smoke is ... a statistical creation of EPA activists who felt ...reducing smoking was important enough to (produce) what amounts to... an outright lie.

(If you'd) like to learn more... visit Web sites such as forces.org and the various links from it...

--Michael J McFadden. *The Free Lance-Star*, 07/12/20

Figure 21

Entry in ANRF's "Tobacco Industry Tracking Database":

McFadden, M.J.; "'Funny' stats used by anti-smoking crusaders," *Free Lance-Star*, 07/12/01.

This editorial by Michael McFadden of Philadelphia, Pennsylvania, took issue with the assertion that "50 million" Americans die from smoking each year. McFadden asserted that only about three million Americans die each year from all causes. McFadden argued that the statistic that 3,000 people die as a result of secondhand smoke exposure can also be manipulated to represent smaller and truer results. McFadden had particular disdain for the Environmental Protection Agency (EPA) and a statistics based computer program called SAMMEC.... McFadden recommends that people visit www.forces.org.

Figure 22

A corollary type of argument to Ad Hominem is the Appeal To Authority. In the Appeal to Authority the debater will simply seek to have the listeners agree with him or her by pointing to someone's credentials or mentioning the name of someone famous and respected as supporting their argument. The effect is again one of transference: instead of examining the substance of the argument, the audience simply accepts that it must be true because of the "Authority" associated with it.

As noted earlier in the chapter on The Idealists, this sort of argumentation is very common at public hearings on smoking bans. It matters not if the speaker knows anything about the particular point being argued if he or she can hold up an M.D. degree (or the appearance of one) before making a statement.

On an extended level, Antismokers often use this approach when they make such claims as "Every major health agency in the world supports us." That may or may not be true at various times; but if it precludes real examination of the facts it is by no means helpful in the search for genuine truth. Many health agencies may indeed support the concept of secondary smoke being a threat; but if their motivation for that support springs from a desire to reduce smoking through bans rather than resulting from an unbiased application of science and epidemiology, then their support is tainted.

Straw Man Argumentation

One uses a straw man argument by setting up a superficial misrepresentation of the opponent's position that is deliberately weak and easy to destroy. One destroys this "straw man" and then goes on to claim that they've actually destroyed the opponent's argument itself.

A good example of the straw man in this area is the statement "Smokers want the right to smoke anytime and anywhere they choose." While no smokers' rights organization makes such a claim, the misrepresentation of their position in this way makes for an easy attack by a Crusader and for nicely inflated numbers in surveys that purport to show support for widespread bans. Most smokers are quite willing to accept reasonable limitations on where and when they can smoke, and while there may be gray areas, no one is arguing that smokers should have the right to smoke on crowded busses, in premature nursery units, or in businesses or restaurants where the owner has freely decided to ban smoking and has clearly posted notice of such prohibition for entering customers to see.

One particular straw man that I have frequently encountered while discussing secondary smoke and smoking bans with friends and acquaintances is the following statement: "So... you're saying that smoking is GOOD for your health?" Certainly I've never said any such thing: on a personal level I believe the case linking smoking to a number of health problems has been pretty strongly made. (I should note: not everyone agrees with such a position. The references in the Recommended Bibliography to forces.org, Carol Thompson's web pages, and Lawrence Colby's *In Defense of Smokers* all provide arguments in this area.)

Of course once I say, "No, I am NOT saying that smoking is good for your health." my opponent will usually simply assert loudly that they have "won" the argument... despite the fact that the argument was only about the effects of secondary smoke in the first place! But having "won" the argument my opponent will simply dismiss anything else I have to say as unimportant. Thus I am apparently left with an almost unwinnable position... a type of "Catch 22."

Catch 22

This is not usually considered a form of fallacious argumentation in and of itself, but I'm not sure what term would be a better descriptor. *Catch 22* was the name of a novel in which a character wanted to be discharged from the army and sent home from the war on the grounds that he was crazy. However, the very fact that he wanted to be sent home before he was killed proved that he was sane and thus should NOT be sent home! In a sense this type of argumentation is related to George Orwell's concept of "Doublethink" explored later (Joseph Heller. *Catch 22*. Scribner 1996).

In addition to the example in the preceding section one can see this technique used in the following instance: Antismokers will claim in one breath that smoking is an addiction so strong that addicts cannot hope to control it on their own while in their next breath they'll state that smokers should have no real difficulty refraining from smoking for extended periods of time as required by some smoking bans. In truth, the Crusader making such arguments may not even be aware of the inherent contradiction: as noted later, a mind well trained in Orwellian Doublethink can handle such inconsistencies with ease.

What they have done is simply state two straw man premises, knowing that when one is attacked, the other can be brought up as a defense against such attack. If the smoker then switches to attacking the other premise, the first is again raised. If the smoker accepts either premise then its relevance to the other will be soundly denied by the debating Crusader who will then usually either "Appeal to Emotion" or resort to some form of "Switching Bases" as discussed below.

Appeal to Emotion

Out of the sixty or so Antismokers who testified at the New York City Council hearing I attended in 2001, there were three who had laryngectomies and gave their testimony using devices held to their throats that enabled them to have a very disconcerting form of speech. Three out of sixty equates to 5%... far, far higher than the percentage in the general population with laryngectomies, and even higher than the percentage in the population of Antismokers.

Why were these people sought after by Crusading groups to give testimony?   Simply because the emotive appeal of their appearance was guaranteed to win a sympathetic ear.   Councilpeople would then ignore what substance may or may not have been in their testimony itself and instead concentrate on the "desperate need" for rapidly approving the requested bans! As mentioned earlier, the possible contributions of their own long-term smoking habits were usually simply ignored.

At one of the Philadelphia hearings a mother brought in a toddler dressed up in a little gas mask. Surely there was no one smoking at that hearing, but the image had the desired effect of inspiring instant sympathy among almost any mother who saw the news spot with the mother tearfully holding her son up to the cameras while speaking of his extended stays in hospitals after passing by clusters of smokers on the way in and out of doorways.

The fact that the bill primarily concerned smoking bans in bar areas of restaurants, and might have actually made the clustering situation at doorways even worse due to the removal of self-chosen specialized nonsmoking venues, was of course shuffled into the background. The harm to the child of possibly being the victim of the mother's own neurotic fears was likewise ignored.

The Appeal to Emotion can also be quite effective on the individual level if the population is vulnerable. The sweet little old grandmother whose only vice is an after-dinner cigarette with her sherry can be convinced to quit if she can be made to believe that traces of her "poisons" may be killing her grandchildren even if she only smokes outside.

She'll be told, "Think about that sweet baby that loves you more than it loves itself." And if that doesn't work, Crusaders will stoop even lower and seek to convince the elderly soul that she's giving her cats cancer. Love is a powerful motivator (Carole Sanders. www.anmlangls.org/smokers.htm; Julie Marshall. dailycamera.com 01/03/03).

To be sure, positive emotions are not the only ones that can be appealed to. Fear and disgust work just as well in the hands of a skilled manipulator. One Crusader, a feeder at the public trough of Delaware National Guard's Counterdrug Task Force, likes to scare impressionable children by holding up a blackened, bloody, and diseased looking lung in classrooms while explaining that the cancerous thing came from a man who had smoked for just 15 years.

In reality, it is simply a pig's lung shot full of carcinogens and prepared carefully to look disgusting, gruesome, and scary... not a human lung at all. The National Guard Captain explained to the reporter covering the story that his lesson was made stronger *"by not passing along that tidbit of truth"* (James Merriweather. *Delaware News Journal*. 04/05/01).

As stated earlier, "Saving The Children" is a powerful emotional argument. I confess to using a variation of this method when I brought up the effects of smoking bans on psychiatric patients and seniors. I felt justified because those were particularly horrible examples of how unthinking bans can hurt those among us who are most helpless, but I still recognize that to some extent I was "Appealing to Emotion" in my argument. Now if I had a few hundred million dollars to put billboards up across the country picturing 98-year-olds being forced to stand outside in blizzards I might feel a bit more guilty about it...

Switching Bases

As mentioned earlier, it's common to see Crusaders switching numbers and concerns around faster than a Three Card Monte player on Times Square. Secondary smoke is **not** the same as smoking itself. Six-year-olds are **not** the same as nineteen-year-olds. Banning smoking by kindergarten teachers during kindergarten classes is **not** the same as banning a bartender from smoking while working at a bar. Smoking-related or smoking-associated deaths are **not** the same as smoking-caused deaths: the first two terms are carefully specifying only a possibly random statistical association; the latter term denotes a finding of causality. In reality this is actually a quite important distinction and certainly not one that should ever be brushed over as simply a matter of semantics.

A somewhat different form of Switching Bases can be seen when Antismokers criticize studies that show nonsmokers are exposed to very low levels of "cigarette equivalents" while working in a smoking environment. Studies using such measurement have generally come up with exposure figures equivalent to less than a pack or so per year even for many working in smoky restaurants and bars! (Jenkins et al. Oak Ridge National Laboratories, US Dept. of Energy, *Journal of Exposure Analysis and Environmental Epidemiology,* February 2000).

Antismokers will claim that secondary smoke is chemically much different than the smoke a smoker inhales and that this difference renders such studies invalid. But without skipping a beat, these same Antismokers will then go on to base their claims about the danger of secondary smoke upon the argument that it is chemically very similar to the smoke a smoker inhales. Whether such smoke is to be judged as being the same as or different from primary smoke all depends purely upon the particular argument a particular Crusader is pursuing at a particular time!

{Note: Due to the "undesirable" results from personal monitoring studies they're usually funded only by tobacco companies, but their science and accuracy are almost never criticized by Antismokers. They're generally just attacked with Ad Hominem arguments or, as noted above, by "Switching Bases." If the study results themselves were questionable it would be an easy matter for Crusading organizations to replicate the data collection and discredit the research in the normal scientific manner. Of course, because the results themselves are in point of fact quite valid and replicable, such an approach is generally not even attempted, particularly since the Ad Hominem attack is so conveniently powerful in our sound-bite dominated media.}

While referring to Orwell's *1984* is almost as trite a form of argument as referring to Nazis, I have done both in this book where it has seemed appropriate and I will do so again here. "Doublethink," the practice of holding two contradictory concepts in one's mind at the same time without acknowledging their fundamental conflict, was an integral part of Orwell's vision of how a truly mind-controlled population could reconcile itself to a world where "thought-crime" was a punishable offense.

Crusaders are masters of Doublethink: as noted earlier, at one moment they will proclaim the addictive power of nicotine as being worse than that of heroin... then, with barely a pause, they'll launch into an argument for an extra 50 cent per pack tax as a deterrent to smoking and claim that it's not **really** a tax since it's "voluntary" and "people can choose not to smoke" (Eric Weiss quoting Connecticut Gov. Rowland in *Courant* 01/25/02) or, as Gov. Ventura of Minnesota stated it: "If you don't want to pay for it, don't smoke" (*Associated Press* NY 02/20/02). Tax increases are depicted as helping working-class smokers by forcing them to spend more money if they want to continue to smoke, thereby encouraging them to smoke less or even to quit.

The addiction/choice dichotomy was also discussed earlier in the chapter on bans: Antismokers will set their convictions about the addictiveness of tobacco to one side in their thoughts while arguing with seeming sincerity that there's no real cost to smokers when they are forced to refrain from smoking for ten or twenty hours during airline trips and layovers. If smoking is truly such a powerful addiction, then the bans are obviously quite stressful to the smoker and accommodations should be made.

Another form of switching bases arises when Antismokers testify for or against particular bills and use teen smoking rates as part of their argument. A drop in teen smoking is something that's desired by almost everyone. When such a drop occurs it offers a veritable field day for switching bases.

If the bill under consideration relates to advertising, Antismokers will credit the drop to the disappearance of Joe Camel. If the debate is over a large rise in cigarette taxes, a youth smoking rate drop will be credited to past increases. The same claims will be made at different times to support increased enforcement through sting operations, the banning of cigarette vending machines in bars (I'm sure we've all seen the long lines of school children in bars lined up at those machines...), increased smoking bans, increased funding for Antismoking groups and ads, or increases or decreases in just about anything else the particular testifying Crusader happens to be focusing on.

Whatever the particular focus of the current proposed law or regulation, claims will be made that past changes in that particular area were solely responsible for the observed drop and that future changes will produce similar future drops. The role of the other factors will be totally ignored until another law or tax is proposed and then another factor will be held up as the "solution" to teen smoking. The funny thing is that it seems that half the time, even when ALL the different goals of the Antismokers are implemented, the teenage smoking rate simply turns around and increases the following year anyway!

Statistical games

The misuse of statistics by Antismokers occurs in so many different ways that I would need a separate book to cover them all, but there are some that tie specifically into the area of logical fallacies, so I'll largely limit my examination to these.

"*Post hoc, ergo propter hoc*" (After that, therefore because of that) is the fallacy of assuming that simply because one event happens after another event that the two events were causally related. The examples cited above about various factors supposedly affecting teen smoking rates are good examples of this. Another example is the widely used argument by Crusaders concerning California. California enacted extreme smoking bans (including bans in bars!) in the late 1990s. Antismokers claim there was an almost immediate drop of 14% in California's lung cancer rate due to their efforts.

Of course the argument isn't true: lung cancer generally has a lag time of anywhere from twenty to forty years after an exposure to an offending substance. Even the California Medical Association's CEO, Dr. Jack Lewin, has stated, "*As physicians we know that the window of danger with tobacco is four to six decades*" (Sweeney. *Copley News Service* July 2002). In truth, the only way time-line graphs of smoking prevalence and lung cancer rates have supported the link between the two historically is when such time lag considerations are factored in. This reality has been noted in Surgeon Generals' Reports ever since 1964. And, to put the final nail in the coffin of this 14% drop claim: the study from which it comes actually referred to a drop between 1988 and 1996: two full years **before** California banned smoking in all bars and workplaces! (op.cit. *2001 Master Plan For a Smoke-Free California*)

As noted in the earlier chapter on Secondary Smoke, the change in California's cancer rate obviously had far more to do with a changing population base of Mexican immigrants and young yuppie couples and an increasingly stringent set of motor vehicle emissions regulations in previous decades than it had to do with yet-to-be-enacted smoking bans in bars; but the figure is nonetheless quite widely used by Crusaders arguing for bar bans in other cities both in the U.S. and overseas!

Once again, in all fairness, the reader may want to go back to a prior argument where I noted that the use of hard drugs and inhalants by teens had gone up drastically during the past ten years as the Antismoking Crusade has sought to picture tobacco as more dangerous than any other drug. Certainly there's no way of proving that such a statistical increase was caused directly by the Crusade, and I don't believe I made a claim of such proof; but in this case there is at least some sound basis for the argument linking the two. My "*post hoc*" has a good claim to being at least partially "*propter hoc*" as teenage thinking about the relative dangers of drugs was fuzzied and blurred in the 1990s, and there's no forty-year time lag involved.

I also looked earlier at the way a computer program called SAMMEC was able to generate virtually any scary figures the programmer desired. Unfortunately, numbers have a special aura of authority and SAMMEC's misinterpreted claim that "smoking causes 400,000 deaths a year" has become such a basic part of America's belief system that it will be hard to dislodge. The statistical sleight of hand performed by the EPA in its contested report was perhaps even more incredible as it moved studies in and out of its database and distorted its normal standards for statistical significance until it achieved the desired answer to feed to the public.

As Mark Twain is reputed to have said: *"There are three kinds of lies: Lies, Damned Lies, and Statistics."* Unfortunately too many people have forgotten to take their grain of salt after every new study that appears in the news, but I hope that this book will help in some measure to correct that. Never believe a news report about a study without first attempting to look at the study itself, or, at a minimum, at its official abstract.

Such minimum fact-checking is almost absurdly easy in today's computerized newsrooms, but all too often it seems that reporters will simply regurgitate a press release about a study without even having done such a minimum amount of homework. The fact that the press release was paid for by an advocacy group desiring to put a particular spin on that study will all too often be ignored by a lazy, unskilled, or overworked reporter fighting a deadline.

A tip-off when reading a press release is to check whether it was released by an organization through public relations out-lets. These companies will print and release just about anything, as long as the ones who wrote the release are willing to pay a few thousand dollars for the service. When a well-heeled Crusading group wants to make a media splash with a new campaign they'll simply arrange for a cascade of "news stories" to appear through such outlets, highlighting various aspects of an issue or rehash-ing old news as if it were new.

A classic example of this came in the summer of 2002 when the Coalition for World No Tobacco Day (supported by such unbiased Coalition members as Glaxo-Smith Kline, the maker of the stop-smoking aid Zyban) paid for close to a dozen press releases citing the news that fire departments in various cities were banning smoking for the day. In a PR campaign that lasted for over three weeks, timed releases were put out supposedly reporting the news from different fire departments around the country that were planning to ban smoking for that day (See, e.g. Pittsburgh *PRNewswire* 05/28/02, Austin *PRNewswire* 05/06/02, Indianapolis *PRNewswire* 05/21/02 among others).

However, if one bothered to cross check the different stories, one found that **all** the fire officials and health officials in Pittsburgh, Austin, Minneapolis, Indianapolis and other cities just happened to say **exactly** the same boilerplate statements without even a word being changed.   Either our public service departments have all been taken over by identical alien clones or someone was playing very loose with the facts in these "news releases."

Check the bottom lines of news stories to see where they came from.   If they're from a non-profit or government-sponsored group that's been flush with smokers' money from the Master Settlement Agreement, get the extra-large salt-shaker ready.   Of course there's no such red flag when a real, though irresponsible, reporter transmits a by-lined story that's simply based entirely upon such paid propaganda releases.

Bandwagon / Ad Populum

When Regina Carlson of New Jersey GASP (Group Against Smokers Pollution) was debating about open air smoking bans on the earlier-referenced Lynn Doyle show, she repeatedly intoned phrases about how "Everyone is doing this more and more" and "This is the way things are going" and "Communities all over the country are enacting these regulations."   No one wants to be left alone out in the cold while everyone else has hopped on a bandwagon and gone off to have fun.

If a debater can convince an audience that his or her view has been accepted by the vast majority of people, or even just that more and more people are starting to accept their view, it is likely that the audience will find itself swayed without bothering to listen to actual particulars of the arguments. After all, we **all** like to feel we're on the winning side of things!

At City Council hearings on smoking bans Crusaders will repeatedly refer to other cities and towns where such bans have been enacted or are being considered.   They make it sound as though any particular city resisting this imaginary trend will be left behind and alone. Of course they'll never mention that many of the places that have in fact enacted widespread smoking bans subsequently backed down after suffering economic losses or have allowed so many hardship exceptions that the bans were effectively voided though still on the books. They'll also avoid mentioning that many of the cities living with extreme smoking bans are in California and had no choice but to go along with the state ban itself.

The Bandwagon appeal is a strong one when pitched to politicians because any politicians not on the same bandwagon as their constituents are unlikely to be re-elected. Remember, it was not political idealism or his deep love for children that prompted President Clinton to attack Big Tobacco in the 1990s: it was the result of focus groups that showed audiences reacting warmly to politicians opposing Big Tobacco when the issue was framed in terms of "Big Tobacco addicting innocent children to nicotine."

Before those groups latched onto the issue of connecting smoking to children and showed the emotional power of this approach, the Democratic campaign had been very hesitant to say much of anything about smoking for fear of losing the Southern vote. As it turned out, the bandwagon power of "Saving The Children" very definitely saved the day for the Democrats as Clinton and many of his supporters won elections at least partially on this issue.

Unfortunately for the Antismoking Lobby, their attempts to switch the issue to higher taxes and universal bans may have backfired in their heavily financed campaigns in 2002. Although a number of individual states were targeted with as much as five million dollars apiece just for these efforts (e.g. Florida: $5.8 million; Missouri: $4.8 million) they met with mixed results as voters rebelled.

Conservative and angry smokers who might normally have sat out some of these elections showed up at the polls to defend their rights and wound up tipping the political scales in favor of conservative Republican candidates in several close elections. In Missouri for example, supporters of a 300% tax hike on cigarettes outspent opponents by a ratio of 50 to 1 and not only failed to get the tax passed but managed to pull out enough conservative smokers to tilt a very close Senate race to the Republican candidate (Jim Talent) who favored "less Big Government." Increased smoker turnout in Delaware, Maryland, Florida, and Oklahoma may have swung a few other close races as well (*Associated Press* 11/06/02; www.ballot.org; Private emails with local news reporters and activists).

Argument Ad Populum (Appeal to the People) is similar: it basically argues that since "everyone" agrees with something, therefore it must be true. In reality, it's rare that "everyone" actually agrees with something that is being argued; and in any event, what "everyone" believes really has no bearing on whether an argument in and of itself is valid.

The Ad Populum argument is often made by Antismokers in the effort to create a self-fulfilling prophecy: if they picture the world in a certain way often enough, and convince enough people that that's actually the way the world either is, or is becoming…. then perhaps it WILL become that way! This motivation forms a great deal of the impetus behind the efforts to eliminate the portrayal of smoking in both the news and entertainment medias: the Denormalization of smoking in the media is meant to encourage the Denormalization of smoking in life.

Fallacies of Equivocation and False Dilemma

The fallacy of equivocation occurs when one uses the same word in two different ways during the course of an argument in order to produce the desired, and false, conclusion. We saw an example of this in the chapter on Language when we spoke of the "toxic" elements in tobacco smoke. There is the scientific term toxic, which refers to a certain amount of a given element producing harm, and there is the popular definition of toxic, which means "it will kill you," without reference to the amount necessary, and then there is the even looser popular interpretation that toxic simply means "something bad."

Thus, scientifically speaking, salt is toxic to the human body when ingested in unusually large quantities. Popularly, of course, salt is never considered to be a toxin. Conversely, a real scientist would not normally use the term "toxic" to describe the quantity of arsenic in the air when someone has smoked a cigarette. Remember, the quantity a nonsmoker would normally be exposed to is measured in nanograms or even just picograms!

To the popular mind however, arsenic is a deadly poison, and people are not accustomed to thinking of it in any other way, regardless of the dose involved; which, of course, is why arsenic, formaldehyde and similar chemicals are often the ones cited by Crusading groups at hearings on smoking bans. The table at the end of Appendix B shows just how weak those arguments really are when examined with science rather than rhetoric.

Crusaders also use equivocation in several different ways when they speak of "Saving the Children." First, as pointed out earlier, is the simple play on the word "children" itself, which summons up images of 6-year-olds rather than 18-year-olds. The second equivocation occurs when they speak of deaths in the same breath as they speak of children. The deaths that they speak of are not the deaths of children as children, but deaths that largely occur when those children are retired and raising grandchildren themselves! While assuredly no death is ever good, the emotional appeal of confusing the possibility of deaths decades into the future with the present image of childhood's purity and innocence is equivocation.

In a similar vein the decision to use the term "pediatric disease" to describe smoking is pure equivocation, both in the use of the word pediatric to describe a practice that does not generally cause disease in the pediatric population, and also in the decision to label the practice of smoking in teens as a disease while ignoring the more widespread (and far more dangerous for young people!) use of alcohol or the increasing use of inhalants.

As English soccer star Tony Adams has noted, "*At the moment, drinking is acceptable. It is like smoking back in the Sixties...*" (*Reuters.* London 01/10/02). It's truly incredible that such substances, actual real killers of many of our teens from either overdose or accident, are relatively ignored while tobacco smoking is proclaimed a pediatric disease despite its general lack of significant effect on pediatric health.

One particularly popular equivocation at hearings on smoking bans is the false opposition of "The Right To Breathe" with "The Right To Smoke". Politicians are given a false dilemma choice between "air that is safe to breathe" and air that is "contaminated by toxic tobacco smoke." People were breathing quite successfully for decades without the existence of wide-spread smoking bans, and of course air that has a sufficiently diluted quantity of tobacco smoke in it is still generally going to be quite safe to breathe from any rational scientific, individual or even public health standpoint.

Even the air at the top of Mt. Everest will always contain a few atoms that rose from someone's pipe, cigar, or barbeque. "Safe" air does **not** necessarily mean "smoke-free" air. The matter of concern for safety is always one of degree… a distinction universally ignored by Crusaders when they push for total bans: in true Newspeak fashion the goal is to redefine the terms so that it becomes impossible to even think of air as being safe if it might have a trace of smoke in it.

The phrase "safe, healthy, smoke-free air" is deliberately made a unitary term by activists like Joe Cherner of Smoke-Free Educational Services when he pushes for smoking bans in bars because "ALL workers deserve a safe, healthy, smokefree work environment" (www.smokefree.org; Emphasis in original). Using this language and reasoning, and using the absolutist standard of air that is 100% free of any and all wisps of combustion products, one would have to eliminate fireplaces, cooking grilles (with or without exhaust hoods), outdoor fireworks displays at Disneyland, and even birthday candles in McDonalds! Air **can** be safe and healthy for human beings, even with small amounts of smoke in it, and most people with common sense know that.

The confusion of "active smoking" with "passive smok-ing"; the mix up between "smoking related" deaths with deaths actually "caused by smoking" (a very big difference in scientific terms: one is simply a correlation, the other is an actual supposedly determined cause); the difference between "allowing" college-age students to smoke on a campus as opposed to "encouraging" them to smoke; the difference between "targeting children" and advertising in magazines with an 80% over-21 readership; the confusion of unbreatheably smoky air with air that has barely detectable amounts of smoke in it -- all of these are examples of equivocation in action.

Argumentum Ad Nauseum

This final fallacy is really one of the simplest, but it's one that plays a prominent role in public hearings about smoking bans. Antismoking Crusaders very deliberately seek to stack the deck with as many people as possible at City Council hearings, most of whom will simply repeat the same misleading phrases, incorrect arguments, and juggled figures over, and over, and over again.

They have an inherent advantage over those of us who wish to question such mountains of misinformation: they have large numbers of salaried and knowledgeable staffers working for the various groups who are paid to show up repeatedly during the course of normal workdays to testify at hearings that are constantly being rescheduled, postponed, and extended. These paid lobbyists have their numbers buttressed by the frenetic energy and participation of the various Antismoking subgroups as outlined in the first half of this book.

Thus when such hearings finally take place, they are assured of a large majority of speakers. The interconnectedness of the various Crusading organizations and their intimate sharing of sources of information through intergroup conferences also ensure a consistency of terms and message. This consistency translates to repetition and with repetition comes the appearance of legitimacy.

This fallacy is, in a sense, an offshoot of Ad Populum: one is left with the impression that "everyone" believes something, simply because one has heard it repeated so many times. It's reminiscent of the Big Lie technique: repeat an outlandish statement often enough and loudly enough and no matter how bizarre it is, people will eventually believe it. And, of course, if everyone believes it, then it MUST be true!

Conclusion

At this point I will leave the area of Fallacious Argumentation before I am myself accused of Argumentum Ad Nauseum. The reader however, should bear one final thought in mind: never assume that just because you've heard an argument a hundred times that it is therefore a sound argument. Just as with scientific studies and their media-reported interpretations, the facts don't always jibe with what they're made out to mean. I have tried to avoid misrepresentations here, but would never object to anyone cross-checking anything they have doubts about. There are many good information sources out there beyond the hyped up articles you commonly see on TV and in the papers... use them!

While I'm sure my efforts have been far from perfect, I've done my best to generally avoid using the techniques of fallacious argumentation outlined above. I've tried to point out those areas where I might have been guilty of using them so that the reader can take note and decide for him or her self whether my arguments can stand on their own merit. It's hard not to at least occasionally respond in kind when an adversary is making extraordinarily effective use of basically unfair weapons, and I know that I've done some of my own heartstring-plucking with regard to our universal concerns about the welfare of children and older folks. As noted earlier though: at least I'm open about it.

We've now examined the psychology of many of those who make up the Antismoking Crusade, as well as the tricks and techniques they've used on their road to conquest. Conquest never comes cheaply though: in Section 3, The True Costs, we'll take a hard look at some of the prices we have all paid in this War On Smoking (or, as many Free-Choice advocates would put it, this War On Smokers.)

~Summation~

The tricks and techniques of propaganda and language are powerful and persuasive tools in the hands of those who would manipulate us "for our own good" whether that good be a smoke-free world, or a world dominated by the values of whatever country we happen to be citizens of. In today's world those who have control over the media whether by virtue of status or simply money can wield an influence over the rest of us that is frightening.

That influence can be diminished when one knows what to look for and can see the chinks in the armor of a foe who might appear invulnerable at first glance. I hope this section has provided the informational crowbars by which those of us without access to high-profile media weaponry can pry open that armor. Exposing lies and manipulation can do more than eliminate their power: such exposure can be a weapon in and of itself in destroying the success of those who would dominate us.

The following two sections will bring together into a coherent unit some of what has already been examined and also form a basis from which Free-Choice advocates can launch their own drive to restore the balance between smokers and nonsmokers to some reasonable level of sanity. Combined with the information in the various Appendices, any motivated activist should be able to use the body of information in *Dissecting Antismokers' Brains* to stop and reverse the damage the Antismoking Crusade has already done and is planning to do to our society.

The True Costs

From my point of view, anything that stops smoking is good.

--Surgeon General Koop, 1996

This section will be fairly short, as many of the costs of the Antismoking Crusade have already been touched on along the way. It is nonetheless worth gathering some of them together here, and adding a few not mentioned, in order to emphasize the fallacy of the Crusading mantra -- that ever-wider and more extreme measures against smoking produce only a positive good (a physically healthier population) at no real cost to anyone but the tobacco companies.

Some of the costs are societal, such as the creation of a new generation of "rum-runners" who now smuggle vast quantities of cigarettes from state to state and country to country to evade confiscatory taxes or finance terrorism; and some are purely personal, such as the divisiveness sown between individuals and the guilt and pain felt by those blamed unjustly for the illnesses of others.

Some are financial, such as the many hundreds of dollars a year that most smokers are now forced to pour into the public coffers for all sorts of programs that are of little or no benefit (and sometimes actual detriment) to themselves; and some are purely emotional, such as the dislike, anger, and even hate that has been created as a result of this campaign and the resultant alienation and depression felt by ostracized smokers.

Occasionally, as noted in the chapter on Hate, there's even sometimes a cost to human life as deranged individuals have their hatred fanned to the point where they physically attack and even murder smokers.

On an individual level, the personal attacks mounted against the character of smokers have surely had a terrible effect on many. Teen smokers and older smokers with background insecurities cannot help but feel personally assaulted by the thousands of billboards, public transit ads, TV spots and misinterpretations of research studies all of which blend to portray them as lazy, addicted, diseased, dirty, and even criminal losers in a society of nonsmoking winners. News stories about teens beaten to death or pregnant smokers being shot by misguided Crusaders are but the visible tip of the iceberg when it comes to the assaults we've encouraged on this new minority group.

There is no count as to how many teen suicides may have resulted from this sort of thing. Imagine a research study that proposed taking a group of a thousand overweight high school students and deliberately inundating them with four years of television, print, and classroom propaganda that surrounded them with images of fat kids fitting the above stereotypes along with pictures, posters, and descriptions of their hearts and blood vessels being clogged and cloyed with fat. Throw in a program encouraging all their friends to think of them as smelly, undesirable, and stupid.

For good measure, add a clause that would allow for the constant monitoring of their weight and their dismissal from extra-curricular and after-school activities if they gained any additional weight or were caught with junk food or wrappers in their possession. Finally, have special days and programs where the thin students would all wear colorful T-Shirts saying "Thin People are the BEST!" or "Being Fat is STUPID!" while competing for scholarships not available to the fat kids.

Such a study proposal would be immediately vetoed because of the obvious risk of not just a few suicides, but of widespread damage to the psyches of all those individuals. Yet, that is what we have done on a much wider and more invasive scale to teen smokers throughout the last twenty years and there has certainly been a price paid, even if not formally tallied.

Another cost on the personal level is one rarely considered by today's scientific establishment because of Crusaders' pressures against efforts to make cigarettes safer rather than simply eliminate them. It's quite possible that safer cigarettes might actually be ones with higher nicotine levels: those smokers who smoke for the nicotine would smoke less and be less exposed to the carcinogens and monoxide in their smoke. Nicotine itself is relatively innocent as a cause of disease: its main effect in smoking is simply to make the experience more enjoyable for the smoker, serving much the same role as caffeine in coffee and sodas. Higher nicotine cigarettes could very well produce lower, and safer, smoking rates among smokers.

As a side benefit, if government reversed its path and actually encouraged cigarette makers to offer only high nicotine cigarettes we might see a return to the days when kids who tried smoking usually gave it up right away rather than finding it pleasant and continuing. It's quite possible that a significant part of the increase in youth smoking over the past twenty years is a direct result of the Antismokers' success in requiring nicotine content to be displayed in advertising. That requirement set off a "nicotine derby" in which manufacturers raced each other to produce good tasting products with the low nicotine content wanted by most novice smokers. The manufacturers got an extra push in that direction by attempts at graduating taxes based on nicotine content: the government actually has been encouraging the tobacco companies to make **less** safe cigarettes!

On the family level, homes are disrupted as one parent joins the ranks of the Innocents or the Neurotics and comes to believe that the other is attacking the health of their children. This familial destruction can happen even if the offender smokes only outside, as Antismokers frighten worried spouses with the idea that burrowing molecules of "toxic smoke" are carried in on clothing and then leap out to cause "mini lung cancers" in children. One Crusader urged parents to *pretend that smoke carries HIV and clean your home accordingly,*" while expressing concern about new particles carried in on clothing (Message-ID:19980327211 62100.QAA27026@ladder01.news.aol.com).

While few have firsthand experience of the above, many more have seen the damage to extended families as grand-parents, aunts, and uncles are told that they're only welcome for holiday gatherings if they stand outside whenever they wish to carry on the "deadly" habit that they've enjoyed for fifty or sixty years of their lives.   Even sadder, as noted earlier, we've seen children educated to believe that kissing a smoking family member is "like licking an ashtray." Picture a grandmother being rejected with that comment by her formerly loving grandchildren and think about what that does to the quality of **her** life.

On a cold October night in upstate New York, an elderly woman named Pearl huddled in her overcoat on the unlit porch of her adult group home, smoking a cigarette.

"*A lot of us smoke, and we had a meeting about it, but [the manager] told us if anyone was caught smoking inside, he'd throw us out,*" Pearl said.

I asked Pearl if she couldn't move somewhere else, but immediately regretted the question. Even in the dark, I could see her eyes fill with tears as she looked away and shook her head.

                    -- Sara Vossler. "The Resistance." Fall 1999

Figure 23

Interpersonally, friendships that in the past would have formed without a second thought as to disparate smoking statuses are now aborted before they have a chance to begin as this newly enculturated prejudice rears its ugly head. Even among those friends and groups that see past each other's smoking status, public gatherings are often disrupted to various extents as smokers are forced to leave and go to a separate area if they wish to smoke (Remember the Crusaders' Catch-22 here: Antismokers will claim that smokers should simply put off smoking rather than leave, but a minute later they'll claim that smokers are helplessly addicted to their habit... there is no winning in an argument with a true fanatic!)

On the larger societal level we've seen businesses destroyed as regulations banning smoking have driven them over the economic edge and their customer bases declined. The Crusaders' claim that huge numbers of nonsmokers would suddenly materialize to fill the spots vacated by smokers never come true: no surprise to anyone who has noticed that localities imposing smoking bans quickly start calling for wider laws to "level the playing field" as even their unique and supposedly-should-be-wildly-profitable lock on the nonsmokers' market isn't enough to make up for their losses. As Thomas Jefferson wisely observed in his *Notes on Virginia, "It is error alone which needs the support of government. Truth can stand by itself."*

We've also seen the increase in deadly drug use among our children as teens have been encouraged to move from gathering places with adult supervision to gathering places with none, and as our children have been given the message that their own heroin or inhalant use is safer than their parents' use of tobacco. The social fabric has been ripped further asunder by the increase in black marketeering of cigarettes and the widespread popular acceptance of such illegal activity. The increased production of fake ID's for tobacco purchase is even more destructive: those learning the lucrative skills of counterfeiting here may well go on to counterfeit documents that could result in the obliteration of a city someday.

In the area of law, those under 18 caught smoking in some states or adults sneaking a smoke in a no-smoking zone have perforce lost the perception that "the officer is our friend" and have had any inherent disrespect for authority reinforced. Nightmare wisps of Stalinist Russia tickle the consciousness when one hears a San Diego police sergeant openly state to the press that:

> **What we want to do is create paranoia.... We want smokers to be paranoid about being cited for breaking the law. If paranoia gets compliance, I can live with it.** (Sgt. Sam Campbell. As quoted by Tony Perry. "Smoking Ban..." *Los Angeles Times.* 02/21/99)

The good Sergeant backs up his efforts with undercover police who'll chat with patrons at local bars while waiting for one to light up – at which point the luckless smoker will be flashed a badge and "invited" outside to meet the legal consequences.

Disrespect for the law in a democracy is dangerous tinder to intentionally gather, but every no-smoking sign in an outdoor or well-ventilated indoor area does just that. On a still wider level, some writers such as Don Oakley believe that the formal changing of the rules of law so that they simply apply to one specific target may have done irreparable damage to our entire legal system.

Even the overall public health and welfare of people, not just in the U.S., but also around the entire world, has been hurt by the diversion of money that should be going into sound research on disease cures and preventions at a basic level. Such money has all too often been diverted from basic areas like clean water programs and malaria prevention to the purpose of "disease prevention by behavior modification." In countries where a quarter of the adult population is facing imminent death from AIDS infections the World Health Organization is spending scarce money to mount campaigns warning them that second-hand smoke is dangerous to their health!

While children are dying from parasites ingested in their drinking water and incubating in their bloodstream they can rest assured that they'll be taught the dangers of smoking through materials distributed by erstwhile aid workers. Antismokers will claim that the health impact of reduced smoking will in the long run be far greater than the benefits that might have been achieved by research and action around AIDS, TB, and parasitical diseases, but such claims need to be balanced by recognition of the present and very real costs of taking that money from other worthwhile activities. Many of these children will die from diarrhea long before they reach an age where they'd even be **thinking** about smoking.

These claims should also be balanced by recognition of the spectacular lack of success some of these heavily funded programs have had in achieving **any** reduction in smoking levels. Remember that despite millions of dollars of expenditure and an incalculable infliction of harm, the Smoke Free Class of 2000 smoked more than many of the previously graduated classes.

The ultimate assault on world health may come in the stuffy air of the modern smoke-free fleet of airplanes as germs incubate and spread in their nice, clear, recirculated air. It is quite possible that the Antismoking movement at the end of the 20th century will ultimately go down in history as the cause of one of our greatest public health disasters as some horrific airborne pestilence is spread around the world courtesy of the friendly and smoke-free skies.

A final sad example of the toll exacted upon us by the Antismoking Crusade is the story of Rodrick Chiodini, one of the world's most prominent investigators of Crohn's disease. He was fired from Rhode Island Hospital for allegedly violating its no-smoking policy and banned from its grounds. In the process his cultures were destroyed, years of important work toward a cure of this disease were lost, and Chiodini's valued contributions to the field were effectively brought to a grinding halt. On the other hand, the hospital *did* succeed in maintaining its no-smoking policy (Steven Stycos. *Providence Phoenix* 09/02/94; Lisa Chamberlain. "The *Cleveland Free Times* 06/16-22/99).

What is the cost of the disruption of social cohesion, or the cost of needless fears and fouled relationships? What is the cost of countless minor interruptions in social discourse or the cost of family gatherings aborted with lasting rancor? What is the cost of all the millions of little hurts that have been injected into the social bloodstream by those who seek divisiveness as a means to a goal that is questionable both in terms of its attainability and its ultimate desirability? I don't know... I just know it's too high.

> **Experience should teach us to be most on our guard to protect liberty when the government's purposes are beneficial - the greatest dangers to liberty lurk in insidious encroachment by men of zeal, well meaning but without understanding.**
>
> --Supreme Court Justice Louis Brandeis

Figure 24

The costs of extremist Antismoking activity exist, and they can not and **should not** be ignored. The ever-present Crusading pictures of children and flowers have a dark underbelly that people need to be made aware of. The Antismoking Angels tread the earth with heavily tainted feet.

Conclusion

Men stumble over the truth from time to time, but most pick themselves up and hurry off as if nothing had happened.

-- Sir Winston Churchill

We have seen the sorts of individuals who make up the membership of the Antismoking Crusade, and we've looked at some of the tools that they've used to mold the minds and attitudes of the public, but overall, are Antismokers doing a good thing or a bad thing?

On the surface, this is not an easy question to answer. Widely accepted medical theory holds that tens of millions of people would live longer and healthier lives if they didn't smoke or if they were forced to quit. This is something that I myself as an author and activist believe and that belief kept me from being more outspoken on this subject for a good number of years. However, the methods and techniques being used to force such abstinence or quitting have very significant harms in and of themselves, not the least of which is the threat to an individual's choice about how they will live their life and balance its pleasures against its length. As has undoubtedly been made clear through the bulk of the preceding pages I believe that, on balance, the Antismoking Crusade has had an overall negative impact on our lives and social well being.

Very few people would choose to live a life on a diet of nothing but soy and wheat paste supplemented with ground sea-weed and the odd spritz of lemon juice in some low-fat fruit yogurt. But if they DID, they'd probably live a lot longer on the average than by chomping down on Big Macs and Whoppers. In a similar vein, if restaurants were forced to serve mineral water rather than martinis many of us would undoubtedly be healthier. Should government be given the power to make this sort of decision for people? I believe most of us would say no.

Should taxpayer-funded activist organizations use subliminal psychological manipulation through our popular media to change our legal behaviors? Again, I think most people would be against such government-funded diddling with our minds and our lives. Every individual has the right to decide what makes them happy in life and what enjoyments of life they will engage in, despite whatever inherent risk those enjoyments might entail.

When Antismoking Crusaders stick to educating people honestly about the health effects of smoking and the benefits of quitting I think most people would feel they are doing the right thing. But when they push programs designed to alter behavior indirectly by such things as selectively raising taxes, sowing the seeds of hate, or creating and exacerbating neurotic fears of almost imaginary dangers I believe most people would feel they were wrong no matter how worthy the goal. Ends do not always justify means, and unintended consequences can sometimes overshadow intended effects.

When such programs extend beyond the realm of persuasion into the arena of promulgating laws with severe penalties and taxes/fees that literally double, triple, or quadruple the price of a product, they have moved into a realm that approaches criminal interference in the privacy and primacy of individual free choice. America has allowed its policies on smoking to be determined by a handful of strident extremists, many of who may actually be acting out of the drives of undiagnosed mental illness. These policies have turned ordinary citizens into criminals, ripped families apart, and destroyed businesses while at the same time they have increased black market crime, driven a wedge between law enforcement officers and our young, and have helped drive truly dangerous drug use among our children to heights never before seen.

The fact that these fanatics have managed to swell their numbers in recent times by means of their successful campaigns to breed fear, discrimination, and hate does not justify the power we've given them through the granting of hundreds of millions of dollars a year from our taxes. When a single state, California, can spend close to 150 million dollars a year on programs largely designed to negatively target a selected and vulnerable minority, something is obviously amiss (Dougherty. *WorldNetDaily.com* 06/19/02).

For the sake of our country and the world, as well as for the sake of plain human decency, policies on smoking need to be returned to a more reasonable level of dissuasion on the basis of health but with tolerance on the basis of free choice. The promulgation of laws aimed at sowing divisiveness between people without compelling reason should be halted immediately, and those regulations that do more than provide for our basic education and reasonable safety should be repealed.

What can an ordinary individual do to fight the momentum of the leviathan that the Antismoking Crusade has become? How can one hope to fight against hundreds of millions of dollars a year and a belief system that has grown roots deeper than many religions? I don't have an easy answer... I wish I did. Those individuals connected to the Internet can go to sites like FORCES.org, NYCCLASH.com, Smokers Fighting Discrimination, Smokers United, SmokersClub.com, or any of the other sites linked to in the Recommended Bibliography at the end of this book to help battle the rampant lies and hate and connect with other individuals already fighting. Those not connected through the web can speak to and inspire other smokers and sympathetic nonsmokers to realize that this seemingly little corner of injustice in our society is more important than might appear at first glance.

Of course anyone can write letters to the editor, letters to businesses, and letters to local governments that have promoted unreasonable smoking bans. Equally important is confronting politicians who mount up on the sanctified podium of "protecting our children" in order to get votes from the gullible. Don't let them get away with abusing our love of our children this way: Go to City Council meetings and expose them for what they are. The Antismokers may have a huge advantage at public hearings in terms of sheer numbers of paid lobbyists as well as in terms of professionally prepared documentation that they can bring with them, but the voice of the ordinary citizen still has the power of truth.

In addition, the power of the voting booth is not something to overlook here. Smokers make up roughly one-quarter of the voting-age population. Minority groups with far smaller memberships have pressured politicians into taking significant actions based on fear of them as organized voting blocs. If smokers hit by outrageous taxes and unreasonable bans went to the voting booths in November and voted the offending politicians out of office we might see a very different attitude emerge when it came time to consider new taxes and laws. We might even see a rollback of some of the current measures, particularly if the media began reporting some of the background information showing their injustice and if smokers began working together to show their political power.

> # Never doubt that a small group of thoughtful, committed citizens can change the world.
>
> # Indeed, it's the only thing that ever has.
>
> --Margaret Mead

Figure 25

Finally, if a person is a smoker or even just a nonsmoker willing to hold a lit cigarette, he or she can simply perform a Gandhian act of civil disobedience the next time they see an unwarranted no-smoking regulation. Every time a smoker smokes in such an area he or she is sending a message to other smokers that they should also do the same. If that smoker refuses to pay a fine or perform state-sponsored slave labor (euphemistically known as "community service") the state may have no alternative except to release a real criminal in order to make room for the "deadly smoker."

While smokers filling the jails would certainly bring the Crusade grinding to a halt, far lower levels of commitment can also have profound effects. Even if such a smoker extinguishes his or her offending smoke at the first request of an authority, the point has still been made: the system has been forced to respond and recognize that there is a real cost of investment of resources needed to enforce such a ban. When the unjust authority of a state apparatus makes its first encroachments upon individual freedom it depends on the "oil" of public indifference to those moves. Don't be the oil in the machine: be the sand in the gears.

An important side note on resisting unreasonable no-smoking zones: quite often you will find that these are **not** legally designated as such: Antismokers are encouraged by their activist organizations to take it upon themselves to post such official looking notices wherever they desire! Never assume that a no-smoking sign has any vesting of legal authority behind it simply because it's hanging on a wall or posted in a window. However, smokers **should** respect private individuals or businesses asking you not to smoke indoors while on their premises. You are not forced to go there, and if you object strongly enough to the restriction you can simply go elsewhere. If they miss your patronage enough they will change their policies to be more accommodating to everyone.

On the other hand, smokers should do their best not to add fuel to the Crusaders' bonfire: avoid smoking in crowded and un-ventilated situations, don't litter (The one exception to this might be when a "designated smoking area" is deliberately set up without ashtrays!), and don't be rude to nonsmokers who confront you about smoking. Be polite, move a bit if it seems reasonable to do so, smile but remain firm in your right to perform a normal and non-harmful activity in a well-ventilated public place. Don't just angrily confront nonsmokers: talk to them and educate them. If **they** become rude and abusive in front of others, they've helped you all the more in making your point as to the wrongness of their stand and the neuroticism at its base.

Finally, and perhaps most importantly, smokers and nonsmokers who resent the infringements on freedom brought by the Antismoking Crusade need to link up and get involved with the smoking activist groups that already exist. As mentioned above, anyone with a link to the World Wide Web can have easy access to many such grassroots citizens groups.

Those outside the United States do not need to feel that they are alone either: FORCES has chapters in over a dozen diff-erent countries, and there are active grassroots groups forming and fighting as far away as New Zealand. New Zealand's Smokers Of The World Unite, has mounted some large and very im-pressive demonstrations of smokers in front of government offices! See: http://homepages.ihug.co.nz/~jfaulkne/

As a source of information upon which to base activism, those connected to the Internet should also be sure to examine the longest running and largest weekly Free-Choice newsletter in the world: Samantha Phillipe, founder of SmokersClub.com puts together this wonderful resource every week and its mailing list is open to any and all, supporters or detractors! Samantha, a wonderful and enthusiastic activist I have had the good fortune to meet is also quite active online and off in support groups for ADD and ADHD children.

If you are not previously familiar with them I believe you will be quite surprised at the wealth of information these groups offer. They are not Big Tobacco fronts, although even if they were, their information would still stand on its own merit. The two American smokers' rights groups that did have Big Tobacco roots, the National Smokers Alliance and the American Smokers Alliance, have both dissolved with the withdrawal of industry funding.

The Internet message board of the NSA was so popular however, that two dedicated long time smokers' rights activists, Martha Perske and Wanda Hamilton, took over the domain when NSA disappeared, paying for it from their own pockets, and now they moderate the SpeakEasyForum.com where Free-Choice activists regularly gather and exchange thoughts, information, and inspirations. It's a worthwhile and educational visit on the Web: if you visit you may just find yourself drawn into the discussions. If you prefer a more free-swinging online battle with Crusaders, check out the message boards at Yahoo.com and the postings on the alt.smokers Internet Newsgroup.

Most legitimate smokers' rights groups generally speak out quite strongly against any complicity between Big Tobacco and Big Government in targeting smokers while keeping taxes and corporate profits flowing in buckets. For the most part, from what I have seen, these groups are made up of sincere and concerned individuals who are not only concerned about government intrusions on the choice to smoke, but about the wider issues of government control of other behaviors as well. Some of the views and arguments you may encounter there will be considerably more extreme than the ones presented by me, but I'm glad that they're there and that people still have the freedom to present them.

Finally, I should mention FOREST, a very active British Free-Choice organization that has much good information on its web site at www.forestonline.org The reason I list FOREST separately is because, although their work is often excellent, they do receive a good deal of support from the British American Tobacco Company and some would feel that discredits them.

They were independently founded however and some of their stands have been unpopular enough with their tobacco sponsors that some of those companies have cut their funding off outright and disassociated themselves entirely from the group. FOREST is well worth evaluating on their content, not on their connections.

If you want to read further order a copy of Don Oakley's *Slow Burn* or Jacob Sullum's *For Your Own Good*. As noted in the Preface, they both offer a more detailed look at the wider scope of the "Great American Antismoking Scam" than I have given you here. Lauren Colby's *In Defense Of Smokers* is worth examining as well since it offers some interesting criticism of the science around the entire smoking-cancer connection. It is not available in hardcopy, but can be printed out from his web site at http://www.lcolby.com/colby.htm

The psychological aspects of movements like the Antismoking Crusade and the motivations of their Crusaders need to be more fully appreciated so that we can guard against their corruption of our free society. The tools of wartime propaganda are reprehensible enough when used in time of war: they have NO place in altering the minds and thoughts of citizens with regard to legal peacetime activities! And to go beyond simple propaganda to the sort of actual mind-control made possible by corrupting the meanings and nuances of common English words and then using the power and resources of the government to make sure that the new meanings take root in our collective psyche is, without exaggeration, absolutely terrifying.

Remember, this is **NOT** just about smoking: it's about freedom and the unjust singling out of a vulnerable minority for punishment, hatred, and excess taxation. If you accept such a situation as the norm for any group, then you lay the foundations for your own persecution in the future.

If we accept this sort of censorship of history and current reality, this sort of manipulation of our lives, our families, our freedoms, and our choices, this artificial division into opposing and antagonistic groups... what will we ultimately have left to us as supposedly free citizens?

Appendices

The following Appendices contain material that supplements the analyses that have gone before. In some cases the relevance is direct and clear, such as the necessity of showing that fear of ordinary exposures to secondary smoke is not something that is reasonably based in scientific reality.   In other cases the connection is not so clear -- such as the examination of the medical costs of smokers -- but is still important in terms of understanding why the feelings of resentment those smokers feel about their level of taxation are indeed rational.

If a particular appendix would be helpful to a teacher for a class discussion or if sending a copy of a particular appendix to a legislator might swing his or her vote on a ban or tax vote, please feel free to make judicious use of the material I have supplied here. I promise that I won't send undercover police to track you down for a single instance of skirting my copyright for a few pages: I wrote this book in the hope of seeing its ideas spread widely.   However, in most cases, think of the larger benefit to your audience if you provide them with the entire book to read.

Really, I'm serious.

Appendix A

ETS Study Results
and Commentary

A wise man proportions his belief to the evidence.

– David Hume

The details of the codes used in the following table are available in the footnote section at its end. In general, this is as complete a collection of study results on secondary smoke exposure and lung cancer as you are likely to find anywhere.

The studies are divided by type, with workplace and spousal studies generally based on constant daily exposures lasting for 30 to 40 years or even longer. The numbers to pay attention to are in the Relative Risk column and the Confidence Interval column.

As noted earlier, relative risks below 2.0 or 3.0 are generally viewed with suspicion by epidemiologists because of the risk of contamination of the studies by confounding variables or biases, quite aside from simple statistical error. An additional point of importance is the notation in the Confidence Interval column that indicates whether the CI includes the value of 1.0 between its low and high points. If it **does** include 1.0, then the study is **not** statistically significant and is viewed by statisticians as affirming the hypothesis that there is no connection between the hypothesized cause and the speculated effect.

Note: statistical significance in and of itself is **never** considered by scientists to be sufficient evidence to determine cause and effect: it's merely a minimum standard used to determine if the results of a study merit further examination and analysis for such things as bias and confounding variables.

As you go through these figures, even superficially, you will find two points that stand out strongly as contradictions to Crusaders' oft-repeated claims that ETS studies are "unanimous and unequivocal" in their condemnation of secondary tobacco smoke. First of all, the vast majority of the studies are not statistically significant, thus in reality supporting the hypothesis that there is **no** connection between ETS and lung cancer. Secondly, and even more amazing given the publicity to the contrary, each of the studies marked by an asterisk in the Relative Risk column actually indicated tendencies of ETS exposure to **protect against** lung cancer! Of course most of those asterisked studies are also non-significant statistically, but as noted in the finishing abstract, at least one very important study actually came up with the unexpected significant finding that early contact with secondary smoke might protect children from future lung cancers!

Name	Yr	Geo	Type	Sex	Relative Risk	Confidence Interval
Garfinkel 1 (+)	81	US	Spouse	F	1.18	.90-1.54
Chan +	82	HK	Spouse	F	0.80 *	.43-1.30
Correa(+!)	83	US	Spouse	F	2.07	.81-5.25
Correa(+!)	83	US	Spouse	M	1.97	.38-10.32
Trichopoulis(+!)	83	Grk	Spouse	F	2.08	1.20-3.59
Buffler	84	US	Spouse	F	0.80 *	.34-1.90
Buffler	84	US	Spouse	M	0.51 *	.14-1.79
Hirayama (+)!	84	Jap	Spouse	F	1.60	1.00-2.40
Hirayama +	84	Jap	Spouse	M	2.24	1.19-4.22
Kabat 1(+)	84	US	Spouse	F	0.79 *	.25-2.45
Kabat 1(+)	84	US	Spouse	M	NS	0.20-5.07
Garfinkel 2(+)	85	US	Spouse	F	1.23	0.81-1.87
Lam W	85	HK	Spouse	F	2.01	1.09-3.72
Wu(+!)	85	US	Spouse	F	1.40	0.40-4.20

Akiba(+)	86 Jap	Spouse F	1.50	0.90-2.80
Akiba(+)	86 Jap	Spouse M	1.80	0.40-7.00
Lee(+)	86 UK	Spouse F	NS	0.37-2.71
Lee(+)	86 UK	Spouse M	1.30	0.38-4.39
Brownson 1	87 US	Spouse F	1.68	0.39-6.90
Gao	87 Chn	Spouse F	1.19	0.82-1.73
Humble	87 US	Spouse F	2.20	0.80-6.60
Humble	87 US	Spouse M	4.82	.63-36.56
Koo	87 HK	Spouse F	1.64	0.87-3.09
Lam T	87 HK	Spouse F	1.65	1.16-2.35
Pershagen(+)	87 Swd	Spouse F	1.20	0.70-2.10
Butler	88 US	Spouse F	2.20	0.48-8.56
Geng	88 Chn	Spouse F	2.16	1.08-4.29
Inoue	88 Jap	Spouse F	2.25	0.80-8.80
Shimizu	88 Jap	Spouse F	1.08	0.64-1.82
hoi	89 Kor	Spouse F	1.63	0.92-2.87
Choi	89 Kor	Spouse M	2.73	.49-15.21
Hole	89 Sco	Spouse F	1.89	.22-16.12
Hole	89 Sco	Spouse M	3.52	.32-38.65
Svensson	89 Swd	Spouse F	1.26	0.57-2.81
Janerich	90 US	Spouse MF	0.93 *	0.55-1.57
Kalandidi	90 Grk	Spouse F	2.11	1.09-4.08
Sobue	90 Jap	Spouse F	1.13	0.78-1.63
Wu-Williams	90 Chn	Spouse F	0.70 *	0.60-0.90
Liu Z	91 Chn	Spouse F	0.77 *	0.30-1.96
Brownson 2 ^	92 US	Spouse F	NS	0.80-1.20
Stockwell ^	92 US	Spouse F	1.60	0.80-3.00
Liu Q ^	93 Chn	Spouse F	1.66	0.73-3.78
Wu	93 Chn	Spouse F	1.09	0.64-1.85
Fontham ^	94 US	Spouse F	1.29	1.04-1.60
Layard	94 US	Spouse F	0.58 *	0.30-1.13
Layard	94 US	Spouse M	1.47	0.55-3.94
Zaridze	94 Rus	Spouse F	1.66	1.12-2.46
Kabat 2 ^	95 US	Spouse F	1.08	0.60-1.94
Kabat 2 ^	95 US	Spouse M	1.60	0.67-3.82
Schwartz ^	96 US	Spouse F	1.10	0.72-1.68
Schwartz ^	96 US	Spouse M	1.10	0.60-2.03

Sun	96 Chn	Spouse	F	1.16	0.80-1.69
Wang S-Y	96 Chn	Spouse	F	2.53	1.26-5.10
Wang T-J	96 Chn	Spouse	F	1.11	0.67-1.84
Cardenas ^	97 US	Spouse	F	1.20	0.80-1.60
Cardenas ^	97 US	Spouse	M	1.10	0.60-1.80
Jockel-BIPS	97 Ger	Spouse	F	1.58	0.74-3.38
Jockel-BIPS	97 Ger	Spouse	M	1.58	0.52-4.81
Jockel-GSF	97 Ger	Spouse	F	0.93 *	0.66-1.31
Jockel-GSF	97 Ger	Spouse	M	0.93 *	0.52-1.67
Ko ^	97 Tai	Spouse	F	1.30	0.70-2.50
Nyberg	97 Swd	Spouse	F	1.20	0.74-1.94
Nyberg	97 Swd	Spouse	M	1.20	0.57-2.55
Boffetta{WHO}	98 Eur	Spouse	MF	1.16	0.93-1.44
Kabat1 ^	84 US	Work	F	0.70 *	0.30-1.50
Kabat 1 ^	84 US	Work	M	3.30	1.0-10.40
Garfinkel 2 ^	85 US	Work	F	0.93 *	0.70-1.20
Wu ^	85 US	Work	F	1.30	0.50-3.30
Lee ^	86 UK	Work	F	0.63 *	0.17-2.33
Lee ^	86 UK	Work	M	1.61	0.39-6.60
Koo ^	87 HK	Work	F	0.91 *	0.15-5.37
Shimizu ^	88 Jap	Work	F	1.18	0.70-2.01
Janerich ^	90 US	Work	MF	0.91 *	0.80-1.04
Kalandidi ^!	90 Grk	Work	F	1.39	0.80-2.50
Wu-Williams ^	90 Chn	Work	F	1.20	0.90-1.60
Brownson 2	92 US	Work	F	0.79 *	0.61-1.03
Stockwell ^	92 US	Work	F	NS	NS
Fontham ^	94 US	Work	F	1.39	1.11-1.74
Zaridze	94 Rus	Work	F	1.23	0.74-2.06
Kabat 2 ^	95 US	Work	F	1.15	0.62-2.13
Kabat 2 ^	95 US	Work	M	1.02	0.50-2.09
Schwartz ^	96 US	Work	MF	1.50	1.00-2.20
Sun	96 Chn	Work	F	1.38	0.94-2.04
Wang T-J	96 Chn	Work	F	0.89 *	0.46-1.73
Jockel-BIPS	97 Ger	Work	MF	2.37	1.02-5.48
Jockel-GSF	97 Ger	Work	MF	1.51	0.95-2.40
Ko ^	97 Tai	Work	F	1.10	0.40-3.00

Nyberg	97 Swd	Work	MF	1.60	0.90-2.90
Boffetta{WHO}	98 Eur	Work	MF	1.17	0.94-1.45
Correa +	83 US	Childhd	F	NS	NS
Kabat &Wyn ^	84 US	Childhd	F	0.92 *	0.40-2.08
Kabat &Wyn ^	84 US	Childhd	M	1.26	0.33-4.83
Garfinkel 2 +	85 US	Childhd	F	0.91 *	0.74-1.12
Wu (+)	85 US	Childhd	F	0.60 *	0.20-1.70
Akiba +	86 Jap	Childhd	MF	NS	NS
Gao ^	87 Chin	Childhd	F	1.10	0.70-1.70
Koo ^!	87 HK	Childhd	F	1.73	0.60-6.40
Pershagen ^	87 Swed	Childhd	F	NS	0.40-2.30
Svensson ^	89 Swed	Childhd	F	3.30	.50-18.80
Janerich ^	90 US	Childhd	MF	1.09	0.68-1.73
Sobue (^)	90 Jap	Childhd	F	1.28	0.71-2.31
Wu-Will(^)!	90 Chin	Childhd	F	NS	NS
Brownson 2 ^	92 US	Childhd	F	0.80 *	0.60-1.10
Stockwell ^	92 US	Childhd	F	1.10	0.50-2.60
Fontham ^	94 US	Childhd	F	0.89 *	0.72-1.10
Zaridze	94 Russ	Childhd	F	0.98 *	0.66-1.45
Kabat 2 ^	95 US	Childhd	M	0.90 *	0.43-1.89
Kabat 2 ^	95 US	Childhd	F	1.55	0.95-2.79
Sun	96 Chin	Childhd	F	2.29	1.56-3.37
Wang T-J	96 Chin	Childhd	F	0.91 *	0.56-1.48
Jockel-BIPS	97 Ger	Childhd	MF	1.05	0.50-2.22
Jockel-GSF	97 Ger	Childhd	MF	0.95 *	0.64-1.40
Ko ^	97 Tai	Childhd	F	0.80 *	0.40-1.60
Boffetta{WHO}	98 Eur	Childhd	MF	0.78 *	0.64-0.96

Garfinkel 2	85	US	Social F	1.42	0.75-2.70
Lee	86	UK	Social F	0.61 *	0.29-1.28
Lee	86	UK	Social M	1.55	0.40-6.02
Janerich	90	US	Social MF	0.59 *	0.43-0.81
Stockwell	92	US	Social F	NS	NS
Fontham	94	US	Social F	1.50	1.19-1.89
Kabat 2 (^)	95	US	Social F	1.22	0.69-2.15
Kabat 2 (^)	95	US	Social M	1.39	0.67-2.86
Boffetta{WHO}	98	Eur	Social MF	1.03	0.82-1.29

Column 1 codes:

^ = Figures from Final Report CA EPA 1997
! = Difference from Forces' #s (usually slight, no consistent bias)
+ = 1986 Surgeon General's Report
( ) = derived/approximate...
{WHO} = taken directly from WHO study

Unmarked: roughly half the studies noted were not listed in either the California EPA report or the Reports of the Surgeon General. Figures for those are from FORCES (a Free-Choice advocacy group). For the 66 figures in which cross checking was possible a generally high level of agreement was found with CA EPA and the Reports of the Surgeon General so there is no reason to believe the other FORCES figures are incorrect. Limiting the chart to only CA EPA, Reports of the Surgeon General and WHO figures would not significantly change the general tendency of the findings.

Note: in the case of ranges the chart fairly consistently presents the middle range of exposure for these figures so as to avoid any charge that it understates or overstates risk figures. For example: in the Janerich '90 childhood study it uses the figure for up to 25 years of childhood exposure of 1.09 rather than the 2.07 found for more than 25+ years, while in the Brownson 2 1992 study childhood exposure would have shown a significant negative correlation if exposure was restricted to smoking parents. Koo 87 "childhood" (actually co-habitant) figures showed a similar effect: The midrange, which is in the chart, is 1.73, while the "heavy" exposure of two or more smoking co-habitants actually yields a lower figure, 1.35. However in Fontham 94 the lower exposure (1-17 co-habitant exposure) would have yielded a slightly higher (.99) correlation than the higher exposure (18+ years) used (.88). Many of the studies used differing coding schemes and studied different ranges/sources of exposure. The chart generally seeks to highlight the middle, or most reasonable, ranges rather than highlight the anomalies in either direction.

Column 7 codes:

* = Studies indicating a NEGATIVE relationship of exposure to secondary smoke and lung cancer. In these studies, the people that WERE EXPOSED to secondary smoke averaged LOWER rates of lung cancer than those not exposed.

   NS = Reported by authors only as having no significant relationship or a relationship indicating the SAME rates of lung cancer (i.e. RR = 1.00) among those exposed to secondary smoke and those not exposed.

WHO Study (Excerpted Abstract)

Multicenter case-control study of exposure to environmental tobacco smoke and lung cancer in Europe. Authors: P Boffetta et al.

BACKGROUND: An association between exposure to environmental tobacco smoke (ETS) and lung cancer risk has been suggested. To evaluate this possible association better, researchers need more precise estimates of risk,... we have conducted a case-control study of lung cancer and exposure to ETS in 12 centers from seven Euran (sic) countries.

METHODS: A total of 650 patients with lung cancer and 1542 control subjects up to 74 years of age were interviewed about exposure to ETS....

RESULTS: ETS exposure during childhood was not associated with an increased risk of lung cancer (odds ratio [OR] for ever exposure = 0.78; 95% confidence interval [CI] = 0.64- 0.96). The OR for ever exposure to Spouse ETS was 1.16 (95% CI = 0.93- 1.44). No clear dose-response relationship could be demonstrated for cumulative Spouse ETS exposure. The OR for ever exposure to workplace ETS was 1.17 (95% CI = 0.94-1.45), with possible evidence of increasing risk for increasing duration of exposure. No increase in risk was detected in subjects whose exposure to Spouse or workplace ETS ended more than 15 years earlier. **Ever exposure to ETS from other sources was not associated with lung cancer risk.** Risks from combined exposure to Spouse and workplace ETS were higher... but the differences were not statistically significant.

CONCLUSIONS: Our results indicate no association between childhood exposure to ETS and lung cancer risk.

We did find weak evidence of a dose-response relationship between risk of lung cancer and exposure to Spouse and workplace ETS. There was no detectable risk after cessation of exposure. *<Emphases added>*

Note that while the author's interpretation of the childhood figures in the WHO study was simply "no association," the 22% *reduction* in lung cancer among children of smokers was in fact *the only scientifically significant result* found! Imagine the publicity this study would have received if the results had been in the opposite direction!

Note also that exposure from "other sources" {e.g. *bars and restaurants!*} showed *no* association to lung cancer.

Despite this, the WHO study is often trotted out as supporting claims by smoking ban supporters who realize that very few politicians will actually be familiar with the real results of the study.

Figure 26

Appendix B

Secondary Smoke Exposure

Introduction

This Appendix did not exist in the early drafts of *Dissecting Anti-smokers' Brains*.   I had examined the literature concerning smoke exposure as measured by air monitors, blood and urine cotinine sampling, and even hair nicotine analysis, and I felt confident that a simple assertion that nonsmokers would gener-ally inhale roughly a thousandth of a cigarette per hour of normal exposure to smoking situations would be both accurate and sufficient when followed by a couple of citations.

After several friends reviewed those drafts I realized I was mistaken. If I was going to make such a claim I would have to back it up either by extensively analyzing the studies conducted using the different methods that were out there, and discussing in detail their various nuances, defects, and limitations, or I would have to come up with a new model of my own. I have decided largely on the latter approach although I will take a few paragraphs to look first at the work done by others.

In the 1986 Surgeon General's Report, the one that focused on secondary smoke exposure and effects, the major studies examining exposure quantification came from tests of nicotine and cotinine (a nicotine metabolite) in the blood and urine of nonsmokers. Several of these studies compared such levels in smokers and nonsmokers, with nonsmokers generally having a low level even if not exposed to smoke... perhaps from the small amount of dietary nicotine from such things as tomatoes, potatoes, and eggplants.

Feyerbend in 1982 found that non-exposed nonsmokers had about 8ng/Ml (nanograms/milliliter) nicotine in their urine while those with 8 hours of work exposure had 22ng/Ml. That's an increase of 14ng/Ml, due, theoretically, to working with smokers. An average smoker at shift's end had about 1350 ng/Ml. Thus, the increase in nicotine level of the nonsmoker's urine would be equal to about 1/100th of the increase in that of the smoker – indicating that the nonsmoker was exposed to roughly 1/10th of a cigarette during 8 hours of work (assuming the smokers smoked about a pack a day and started out with a clean slate) or a bit over 1/100th of a cigarette per hour or about a pack per year. If, as is likely, smokers had a base level from the previous day, then nonsmoker exposure would be significantly **less** than the 1/100th figure.

Jarvis in 1984 used a similar method to look at hospital clinic patients and found exposed nonsmokers increased their base measurements by about 8ng/Ml while regular smokers had levels averaging 1750ng/Ml. In this case the increase would indicate the nonsmokers were being exposed to levels of 8/1750 or about 1/200th that of the smokers. Again, in concrete terms, if the smokers smoked a pack a day, that would mean the regularly exposed nonsmokers were absorbing about 1/200th as much as the smokers: about 1/10th of a cigarette per day or 1/100th of a cigarette per hour or about a pack a year; a result very similar to that found by Feyerbend.

Wald in 1984 did a study of clinic patients that examined cotinine levels and found levels somewhat higher: an increase of about 25 ng/Ml in nonsmokers exposed to an average of 50 hours of secondary smoke per week while smokers themselves had levels of about 1650 ng/Ml. If the smokers averaged 20 cigarettes per day that would indicate that the nonsmokers were exposed to (25/1650)x20 or about 3/10th of a cigarette per day or about 1/50th of a cigarette per exposure hour for 16 hours of active contact with secondary smoke. Wald's study definitely represents the high end of reported exposures and even so would equal only about a pack of exposure every two or three months (*1986 Report of the Surgeon General.* pps. 209 – 212).

The above results would indicate that in work or clinic settings where nonsmokers were generally exposed to smoke they were inhaling roughly the equivalent of $1/25^{th}$ to $1/100^{th}$ of a cigarette per hour. It's important to remember however that these studies were done in the early 1980s, before the concern about secondary smoke was widespread and before the advent of modern ventilation and filtration technologies. Similar studies carried out today would yield results far lower. In addition, it is possible that the blood and urine readings of a nonsmoker might exaggerate the degree of exposure if the readings of smokers reflect some degree of protective deflection of nicotine as it reaches higher levels in the body.

A major defect of many ETS studies is that they depend partly on the memories, awareness, and prejudices of the individuals tested in determining the actual amounts of exposure reported. An individual with very little exposure who happened to be intensely fearful of smoke might report a much higher level of exposure than an individual who wasn't concerned and who might not notice people smoking around him or her. Somewhat elevated levels of nicotine and cotinine in the sera of nonsmokers who were actually occasional smokers might also be missed and lend to higher exposure estimates. To be fair, it should also be noted that an argument can be mounted from the opposite direction: those labeled as non-exposed nonsmokers may indeed have had exposures that were insignificant enough not to be noted.

In the 1990s another method was tried, one based a bit more on physics than on biology. This approach used air monitors carried by nonsmokers who lived and/or worked with smokers to actually measure individual levels of exposure. These studies had the advantage of hard data measurement that was not based in any way on anecdotal memory reportage of exposure. Their results were also easily replicable by other researchers. And finally, they were sensitive to the actual moment-to-moment changes in physical exposure such as might be experienced by a nonsmoking bartender who got cornered by a chain-smoking customer at the end of his or her shift.

These air-monitor studies generally gave much lower estimations of exposure levels than did the earlier blood/urine analysis studies. According to air monitors worn by hospitality workers it seemed that ordinary bartenders and waitpeople in Free-Choice smoking-allowed pubs and restaurants might be exposed to notably less than a pack of cigarettes during the course of an entire year... a far cry from the half-pack per shift claimed by New York's Mayor Bloomberg or the absurd four packs per shift claimed by Arizona Crusaders while seeking petition signatures for a ban (www.petitiononline.com/modperl /signed.cgi?azsmoke).

The main problem with the air-monitor studies is that despite the fact that they have been carried out by very reputable scientists (some of the most famous of these studies come from the Oak Ridge National Laboratories of the U.S. Department of Energy) the money to carry them out usually came from sources like the Center for Indoor Air Research (CIAR) or, in England, Covance Laboratories. CIAR and Covance both have funding connections at some level with tobacco companies so it's true that the results of any research sponsored by them should be examined with that in mind. However, if the science is sound, the question of who funded it is objectively quite secondary to the actual findings.

Why did the tobacco industry fund these studies? Probably because they knew from their own previous research that the results found would show very low levels of exposure and thus help the industry in fighting smoking bans. Does that motivation mean the research is defective or the results false? No. If that were true then the Antismoking Lobby would quickly have funded its own air-monitor studies to show the fakery involved.

Instead, the response of the Crusading community to these studies has almost always been, not to criticize their science, but rather to simply dismiss them because of their funding source: an argument Ad Hominem. The study results are accurate; they just don't show what the Antismokers wish.

As the new millennium rolled in, Antismokers found a novel method which gave results much more favorable to their cause. For some time it had been known that nicotine levels could be measured over a long-term period by analyzing the hair of smokers. There had even been more recent research showing trace levels of nicotine in the hair of infants born to smoking mothers. (http://news.bbc.co.uk/hi/english/health/newsid_172 0000/1720128.stm).

On March 9th of 2001, the New Zealand Medical Journal published an article titled "Hair Nicotine in Hair of Bar and Restaurant Workers" by Wael Al-Delaimy et al. Dr. Al-Delaimy claimed that workers in venues that allowed smoking had close to the same levels of nicotine in their hair as workers who smoked a half pack a day themselves.

Unfortunately for Crusaders the very success of this method sowed the seeds of its failure. If in truth nonsmokers were inhaling a half pack of cigarettes per shift they would be expected to become just as fond of nicotine as most smokers and they'd all be running out to buy cigarettes on their days off rather than complaining about secondary smoke. We'd also be seeing lung cancer rates among such workers at levels several hundred percent higher than what they are; unless the figures on lung cancer and smoking itself were all wrong to begin with.

The model, despite the fondness lavished upon it by New York's Mayor Bloomberg, is obviously defective, perhaps because of absorption of nicotine through the hair shaft, perhaps for some other reason. For whatever reason, its main use is only as a tool of the Crusade, not as a serious scientific comparator of the relative exposure to smoke of smokers and nonsmokers: its conclusions stand alone in claiming such massive exposures.

Despite this, in the months leading up to the New York City ban, the idea that an ordinary barkeep or waitress was inhaling a half pack of cigarettes a day was constantly repeated in papers ranging from USA Today to the New York Times.

One spokesman for the ALA in Chicago stretched it a bit (a bit?) and stated that the equivalent workday exposure ranged up to forty cigarettes a day, while the previously mentioned petition aimed at pushing a ban through the Arizona legislature led off right at the top of the page with the outrageous claim that an eight hour bartender's shift was equal to smoking **EIGHTY** cigarettes a day! (Bruce Lambert. *New York Times* 10/08/02; Rick Hampson. *USA Today* 10/21/02)

We've seen three approaches to the measurement of nonsmokers' exposure to smoke and we've seen some criticism of each of them. What I propose below is a model clearly based on physical and biological measurements and which allows for reasonably estimated adjustments to be made for various real world environments. The general, middle of the road, average exposure of a normal nonsmoker exposed to secondary smoke is found to be about 1/1000th of a cigarette per hour in most reasonably populated and well-ventilated situations, a level far below anything ever responsibly theorized to represent any sort of a health threat.

The Bio-Physical Models

These models are based primarily upon two figures: the actual amount of air breathed in and out by nonsmokers in normal situations, and the concentration of smoke in a given volume of air in such situations.

The base rate for the volume of air that an average person breathes while at a state of rest is generally accepted to be about six liters per minute. A person working at a low level of activity, such as a bartender during a slow day at the bar, might double that; a person working at a higher level of activity, such as a waiter with a steady stream of populated tables, might triple it. For ease of calculation this model will generally examine exposures at a rate of breathing 10 to 20 liters per minute, giving a significantly higher exposure than would be experienced by someone at rest (Domino et al. *New England Journal of Medicine* 08/05/93).

The air volume of a given environment is calculated using the actual physical dimensions of that space and also takes into account the ventilation present in terms of air changes per hour. To keep things simple I will approximate three feet as being equal to one meter... not exact, but not significantly different for general figuring. Thus, a room that's 15 ft. x 15 ft. with a fairly high 12 ft ceiling would have a metric volume of roughly 5 meters by 5 meters by 4 meters for a total of 100 cubic meters of air. A cubic meter is equal to 1,000 liters, so such a room would hold 100,000 liters of air.

However, unless one happens to be sitting in the middle of a biohazard-sealed-airlock type room, there's going to be a certain amount of air exchange. In a normal house there's a lot more air infiltration around windows and such than most people realize. Even a very tightly sealed house generally exchanges its total air volume with fresh air from outside once every two hours or so, while most normal houses are more likely to have air exchange rates of once, twice, or even three times per hour; potentially even much higher in nice weather with open windows.

If our model room were in a house with a 2x/hour air exchange rate and the room's doors and windows were closed but no better sealed than the rest of the house we would expect a similar level of air exchange -- giving our room a total effective hourly fresh air volume of 2x that original 100,000 liters: 200,000 liters of air. Similar calculations can be made for any space once the room size and an air exchange rate is determined.

Most modern commercial establishments that allow smoking have fairly high air exchange rates. The norm is probably about six to eight air exchanges per hour, and in very well-ventilated places this figure can toward twenty air changes if the venue is one that expects a lot of smoking (e.g. a bar or casino). Dover Downs in Delaware for example boasts a ventilation rate of 19 air changes per hour (personal communication, DEUSA).

Antismokers try to expand their estimate of deaths due to secondary smoke by arguing that convincing evidence shows such smoke hurts the heart as well as the lungs.

What is this evidence? It's evidence like the study titled, "Unfavorable Effects of Passive Smoking on Aortic Function in Men" published in the *Annals of Internal Medicine* on 03/15/98. That study claimed subjects suffered unfavorable elastic reactions in their aortas after secondary smoke exposure. The exposure level was set at 30 ppm of carbon monoxide.

Was that a reasonable level? Consulting the *1979 Report to the Surgeon General* we find that 30 ppm is:

>about 1500% the level on a smoking air flight
>about the level on a bus carrying 200 smokers
>about the level in our small model room if our
    smoker smoked 100 cigarettes an hour.

With exposure levels like that, the only surprising thing is that the nonsmokers still HAD aortas to measure.

Figure 28

We will examine four different situations:

1) A one-room space as described above with one smoker and one nonsmoker.

2) An average house lived in by one smoker and one or two nonsmokers.

3) An average sized neighborhood bar.

4) A slightly less than average sized restaurant.

For each situation we will postulate figures for five variables:

1) Total air volume accounting for air exchange rates.
2) The average number of smokers.
3) The amount of smoking they are likely to engage in.
4) The total amount of smoke emitted.
5) The exposure time of the nonsmokers.

Finally, we will examine within each model the likely effects of air-cleaning or directed ventilation technology.

One Room Model:

Let us start with the one room model as was described above. The average smoker smokes roughly a pack a day, or just a bit more than one cigarette for each waking hour. For ease of calculation, we will assume the actual smoking rate in our model to be one cigarette per hour.

According to the figures on page 133 of the *1986 Report of the Surgeon General on the Health Consequences of Involuntary Smoking* the ratio of sidestream smoke to mainstream smoke for the three major components (tar, nicotine, and carbon monoxide) showed sidestream smoke giving off a bit less than twice what exists in the mainstream smoke of a standard nonfilter cigarette and a bit more than three times that of a standard filter cigarette. It should be noted that for selected components of the chemicals in smoke some will be higher in sidestream than in mainstream and some will have the reverse tendency. Cherry picking particular components in the pico- and nanogram range that would support our arguments is a Crusader trick I will not indulge in here: the three components noted above are generally considered the major constituents of ETS.

Taking the main three elements noted above as our standard it is fair to say that sidestream smoke produced by a normal cigarette is about two and a half times what is inhaled directly by the smoker in the form of mainstream smoke. In addition, the smoker him or her self will exhale some of their mainstream smoke back into the air. Thus, if a nonsmoker inhaled *all* of the smoke from the end of the cigarette and added to it the smoke exhaled by the smoker, it would be roughly equivalent to that nonsmoker smoking three cigarettes.

Let us return to our model room. While sitting in that room for an hour our nonsmoker would be breathing 10 liters of air or less per minute, or about 600 liters in the course of that hour. With an air exchange rate of 2x per hour the total room air volume would be equivalent to 200,000 liters of air. Thus our nonsmoker would be breathing 600/200,000 of the total amount of air and smoke in that room. 600/200,000 is equal to 3/1,000ths of the air, or 3/1,000ths of the equivalent mainstream smoke from three cigarettes: 9/1000ths or about 1/100th of a single cigarette. Over the course of an 8-hour day, 5-day week, our nonsmoker would "smoke" roughly one pack of cigarettes per work-year.

What would be the effect if air-cleaning technology or increased ventilation were employed in this situation? It would of course depend upon what type of air cleaner was being used and how powerful it was. A standard $150 ten pound Honeywell HEPA model promises to remove 99.9% of particulates and would cycle through all the air in our model room about six times an hour. This would reduce our nonsmoker's exposure to a bit over 1/1000th of a cigarette per hour, or about 2 cigarettes per year, at least as far as particulate matter was concerned.

Alternatively, what if a window were opened in the room and a standard small window fan were turned to exhaust? Increasing the air change rate from 2 air changes per hour to 12 air changes would reduce the nonsmoker's exposure to about the same level as the air cleaner scenario above, with the added advantage that gas phase components of the tobacco smoke would be exhausted as well. If the smoker sat near the fan obviously the effect would be greatly increased, as the fan would tend to pull much of the smoke directly out the window before it had a chance to circulate into room air. Even if such positioning only helped by 50% we'd see the nonsmoker's exposure go down to about one cigarette per year.

A somewhat funny but nonetheless true observation about the one-room model is the comparison between sharing such a room every day with one smoker or with two nonsmokers. While the long-term health risk from the smoker's smoke is quite questionable, the short term health risk from exposure to the germs of the two nonsmokers is not: infectious disease unquestionably passes from person to person, is unquestionably capable of killing quickly, and is twice as likely to be passed to you by two people as by one. You might actually be much safer in the room with the single smoker!

Average House Model

While house sizes certainly vary enormously, let us take an average small American row house for a couple or a couple with a child as being 15 feet wide, 60 feet deep, and having two stories with 10 foot ceilings. Again, approximating English to Metric this would give us a total air volume of 5 meters x 20 meters x 3 meters with that result being doubled to account for two floors: 600 cubic meters or 600,000 liters of air. As with the Room

Model above we will assume an average air exchange rate of 2 air changes per hour giving a total fresh air volume of 1,200,000 liters.

We will assume that one spouse smokes and the other does not. For this model to make sense we need to make some sort of accounting for the fact that at some points the non-smoking spouse or child may be in close proximity to the smoker and at other points they may be in a totally different and closed off part of the house. We also need to account for the fact that it is unlikely that either the smoker or the nonsmokers will be in the house for the entire day and that all smoking will be done in the house.

We will deal with the first difficulty by assuming that all the smoke produced will always be evenly distributed around the house. Additionally, if any effort was made to restrict exposure by the nonsmokers by such means as restricting the smoking to the smoker's bedroom with the door closed, then such a model would greatly overestimate the nonsmokers' exposure. Contrariwise, if the smoker spent most of his or her time smoking in the same room as the nonsmokers their exposure would be greater. The fairest approximation is to assume the even spread of smoke throughout the air volume of the entire house.

For the second difficulty we will assume that the smoker smokes roughly half their cigarettes at home, for a total of ten cigarettes. Just as in the Room Model above, we will use the figure of one cigarette smoked actually giving forth into the air the equivalent of what a smoker would get from smoking three cigarettes.

Using those assumptions we would then see the smoke equivalent of 30 cigarettes being put into the air over the course of a standard day. The hourly air volume of the home as noted above at 1,200,000 liters would give a total air volume per day of 24 x 1,200,000 or 28,800,000 liters of air. At 10 liters per minute for 12 hours of exposure per day, our nonsmoker would breathe in (10x60x12)/28,800,000 of the total air and smoke volume.

Converting that fraction to decimal form gives us .00025, which, when multiplied by 30 yields .0075 or three quarters of one one-hundredth of a cigarette per day. In the course of a year the nonsmoker would breathe 365 times that amount, or about two and a half cigarettes.

Of course, as noted above, if any attempt were made to minimize the exposure of the nonsmokers, such as might be the case if one of them were a young child, that exposure rate would decrease enormously. If the smoking were confined to a room with a small exhaust fan in a window or if the house had a high efficiency air cleaner, the exposure would simply disappear in terms of any realistic measurement.

While a nonsmoker might well claim that there's no reason for them to be "forced" to inhale the equivalent of even two cigarettes a year, such a concerned nonsmoker would be unlikely to spend an average amount of time in the presence of the smoker while smoking was going on: thus their actual exposure would reflect the latter situation above. Concerns about inhaling a fraction of the smoke from a single cigarette over the course of a year are pretty much just plain silly given the contributions of other pollutants in the air caused by cooking, heating, pets, rugs, furniture, and various building materials. Remember: a single dinner cooked at a gas stove produces as much formaldehyde as 100 cigarettes!

Model Bar/Restaurant

Rather than devise two totally different models, I am going to assume that an average neighbourhood bar has roughly the same floor space as the average small restaurant (excluding sealed off kitchen area). The two situations will still be somewhat different however due to different smoking patterns and crowd intensities of bar and restaurant customers.

We will begin with a bar since the model is somewhat simpler than the case of a restaurant. The old classic picture of a neighbourhood bar always involved a cloud of thick blue smoke hanging in the air. Today, very few bars would sport such a cloud due to improved ventilation and the frequent addition of "Smoke Eater" type air cleaning devices.

Bars had a tendency to get smoky because people who drink tend to smoke more often than people who don't, and smokers tend to smoke more while drinking than when they are not. Thus bars generally had a higher density of smokers and those smokers were smoking more intensely than one would find in a comparable situation in a restaurant. Because of this, most bars catering to a concerned clientele today will have air exchange rates **far** higher than would ever be seen in a private home, or even in most other types of smoking-allowed commercial establishments.

ASHRAE is an organization that sets standards for good practice in the fields of heating, air conditioning, and refrigeration. In recent years they've been under pressure from Antismoking Lobbyists who have sought to have them declare that "zero-tolerance" for tobacco smoke was the only acceptable standard. Historically, ASHRAE has generally set a standard based on the number of cubic feet per minute of fresh air per minute per person (cfm/person) that would be required to meet good standards of air quality in commercial establishments under varying conditions.

ASHRAE's standards for nonsmoking establishments generally called for fresh air input of about 15 cfm/person, while those for spaces occupied heavily or exclusively by smokers called for 30 or even 60 cfm/person. While this measurement of air exchange is a bit different than the total air changes per hour used above, the two can be readily compared if one knows the average population density of smokers and nonsmokers in a given space.

I chose my bar model from reality: a nice little Irish bar called O'Donnell's near Philadelphia. On Saturday nights, the two halves of the bar/restaurant blend into one unit as food is no longer served and the side room area fills up with folks listening to Kenn Kweder and other popular musicians. The full bar is approximately 30 feet wide, 60 feet long, and 12 feet high, (10 meters wide, 20 meters long, and 4 meters high). On a crowded Saturday night there might be as many as 80 people in the bar, with roughly half of them being smokers. Those smokers, as noted earlier, tend to smoke more heavily in a bar situation than they might do elsewhere, so we will assume that each smoker smokes two cigarettes per hour rather than the single cigarette assumed in earlier models.

In that crowded period, ASHRAE standards would call for about 20 cfm of fresh air for each of the 40 nonsmokers, and about 60 for each of the smokers.... an average of 40 cfm/person. For our crowd of 80 people that would be a requirement of 3,200 cfm in total or 192,000 cubic feet of fresh air in an hour. Taking our bar measurements from above we see that the bar contains a volume of 30x60x12 cubic feet of air, or 21,600 cubic feet of air (in fact a bit less since the people and furniture displace some air volume). To meet ASHRAE standards the bar would need just about 10 air changes per hour.

So if the bar was *always* filled to such a peak capacity, and *never* used its side room as a restaurant, and threw its SmokeEater devices out the back window, how much smoke would a waitperson or bartender be exposed to during a shift or during the course of a year's work?

Remember that a person at rest consumes about 6 liters of air per minute. For our working bartender we will assume a little more than triple that consumption, or about 20 liters per minute. The metric measurements above give us a bar air volume of (10x20x4) or 800 cubic meters: 800,000 liters. The 10 air changes per hour gives us a total of 8,000,000 liters of air volume. The 40 smokers, each smoking 2 cigarettes per hour, gives us 80 cigarettes, and correcting for the fact that each cigarette produces a total of smoke roughly equal to three times what the smoker inhales directly we see the mainstream smoke equivalent of 240 cigarettes per hour in the air of that bar. 240/8,000,000 = .00003 cigarette-equivalents per liter of air. The bartender would breathe (20 liters per minute x 60 minutes) 1200 of those an hour. 1200 x .00003 = .036 or about one-thirtieth of a cigarette per hour.

In the real world the average exposure of our bartender would be far less than that: the average population of the bar is probably a good deal under the 80 folks who were jammed in there on a Saturday band night, and during the day the restaurant side of the bar/restaurant aspect of the establishment probably cuts down on the amount smokers smoke since very few smokers actually take puffs between forkfuls of food.

A realistic figure for our bartender would be at most perhaps one-sixtieth of a cigarette per hour, or one-seventh of a cigarette per 8 hour work shift. Our nonsmoking 5-day a week, bartender would inhale an annual total of about 35 cigarettes.

Of course, since the bar *does* have an air cleaning device in addition to the aforementioned ventilation, actual exposure to the tar, nicotine, and other pollutants could be less than 20% of that: perhaps 5 or 10 cigarettes per year. As noted earlier, a ventilation/air cleaning system that was properly sized and maintained could essentially produce air in a Free-Choice bar that would be cleaner than the average air in a smoking-banned bar or even cleaner than the "fresh air" outside.

An important thing to note however is the fact that we are assuming good ventilation in this model bar. One, or even twenty, cigarettes a year are not going to pose a significant threat to the long-term health of a nonsmoking bartender, but if the bar is poorly ventilated and the amount rose to several hundred there could at least be the beginnings of a cause for concern.

In a nondrinking restaurant of the same rough size we'd see several differences. First of all, there'd be more families with children in attendance. Adults would likely make up no more than 80% of the population. Secondly, there wouldn't be the great numbers of people standing and moving around: the overall population density would probably be lower... perhaps a maximum peak of 60 people and an overall average of 32 adults and 8 children in such a space for a reasonably successful restaurant.

Of the 32 adults, only about ¼ would be smokers, representing the average of the adult population, giving us a total of only 8 smokers. And those 8 smokers, since they would be spending a fair amount of time eating, would rarely average more than one cigarette per hour, particularly since one or two of them might refrain from smoking altogether if out with their children. This gives us a likely maximum average of about 8 cigarettes per hour, corrected as above for sidestream smoke to a total of 24 cigarette-equivalents: much lower than in the crowded bar environment examined above.

In such a case, if the air change rate was held constant at 10 air changes per hour we'd see our waitpeople breathing roughly 10% of what our bartender did: less than one half of a single thousandth of a cigarette per hour, less than one one-hundredth per 8 or even per 12 hour shift. Such a waiter or waitress would inhale the equivalent of less than 3 cigarettes per year, although if the restaurant had an efficient air cleaner or directed ventilation system, or had slow periods between mealtimes, the figure could be far lower.

As for customers, even an avid diner eating three meals a day at the restaurant and staying for an hour or more for each would breathe less than half that amount. Indeed, since they would be relatively at rest they might breathe the equivalent of far less than a single cigarette in the course of that year. Again, such things as the presence of SmokeEaters or seating arrangements that sat the smokers near vents exhausting the air would reduce our nonsmoking thrice-daily diner's exposure to a level that's equivalent to nonexistent.

As noted earlier, when the level is reached where exposure levels are down to less than a dozen cigarettes per year, the other factors in indoor air pollution begin assuming a much more important role. Just as happened with airplanes, venues that ban smoking may wind up with air that is less healthy due to reduced fresh air exchange: diseases and long-term health problems may actually increase in severity! In such a situation it is the Surgeon General, rather than smoking, that poses the most danger to a nonsmoker's health.

Exposure Conclusion

The different models examined above yield different results, but it seems fair to say that the average exposure in today's environments mixing smokers and nonsmokers is likely to be a good deal closer to 1/1000ᵗʰ of a cigarette equivalent per hour than to 1/100ᵗʰ. Thus that is the figure that was used in the main body of *Dissecting Antismokers' Brains* in any discussion of exposure to secondary smoke. In the past air change rates of 10 or 15 times an hour would have been relatively rare. Today they are seen as necessary in maintaining an atmosphere in which nonsmokers will be content in sharing space with smokers.

Even without such high levels of ventilation, concerns about contact with the "poisons" in tobacco smoke are obviously greatly exaggerated. It would be extremely difficult for any of the elements in secondary smoke to reach levels that the EPA or OSHA normally consider to be of concern. Such levels, called Threshold Limit Values (TLVs) or Permissible Exposure Limits (PELs) would never even be approached in real world situations. The table below illustrates this by looking at a number of these chemicals of concern in an old-fashioned and poorly ventilated small neighbourhood bar.

Our model here will be only half the size of our previously used bar model: just 15 feet wide, 60 feet long, with a 12 foot ceiling -- a small bar with a total volume of just 400 cubic meters. We'll set the ventilation very low, far lower than would normally be found in any modern establishment concerned with ventilation, smoke, and customer comfort: just three air changes per hour. Thus our 400 cubic meter bar will average a total air volume of 1200 cubic meters of air each hour.

There are many elements in tobacco smoke that could be measured and are possibly of concern for people's health. To show that I have not simply selected ones that support my case I have deliberately chosen seven of the more commonly cited chemicals that begin with the letter A and added three others often given a high profile by Antismoking groups in their literature and TV ads.

The ones I have chosen have all been assigned Threshold Limit Values (TLVs) or Permissible Exposure Limits (PELs). TLVs and PELs are the cut-off points at which government agencies such as OSHA believe there first begins to be a health concern for workers exposed to such levels eight hours a day, five days a week, for their entire working lives. Measurements of chemicals below these values are considered to be below levels where threats to health or safety exist.

Table 1 has four columns.

The first column is the chemical name.

The second column shows the TLV or PEL for each chemical. Most TLV/PEL figures come from the State of California website at: www.dir.ca.gov/title8/5155ac1Frame.html, and express the concentration of chemical safely allowed per cubic meter of air, or m^3.

The third column shows the total amounts of the chemicals emitted, both sidestream and mainstream, by standard cigarettes as noted in the 1999 Massachusetts Benchmark Study and the 1979 and 1986 Surgeon Generals Reports. Those figures are measured in thousandths of a gram (mg), millionths of a gram (mcg), and billionths of a gram (ng). The abbreviations stand for milligrams, micrograms, nanograms.

Finally, the fourth column shows the number of cigarettes that would need to be smoked in our small bar each and every hour before the levels of that chemical reached the TLV or level of concern for that chemical. You'll see that the numbers here are so large as to be outright ridiculous in any real-world scenario.

CHEMICAL	PERMISSIBLE EXPOSURE LIMIT (PEL) OR THRESHOLD LIMIT VALUE (TLV)	TOTAL EMITTED PER CIGARETTE, SIDE-STREAM AND MAINSTREAM	NUMBER OF CIGARETTES NEEDED PER HOUR TO REACH TLV OR PEL IN THE AIR OF A SMALL TAVERN
Acetaldehyde	45 mg/m^3	4 mg	13,500
Acetone	1780 mg/m^3	1.7 mg	1,256,470
Acetonitrile	70 mg/m^3	.6 mg	140,000
Acrolein	250 mcg/m^3	634 mcg	473
Ammonia	18 mg/m^3	5.7 mg	3751
Aniline	7,600 mcg/m^3	11.2 mcg	814,286
Arsenic	10,000 ng/m^3	32 ng	375,000
Cyanide	5,000 mcg/m^3	716 mcg	8,380
Formaldehyde	940 mcg/m^3	856 mcg	1317
Toluene	188 mg/m^3	.7 mg	322,286

TABLE 1

It should be noted that if our model neighbourhood bar were a modern yuppie establishment the ventilation figure would be more like twelve air changes per hour than three. In such a bar we'd have to jam about 5 million smokers through the doors to reach the safety limit for some of the elements cited above! Remember the dimensions of the bar: 60 feet long by just 15 feet wide. In such a bar 40 people would be considered more than a good crowd. Even if five times that number were somehow crammed in and they were ALL heavy smokers, we still wouldn't reach the permissible exposure limit of even one of the above compounds --- not even at the poorer ventilation level.

In addition, it's worth remembering that the values in Table 1 are based upon continuous eight hour a day, five day per week worker exposure. OSHA standards regularly allow for these limits to be safely exceeded for certain periods during a workday (such as might occur during a heavy crowding at a bar.)

The concept for the table above came from a similar modelling of a closed 100 cubic meter chamber outlined in a paper by Gori and Mantel available at FORCES.org. However the particular elements chosen, the incorporation of air exchanges and real world modelling, and all mathematical computations are mine.

****

A final humorous note on secondary smoke exposure: a cigarette puts off a bit less than 40 micrograms of cholesterol in both sidestream and mainstream smoke. At 1,000[th] of a cigarette per hour a nonsmoker would have to work with smokers for over 600 years for in order to get one day's recommended dietary value of 600 milligrams.

I'd recommend a good prime rib instead... provided no one's made it illegal.

Appendix C

Taxes, Social Cost, and the MSA

Gesundheit ist Pflicht! {Health is Duty!}

– Nazi Party slogan from the 1930s

The pure hard numbers of dollars and cents should be about as far away from the value judgments, psychological theories, and slipperiness of mutating word definitions as one could hope to travel. Even here though the arguments in the conflict between smokers and Antismokers are more open to varying interpretations than would be ideal.

In the 1970s and 1980s Antismoking groups claimed that cigarette taxes should be raised because nonsmokers were being unfairly forced to pay extra taxes to care for old and sickly smokers. The argument of fairness is a powerful one and many smokers resigned themselves to a future of doubled or even tripled taxes. The spectre of cigarette taxes rising from the 20 cents or so that was common then to levels of 40, 50 or even 75 cents was daunting, but seemed in fairness to be unavoidable.

As the 1980s drew to a close however, new information began to emerge. An article in The Journal of the American Medical Association looked at the social costs and taxes related to drinking and smoking and arrived at an unexpected conclusion. The analysis showed that to reflect true fairness smokers should actually get **paid** between 22 cents and $1.28 by nonsmokers for every pack smoked in order to equalize the societal costs and savings from their habit (Manning et al. "The taxes of sin; do smokers and drinkers pay their way?" *JAMA*: 261:1604 1989).

The factor that had previously been ignored by Crusaders in their push to raise taxes that would pay their own salaries was the fact that, while statistics pointed toward smokers getting cancer and heart disease at younger ages and then requiring expensive care, those same statistics stated that smokers were dying earlier and thus were not running up long-term nursing home and geriatric care bills, or even collecting their fair share of pension and social security payments!

Manning's paper is not alone in its conclusions. The U.S. Office of Technology Assessment noted in 1993:

> *Reduction or elimination of smoking would improve health and extend longevity, but may not lead to savings in health care costs. In fact, significant reductions in smoking prevalence and the attendant increase in life expectancy could lead to future increases in total medical spending, in Medicare program outlays, and in the budgets of Social Security and other government programs.*

And again in 1997 the economist W. Kip Viscusi found that "*on balance there is a net cost savings to society even excluding consideration of the current cigarette taxes paid by smokers.*" When those taxes were included, at the much lower tax rates of the time, Viscusi's figures concluded that smokers were paying $0.85 cents more per pack than their ultimate social and medical costs. Based on these calculations, he noted, one could argue that "cigarette smoking should be subsidized rather than taxed" (W. Kip Viscusi. "From Cash Crop To Cash Cow." *Regulation* Vol. 20, No.3 1997).

These conclusions were similar to those reached in 1995 by a Congressional Research Service inquiry into the issue, and most significantly were strongly endorsed in 1997 in an editorially headlined study in the prestigious New England Journal of Medicine that concluded health care expenditures would actually rise if everyone quit smoking (See Figure 29).

The only well-designed study prior to 2002 that ever attempted to dispute these conclusions was one conducted by Dutch researchers and reported in the Journal of Epidemiology and Community Health. The way they arrived at a contrary finding was by assuming that smokers, instead of dying three to eight years earlier than nonsmokers as is usually claimed by Crusading organizations, actually live to virtually the same age as their nonsmoking counterparts (W. Nusselder. *JECH* 07/ 08/00 - as reported by Andre Picard, *Public Health Reporter*).

Dr. Nusselder claimed that while nonsmokers would live to an average of about 81.6 years, smokers would live to be 80.8 years themselves! That's a difference of less than ten months... far less than any figures used anywhere else by Antismoking organizations or researchers when speaking of the effects of smoking. This study stood alone in its conclusions and seems to have been tailor-made to use before public bodies voting on tax increases. It certainly does not serve in any way to negate the other studies cited above, but for completeness it should be noted.

This brings us up to the latest study to hit the news: In May of 2002, just after New York City proposed a 1700% city tax increase that would raise the price of a pack of cigarettes to over $7, the Centers for Disease Control, with great fanfare, released a study claiming that smokers cost society $150 billion a year... or, not surprisingly, just about $7 a pack (http://www.cdc.gov/tobacco).

They arrived at that figure by using several tricks. About half the "cost" is from what they calculate as lost production for the state: something that used to be calculated only by communist and fascist governments. In order to arrive at $75 billion as a figure for that though, they had to make an assumption in the **opposite** direction to that made by Nusselder in the preceding study cited: they assumed that smokers die an incredible *fourteen* years earlier than nonsmokers!! (And of course the main or even the only cause of all these premature deaths is assumed to be purely the habit of smoking.) The other $75 billion is made up largely of fantastical projections of health care costs while simultaneously ignoring any decrease in costs due to those projected early deaths. As a coup-de-grace, the $50 - $75 billion that smokers ultimately pay in cigarette taxes and fees is completely ignored.

It would seem obvious that the entire argument of simple fairness would dictate not just a reduction of the onerous tax burden now being borne nationally by smokers, but its total elimination. Clearly such a conclusion obviously does not sit well with the Antismoking organizers whose paychecks are flowing from those taxes. But how could they argue against the cold actuarial reality of economic fairness? Always resourceful, never hamstrung by facts, the Crusaders have found a way – actually, several different ways.

The first, and boldest, was simply to ignore reality and continue to claim that smokers were still costing society money. When the facts presented above would be raised against them, they simply claimed that such reasoning was based upon "immoral economics," since it included the savings to health and social care systems that accrued when smokers died prematurely. "Immorality" and "Big Tobacco" go hand-in-hand in the public eye so this approach to what had started out as a purely economic question has been widely accepted and touted by the media.

"Health care costs for smokers at a given age are as much as 40 percent higher than those for nonsmokers, but in a population in which no one smoked the costs would be 7 percent higher among men and 4 percent higher among women than the costs in the current mixed population of smokers and non-smokers.

If all smokers quit, health care costs would be lower at first, but after 15 years they would become higher than at present. In the long-term, complete smoking cessation would produce a net increase in health care costs,"

--The Health Care Costs of Smoking. Barendregt et al. *New Engl. Jour. of Med.* 337(15):1052-7 10/09/97

Figure 29

Even the courts, normally expected to confine themselves to facts and law, have been drawn to the moral argument. One of the very first cases that Big Tobacco lost against the states was heard before Judge Fitzpatrick in Minnesota. According to an article in the *Minneapolis - St. Paul Star Tribune* on Feb. 24th 1998:

> *Ramsey County District Judge Kenneth Fitzpatrick reiterated Monday he will not let the defense <Big Tobacco> claim, or hint, that the plaintiffs <Minnesota> benefit financially from the fact that smokers tend to die prematurely.*

Judge Fitzpatrick also refused to allow the tobacco companies to bring up the fact that smokers were already paying into the state's coffers through their taxes. In effect, the only thing he allowed to be brought before the jury was the calculation of the increased medical costs of sick smokers, without any consideration of the extra taxes they paid or the money saved by the state in geriatric and nursing home care. Legal economic considerations in court had been replaced by a judge's sense of morality and his prejudice against Big Tobacco.

Faced with fighting a case based upon a "Let's Pretend" Alice-in-Wonderland type world such as this, the tobacco companies realized they had no chance of winning. They chose instead to let smokers pick up the tab for them and agreed to pay almost seven billion dollars to Minnesota while also renouncing all rights to privacy and attorney-client privilege with regard to their corporate documents and memos.

Eventually Big Tobacco cut a deal with the Attorney Generals from all the states that it had not already settled with in courts and agreed to pay a fee, passed directly on to smokers, for every pack of cigarettes sold in the United States. This fee, currently equal in practical terms to roughly 60 cents per pack, acts as a direct federal tax upon smokers without ever having had to go through the legislative process of a tax increase. Indeed, virtually every newspaper article and network news mention of the money paid in the Master Settlement Agreement speaks of it as money coming "from the tobacco industry." It's never noted that the industry itself is in actually paying nothing: **every** penny comes directly from the pockets of smokers without their input, choice or legislative consent.

Amazingly, despite the seemingly clear figures indicating otherwise, the tobacco industry gave in to demands that it should be held responsible for government health care costs without recognition of how those costs are balanced and more than balanced by pre-existing taxes and long-term savings. Why did they do this? Simply because, as noted above, it cost them nothing: they were allowed, even in a sense required, to pass all costs directly on to the consumers of their products. In return, they were guaranteed immunity from many future lawsuits and were also afforded guarantees that new and smaller tobacco companies would not be allowed to undercut their prices simply by being honest in their business practices. Finally, as a little noted side bonus, the massive overhead of the taxes passed on to smokers have allowed the tobacco companies to hike their profit margins to levels never dreamed of before the settlement: who will notice or care much about an extra 10 or 15 cents added on to a product that already carries a $5 price tag?

The second weapon deployed by the Antismoking Crusade in pushing for higher taxes has been to make use of the "Save the Children" argument examined earlier. Antismokers have claimed that every ten percent rise in cigarette taxes would result in a seven percent decline in teen smoking. This argument was heavily used in the 1989 California referendum that brought a 50 cents per pack increase to smokers and a 100 million dollar windfall to Californian Antismoking Lobbyists. It was also being used in 2002 as state-by-state polls paid for by Crusading groups purported to show widespread support for raising cigarette taxes.

The polls were cleverly slanted by starting out with questions that have obviously emotive answers ("Are you concerned about smoking by young people?"), and then moving on to budget choices dealing with such things as cutting valued programs for children and the elderly, and finally including the specific image of children in the final question: "Do you favor or oppose a one-dollar per pack increase in the tobacco tax as part of an effort to reduce tobacco use, **particularly among kids...?**" <Emphasis added> In Pennsylvania 75% of the voters favored the increase mentioned in that final question, in a classic "three wolves and a sheep voting on the dinner menu" split (http://www.taxtobacco.com/Docs/Poll_Results.pdf).

One has to wonder if social justice might have made a better showing if the poll was not so cleverly designed to play the "protect the kids" card. What if the wording had more honestly been "Do you favor or oppose a one-dollar per pack increase in the tobacco tax as part of an effort to reduce tobacco use particularly among lower income adults...?" A poll worded in that way might well have yielded a result in which 75% of the voters voted **against** the tax increase rather than in favor of it despite the wolves and sheep motivation.

In any event, despite the enormous tax rises of the last 15 years we've seen youth smoking rates increase by as much as 50% although there's been some downturn in the last three years or so among teen boys. If the statistics of the Antismokers were true teen smoking would be virtually non-existent at this point. Of course they're not true and teen smoking is still higher than it was back in the 1970s and 1980s when taxes were enormously lower, Antismoking ads on TV were almost non-existent, schools had smoking areas for student breaks, and the Antismoking budget was more like $9 million a year rather than $900 million.

This general experience of rising youth smoking rates was duplicated in state after state throughout most of the 1990s, despite the fact that the massive tax increases were also accompanied by a truly fantastic increase in government-sponsored Antismoking media propaganda, widespread smoking bans, and hitherto unparalleled enforcement of underage sale penalties.

The extra billions that smokers have been forced to pay to Antismoking efforts to vilify and ridicule themselves on billboards and in TV ads has generally done little other than enrich the Antismokers and impoverish the smokers. To add insult to injury, Antismoking organizations are now using that same money to crusade for even higher taxes in order to save even more of the children. As for the adult smokers who buy 95% or more of the cigarettes sold, they're expected to simply grin and bear it… or even welcome the higher taxes as a blessing from Antismokers who are helping them give up their nasty habit!

The third argument for further increasing the tax burden on smokers is not widely publicized outside of circles where a sympathetic ear is expected. That argument is simply that massive increases in the tax rates will force poorer smokers to give up the habit or sacrifice basic life necessities in order to pay for it. Once again the technique of doublethink is employed by Antismokers as they argue that an extra dollar or two a pack will make smokers quit while at the same time they continue to argue that smoking is an addiction worse than a two hundred dollar a day heroin habit. If their perception of the addictiveness of smoking were even *slightly* true, all that the extra dollar a pack would accomplish would be to make poor people who smoke even poorer while affecting wealthier people not at all and leaving the smoking rate absolutely untouched.

There is one further argument that has become increasingly common since the late 1990s. This argument is based upon the obvious fact that when you have 50 different states with many different tax rates, about half those states will be below the average and about half will be above. This basic statistical reality has opened the doors for Antismoking organizations to pummel legislatures with demands that state taxes be raised to at least that "average" amount, while ignoring the fact that as soon as they are, the "average" will have then increased to a new and higher level.

On the high end of the scale, Antismokers will point to states like Alaska, California, and New York, and point out how well they are doing with all the money they are raising from their incredible tax rates, while ignoring the fact that in most cases those states with the highest tax rates are also losing an incredible amount of money to black marketeering and the crime that cigarette smuggling generates. At well over $5 an ounce, cigarettes in many states are now more valuable by weight than pure silver ingots! This is clearly reflected in the increased crime spiraling out of control as convenience stores are robbed, not of money, but of cigarettes. It is reflected as well in the social fracture that accompanies such crime and its acceptance by otherwise law-abiding citizens.

Greedy tax grabs in the name of public health have resulted in similar disparities across borders overseas. Cigarette smuggling, and the human and economic costs involved in its control have now become a significant factor on the international crime scene. Individual "busts" have now reached the level of almost twenty million dollars apiece ("Irish Customs Makes Largest Cigarette Seizure" *Reuters* 12/11/01), and in China cigarette smugglers have even been executed ("China Executes Seven…" *Reuters* 02/23/01). Meanwhile, as national authorities were focusing on the multiple "Beltway Sniper" shooting investigation in October 2002, the FBI was being chastised for not devoting enough of its energy to stopping smokers from buying tax-free cigarettes on the Internet (Mike Godfrey. *TaxNews.com* 10/14/02).

Overall, the push to increase cigarette taxes comes down to two basic motivations: Greed and Control. The greed of governments for increasing income without the negative repercussions of generalized tax increases, and the increased control over the poor by making smoking too expensive for them to regularly indulge in, have combined to create a tax monster that is out of control and growing stronger every day. Current efforts by international Crusaders are aimed at getting worldwide laws setting extortionate tax rates levels on cigarettes in every country that depends in any way on United Nations aid or benefits from the World Health Organization's other activities. Anyone resisting these efforts is instantly branded as a tool of Big Tobacco.

In August of 2000 a 500 page WHO report argued for a worldwide tax increase on tobacco products, using basically the same argument that American Crusaders used: tying the increase to a theoretical reduction in smoking rates "particularly among children."

One item of note with regard to this report: in terms reminiscent of a slur that's been made against American tobacco companies (*"We target the black, the poor, the young, and the stupid"* – often cited by Crusading groups as being a quote from a tobacco executive) the UN report noted, in more politically correct language, that these Third World tax increases were important because "youth, poor people, and the less well-educated (Third World people) are more likely to respond to an increase in price." Unlike the apocryphal tobacco executive quote, the UN focus is well documented (N. Koppel. *Associated Press* 08/08/00).

A rose is a rose is a rose.

Appendix D

Deaths Due To Eating

In recent years doctors have been increasingly encouraged to enter "death due to smoking" on the certificates of virtually any smoker of any age who dies of almost any condition speculated to have a statistical relationship to smoking. Sometimes the choice is made especially easy by the existence of a special check off box indicating that smoking "contributed to" the death. Thus, in the case of a smoker who dies of cancer or heart disease at 95 years old, smoking may well be listed as the cause of death, almost as if no nonsmokers ever die of either of these conditions. Such an idea is utter nonsense of course, but that hasn't slowed the effort.

If similar post mortem criteria were actually applied with scientific impartiality rather than political correctness, the diagnosis of "deaths due to eating" would far outstrip "deaths due to smoking." In December of 2001, Surgeon General Satcher announced that 300,000 Americans die each year from obesity and said "major steps" were needed, including federal rules restricting youth access to junk food, to fight this "epidemic." Just as the FDA sought jurisdiction in the war on smoking, the USDA now seeks "wider authority" to fight improper childhood eating habits (*Associated Press* - NY – 12/13/01).

This figure of 300,000 is smaller than the 400,000 claimed for smoking; however obesity is not the only eating-related cause of death. The 1996 Harvard Report on Cancer Prevention estimated that 30% of all cancer deaths are diet related. Given the national cancer toll of 750,000 that adds an additional 225,000 eating-related deaths to Satcher's obesity estimate.

There's more though: over one million Americans die annually from heart disease with almost half of those deaths blamed on the fat and cholesterol so prominent in our meat rich diet. That gives us a total of more than 900,000 "deaths due to eating" in America every year (partially cross-counted perhaps), without even enumerating the toll from diet-related diabetes, food poisoning, and other less common conditions. This body count almost makes smoking look benign by comparison.

The obvious counterargument to this contra-position of smoking and food as causes of death is that eating is necessary for human existence while smoking is not. This counter-argument is weak however: it is not simply eating that kills but rather the act of eating improperly.

If a socially responsible program of mass behavior modification aimed at eating was implemented to the same extent as has been done for smoking, many of these premature deaths could be avoided. An enjoyable diet of wheat and soy paste, supplemented by Brussels sprouts, seaweed sprinkled with lime juice, and an occasional dollop of fruit, would give us more productive American workers and significantly cut short term health care costs.

With just $500 million (half the current government Antismoking budget) procured through targeted taxation of meat and junk food, vast changes could be made in the way Americans eat and think about their food. Pictures of diseased animal organs, TV animations of cholesterol choked hearts, and school programs teaching children that their parents are killing them with meat rich dinners could all be combined effectively into a coherent program to promote the idea that "Big Macs kill when used as directed by the manufacturer."

The above-mentioned taxation is the simplest tool of social engineering. Taxing Big Macs and Whoppers at a profit/product to tax ratio similar to that of tobacco would create a market in which a "Happy Meal" would cost roughly $25. A family enjoying a fast-food-night-out would find themselves hit for more than a C-Note while shoveling their children toward an early grave. This would not be a regressive tax: the poor would benefit the most as their diets suddenly improved, and properly worded and conducted surveys could easily show how many of them appreciated the health benefits of the increased costs.

To paraphrase Surgeon General Koop's commentary on smoking: eating is clearly a pediatric disease, aggravated by happy clowns and characters on TV urging our children to adopt the meat and sugar habits. There's little question as to what age group is targeted by fast-food and sugary-cereal advertising during Saturday morning cartoons and after-school programming. How many parents hear "McDonalds" or some hackneyed derivation thereof as one of baby's first words during a tantrum sparked by passing, rather than stopping at, the local slaughterhouse outlet? Depictions of fast food consumption and logos should be forbidden in movies and sports stadiums and its advertising limited to plain print ads and late-night TV after the children are abed. And of course hot dogs, given their claimed association with a 9,500% increase in leukemia risk will never see the light of day at a baseball game again (Steven J. Milloy. *Science Without Sense*. Cato Institute 1995).

Would I really support such a program of social engineering? Of course not; but it could easily lie in our future. Antismoking fringe groups were once widely ignored by main-stream America. Such groups as the Animal Liberation Front and People for the Ethical Treatment of Animals enjoy a similar status today. But while Antismokers had to blaze a trail through such American traditions as equal justice under the law, free speech, and fair taxation in order to target smoking, groups like PETA and ALF will now have a much easier path to travel in controlling our other undesirable behaviors.

When they're knocking over there friend, they're knocking for you... ignore injustice and tolerate oppression at your own risk. Think of that next time you pass a "smokers ghetto" or vote for higher taxes.

Appendix E

Chemicals In Our Foods*

Cigarettes and cigarette smoke contain a multitude of toxic chemicals, according to Antismoking zealots. Therefore, the public must be protected from evil smokers who would threaten the health of nonsmoking men, women and children in places like restaurants and bars.

But what exactly are those helpless victims eating and drinking in their smoke-free, toxic-free nonsmoking section of the restaurant? You might be surprised.

The chart that follows lists chemicals found in the food and beverages served even in the nonsmoking sections of finer restaurants around the world. Holding your breath while you eat might protect you from toxic secondhand smoke, but don't swallow that food!

Many thanks to Dan Hass of FORCES Duluth for allowing me to freely adapt his wonderful work for this Appendix. Most of the text has been directly plagiarized with his permission from "Bon Apetite!" at ForcesDuluth.com while the listing of chemicals in individual foods is reprinted with the gracious permission of The American Council on Science and Health at acsh.org and HealthFactsAndFears.com

CHEMICAL
Where is it?
What is it?

ACETALDEHYDE
Apples, tomatoes
Mutagen and rodent carcinogen

AFLATOXIN
Nuts, Peanut Butter
Mutagen, rodent carcinogen, human carcinogen

ALLYL ISOTHIOCYANATE
Arugula, broccoli, mustard
Mutagen, rodent carcinogen

ANILINE
Carrots
Rodent carcinogen

BENZALDEHYDE
Apples, coffee, tomatoes
Rodent carcinogen

BENZENE
Coffee
Rodent carcinogen

BENZO(A)PYRENE
Bread, coffee, pumpkin pie, rolls, tea
Mutagen and rodent carcinogen

BENZOFURAN
Coffee
Rodent carcinogen

BENZYL ACETATE
Jasmine tea
Rodent carcinogen

CAFFEIC ACID
Apples, carrots, celery, coffee, pears, grapes, lettuce, mangos, potatoes
Rodent carcinogen

CATECHOL
Coffee
Rodent carcinogen

D-LIMONENE
Black pepper, mango
Rodent carcinogen

1,2,5,6-DIBENZ(A)ANTHRACENE
Coffee
Rodent carcinogen

ESTRAGOLE
Apples, basil
Rodent carcinogen

ETHYL ALCOHOL
Bread, rolls, wine, spirits, beer, tomatoes
Rodent and human carcinogen

ETHYL BENZENE
Coffee
Rodent carcinogen

ETHYL CARBAMATE
Bread, rolls, red wine
Mutagen and rodent carcinogen

FURAN AND MANY DERIVATIVES
Bread, onions, celery, mushrooms, sweet potatoes, rolls, cranberry sauce, coffee
Mutagens

FURFURAL
Bread, coffee, nuts, rolls, sweet potatoes
Rodent carcinogen

HETEROCYCLIC AMINES
Roast beef, turkey
Mutagens and rodent carcinogens

HYDRAZINES
Mushrooms
Mutagens and rodent carcinogens

HYDROGEN PEROXIDE
Coffee, tomatoes
Mutagen and rodent carcinogen

HYDROQUINONE
Coffee
Rodent carcinogen

METHYLGLYOXAL
Coffee, red wine
Mutagen and rodent carcinogen

PSORALENS
Celery, parsley
Mutagens, rodent and human carcinogens

QUERCETIN GLYCOSIDES
Apples, onions, tea, tomatoes
Mutagens and rodent carcinogens

SAFROLE
Nutmeg in apple and pumpkin pies, black pepper
Rodent carcinogen

SYMPHYTINE
Comfrey tea
Rodent carcinogen

So what's on the menu tonight?

      Want to start with some appetizers? Don't serve cream of mushroom soup. That contains hydrazines.

How about a fresh relish tray? Sounds delicious, but be careful of carrots. They contain aniline and caffeic acid. And don't bother with the cherry tomatoes unless you have an appetite for benzaldehyde, hydrogen peroxide and quercetin glycosides. Celery is out, too. That contains caffeic acid, furan derivatives and some psoralens.

A big fan of the nuts? Stay away from the mixed roasted nuts. They're chock full of aflatoxin and furfural.

How about a nice green salad? Say something like a tossed salad and arugula with a basil/mustard vinaigrette? Use lots of dressing to mask the taste of the allyl isothiocyanate, caffeic acid and estragole.

Maybe we should head straight to the entrees?

Everybody likes roast turkey, especially when the whole family is around the table. Hope they like heterocyclic amines, too.

And how about some bread stuffing? Nothing goes better with turkey than some bread stuffing with onions, celery, black pepper and mushrooms. Save room for the ethyl alcohol, benzo-(a)pyrene, ethyl carbamate, furan derivatives, furfural, dihydrazines, d-limonene, psoralens, quercetin glycosides and safrole.

Nothing says "Happy Holidays" like cranberry sauce, unless it's the furan derivatives that go with it.

Not a turkey fan? How about some prime rib of beef with parsley sauce? Use lots of ketchup unless you have a taste for heterocyclic amines and psoralens

You might not care for the flavor, but everyone needs vegetables. How about some broccoli spears? The allyl isothiocyanate ought to kill the taste.

Who doesn't like a nice baked potato? Can't have too much ethyl alcohol and caffeic acid, I suppose. Perhaps you prefer a sweet potato instead. You'll still get your dose of ethyl alcohol, but with a shot of furfural to boot.

No meal is complete without rolls and butter. Or the ethyl alcohol, benzo(a)pyrene, ethyl carbamate, furan derivatives and furfural that come with it.

Save room for dessert!

We all love pie, don't we? Pumpkin pie is good, even with the benzo(a)pyrene, coumarin and safrole inside. Apple pie is my favorite, though I'd rather not think about the acetaldehyde, caffeic acid, coumarin, estragole, ethyl alcohol, quercetin glycoside and safrole that go with it.

If you're not a pie person, which we find hard to believe, how about something from the fresh fruit tray? Fresh apples, pears, grapes or mangos? They're always good, even with the acetaldehyde, benzaldehyde, caffeic acid, d-limonene, estragole and quercetin glycosides.

Anybody else need a drink after all that?

If you drink enough red wine, you won't notice the ethyl alcohol and ethyl carbamate. If you drink so much that it's time for a cup of coffee, the benzo(a)pyrene, benzaldehyde, benzene, benzofuran, caffeic acid, catechol, 1,2,5,6-dibenz(a)anthracene, d-limonene, ethyl benzene, furan, furfural, hydrogen peroxide and hydroquinone might do you some good. Or not.

If tea is more to your liking, you might need some sugar to mask the taste of the benzo(a)pyrene and quercetin glycosides. And for you health-conscious types who prefer only herbal teas, have some symphytine with your comfrey tea. Or some benzyl acetate with your jasmine tea.

A cigarette might taste good after such a meal ...

... just as a finishing touch.

--Dan Hass

Appendix F

Into The Smoke Of Battle

Unless someone like you cares a whole awful lot, nothing is going to get better. It's not.

-- The Once-ler, from *The Lorax*, by Dr. Seuss

Undoing the mythology of the Antismoking Crusade and returning laws and taxes to some semblance of reason will not be an easy task. Unfair as it is, Free-Choice activists have to accept the fact that we will never have the monetary resources of the opposition. Even if the big tobacco companies (who are very aware of smokers' anger over the sweet deal they cut with the government in the MSA) were willing to give Free-Choice activists millions to fight the Crusaders it would be the kiss of death.

Big Tobacco lied for years about what they knew and they were stupid to do so. Their grounds for claiming lack of hard proof of the causal relation of smoking to cancer and heart disease may not have been strong but they were defendable in the strict scientific sense because cancer and heart disease are multifactorial illnesses: there is no way to know for certain if a given individual died from lung cancer or a heart attack simply because they smoked. If the tobacco companies had come out even twenty years ago with an open admission that the bulk of the science pointed to links between smoking and these diseases, if they had offered to work with government to develop safer products, if they had opened their own scientific research to the world... they **might** have escaped the label of total villainy that was eventually firmly attached to them.

They didn't though. They took the advice of their overpriced lawyers and stuck to the principles of capitalist companies in a capitalist world that dictated their main responsibility was to shareholders rather than to the common good. While supposedly those principles should have provided them some shielding in a society openly committed to capitalism, it did not. The lies, secrets, misdirection, and American political games they played along the way with their lobbying efforts eventually led to their downfall.

Not even smokers will trust Big Tobacco anymore since it became clear that they were quite happy to cut a deal with the government that would target smokers rather than themselves and their shareholders. For years smokers sat back and depended on Big Tobacco to rein in Antismoking extremists, comfortable in the notion that the American system and old fashioned political money would work together in the long run to protect the interests of Big Tobacco's customers. Smokers were wrong, and now they are paying for it. To regain fair treatment in today's America (and increasingly in other American-influenced countries as well) smokers will need to stand up and fight for themselves, to act as a political group, and to take an active role in answering the lies and misinformation that is so pervasive in the media.

There are three decisions that smokers need to make in order to win their fight: the personal decision to stand up against unreasonable regulations and taxes, the political decision to fight City Hall at public hearings as well as at the voting booth, and the interpersonal decision to educate those around them who are misinformed. Money might be helpful, but it's not necessary... and if it came from Big Tobacco it would be more hurtful than helpful unless it were given openly and in quantities that would put Free-Choice advocates on the same footing as Antismoking

Crusaders.   While such a possibility might be conceivable in some political fights at the local level it is obviously not going to happen on a global scale.

This Appendix will look at these three roads to change, followed by an Appendix examining the sort of resistance smokers often face from Antismoking-dominated political bodies.   Anyone who smokes or who feels that the injustices being perpetrated upon smokers need to be addressed can do something at some level, no matter how small.   No one needs to feel intimidated by the size and money of the opposition.   Truth, in and of itself, is ultimately more powerful than any special interest group based on untruth... no matter how much money or political power that group may start off with.   All that's needed is to get the truth heard.

The Roads To Change

The difficulty lies, not in the new ideas, but in escaping the old ones, which ramify... into every corner of our minds.

– John Maynard Keynes

We've already touched on resistance to unreasonable smoking bans on the individual level. If there is a particular ban you want to fight and if you are fortunate enough to have at least a few other people willing to take action with you there are some basic tactics that can increase your chances of success.

For anyone who is serious about mounting organized nonviolent resistance aimed at overturning smoking bans I would strongly recommend reading Gene Sharp's *The Politics Of Nonviolent Action* (Porter Sargent. 1974) and Saul Alinsky's *Rules For Radicals* (Random House. 1971). Achieving change through nonviolent action involves a lot more than just having a march and carrying signs. Activists need to be prepared to react properly to provocation in order to avoid incidents that would rebound unfavorably upon the cause when presented through a biased media. Proper attention needs to be paid to interacting with the media in such a way as to encourage maximum coverage and presentation of your information and viewpoints. This can include such a seemingly nitpicky thing as timing your event so that it will either be covered live by the 6 o'clock news or will be held enough in advance of that time that the crews can cover you and then get on to whatever their main story of the day will be. Having one or two designated articulate people whose job will be purely to interact with the media, answer their questions, and make their job easier can be important too!

If your planned activity might involve any sort of confrontation with authority or the breaking of any laws, the participants need to be well prepared as to what to expect and the authorities need to be communicated with beforehand to relax tensions and ensure that they understand the peaceful and organized nature of your activity. As pointed out earlier in *Dissectings'* concluding chapter there are many levels of resistance and no one should ever allow themselves to feel pressured into committing to actions beyond their level of comfort.

I strongly recommend that if you are planning open defiance of a law that you take that route only after careful planning and preparations, after reasonably exhausting other alternatives, and with the participation and guidance of people who have been involved in such actions before. Remember, there's an awful lot of productive resistance that can be accomplished at lower levels of commitment.

If you've decided to mount a protest involving civil disobedience, be sure to pick a venue where the smoking ban will be seen as clearly unreasonable, where it clearly hurts people's lives or jobs, and where you'll be able to gather sufficient numbers to present an image of widespread concern. When speaking to the media, take a page from the Crusaders' handbook: be sure everyone has a short list of statements and sound bites catching the essence of the message and be sure to have something, whether **large** colorful signs or people in costumes, for the visual media to picture while reporting their story.

Finally, make sure you've got a formal statement or press release to hand to every media person who shows up as well as a background "fact-package" with points about smoking bans that may not be covered in your actual statement.

For the demonstrators themselves, be sure that you've got sufficient literature to hand out to any who may show up, and be sure that the literature contains information that new activists can use to buttress their feelings about the issue. If you're planning civil disobedience be sure that any who participate are fully aware of what the consequences may be and are comfortable dealing with those consequences. Preparation is key for this last point: pre-demonstration training for those planning to face possible arrest is **vital** in order to avoid scenes portraying smokers as undesirables and to ensure that no one finds themselves facing unexpected consequences for their actions.

A final note for those planning any sort of rally or demonstration: Just as important as planning for the event itself is doing proper planning for what happens **after** the event. If it's a small affair, plan for what happens right at its ending: A get together at someone's apartment? An impromptu meal and discussion at a Chinese restaurant? Or just a big cheer and everyone going home? Whatever it's going to be, don't just let things peter out without direction or ending: **always** end on an upbeat and organized note.

>> AND... GET PEOPLE'S NAMES!!! <<

And emails, or phone numbers, or whatever is necessary to ensure that the work you put into gathering folks together and attracting new folks from passers-by doesn't go to waste. Bring clipboards for people to sign, with headings indicating what information you want. Have your own folks sign up first to show what's expected so that you don't wind up with dozens of monkey-see-monkey-do columns of "unlisted" emails and phone numbers.

Building a movement is a serious business: it needs planning, preparation, and follow up work to every action undertaken or else you're just frittering away time and energy. As noted elsewhere: if you're serious about this, do some reading and talk to people who've done it before!

Working within the system through City Councils and state legislatures can be just as effective as demonstrating, waving signs, or defying regulations. While testifying at a City Council hearing or voting and campaigning against a candidate running with the backing of the Antismoking Lobby may not be as glamorous as being arrested on the six o'clock news, it can be fully as valuable in the long run. Smokers in America represent a voting bloc that is probably twice as large as the black population, three times that of homosexuals, and probably five times as large as the handicapped. Yet all three of those populations are today far more respected by politicians than are smokers.

If smokers began voting in their own self-interest to the same extent as these other population groups we would soon see some very significant changes in political behavior. Remember: most nonsmokers are **not** Antismokers: if ventilation and seating arrangements are provided for in such a way that they are not made uncomfortable by clouds of smoke most of them would not seek to exile smokers to the streets or punish them with extortionate taxes.

Supporting political candidates can be a tricky business. While Republicans are generally slightly more supportive of the sort of individual freedoms and rights that many Free-Choice advocates cherish, when it comes to this issue most of them are as scared of the Antismoking Lobby as the Democrats. You can't blame politicians for being daunted by the propaganda power that enables Crusaders to successfully condemn Big Tobacco for the $150 thousand they spend each year to lobby **all** the politicians in Florida while simultaneously convincing Floridians to ignore that Antismokers spent an outrageous **$5.8 million** just for a single smoking ban referendum in that state! (www. nosmoker.org/ANRF_13_(florida_ad).pdf;www. ballot.org).

As a general rule, the only major political party that has allied itself firmly with the smokers' cause is the Libertarian Party. A good rule of thumb for Free-Choice advocates at the voting booth is to vote for the candidate most likely to defeat a known shill for the Antismoking Lobby in close races, but throw your support to the Libertarians in any other race.

The politicians won't know smokers are concerned and active unless they hear our voices: call them, write them, go to hearings, and be visible in letters to the editor columns in your local newspapers whenever Antismoking editorials and articles appear. Most papers will print well-written contrary points of view if they get enough of them, even if the paper's policy is firmly Antismoking. (The New York Times *may* be an exception in this regard. Their editorial policy favoring New York's smoking ban seems to heavily affect their choice of letters... though it's possible that such is merely my perception.)

The final approach to change, educating those around you, can be both the simplest and the most difficult. Educating oneself as to the facts is easy: if you've actually read this far you already know far more than almost anyone you're likely to speak to. If you want to learn more, the entries in the Recommended Bibliography will open as many doors as you could wish.

The difficult part lies in the type of reactions you're likely to encounter when discussing this issue. The vast majority of those exposed to American media and influence will have absorbed a good bit of the Antismoking mythos into their background world view and will be strongly resistant to having those beliefs disturbed. Even if they are not actively Anti-smoking in their general life, the challenging of this settled "knowledge" will be emotionally upsetting and will often stir not only resistance to change but also outright anger and hostility toward the one doing the disturbing. You'll find an almost comical tendency among many people to react with versions of "I know the truth already. Don't confuse me with the facts!" The proper psychological term for this is "Cognitive Dissonance": people are made uncomfortable when they are forced to concurrently hold conflicting ideas: a "Doublethink Deficiency."

If you're simply dealing with a momentary acquaintance it's easy enough to hand them one of the printable handouts found at www.Antibrains.com and move the discussion onto another topic. Maybe they'll read it later and investigate further and maybe they won't, but you'll have done your bit. If they take the time to read it on the spot you can at least avoid baseless emotional arguments by challenging them to argue simply about the facts they've been presented with.

For closer friends or family members who are in profound disagreement with the Free-Choice position the only thing I can recommend is that you give them a copy of this book, Don Oakley's *Slow Burn*, or Jacob Sullum's *For Your Own Good*, and ask them to read it before taking up the argument with you again in the future. You may find that simply reading another point of view on the subject will be enough to moderate their views, and if not, at least the fact that they've seen some of the arguments and facts on the smokers' side of the issue will make future discussions better based and less likely to degenerate into name-calling.

Appendix G

Fighting City Hall: a Case Study

No man is good enough to govern another man without that other's consent.

-- Abraham Lincoln, October 16, 1854

The following pages bear a shortened but illustrative example from real life of the sort of response Free-Choice advocates are likely to get as they face the entrenched political powers of Anti-smoking Crusaders. Not every City Council will be as dismissive of its smoking citizens as Philadelphia's, and some, such as I found to be the case at a hearing in New York, may actually provide a fair and equal platform to all who show up, whether they flew in from California on tax money or rode in on a subway train with a token from their own pocket.

In general though, from the stories I have heard over the past few years from various people fighting smoking bans around the U.S., it's rare that as fair a structure as New York's is to be found. I want to give a special credit here to Vincent Robles, who chaired the Health Committee in New York: although I believe he is more sympathetic to the Crusaders' side of the argument than to that of the smokers, he made a sincere effort to be fair to all at the February, 2000 hearing I participated in.

Note: there are some misspellings/errors in the emails and testimonies that follow. They are reproduced without alteration.

On the following pages you will find:

1) An excerpted version of the written testimony I submitted to Philadelphia City Council. The excerpted version represents roughly what I was able to include by slightly stretching the limited time span of two minutes apiece afforded the plain ordinary citizens who were not connected to a lobbying group.

2) A letter of complaint about the proceedings to all the members of City Council and copied to the Mayor.

3) A summary of the exclusionary nature of the processes involved in the formation of the Council's Smoking Task Force. This summary, a formal procedural complaint, and a note on non-responsiveness were given to Councilors and the press when the Council reconvened to hear the Task Force results.

4) A handout to City Council and the press during a follow-up hearing. After this hearing the proposal was tabled and has not been acted on in the following two years.

Testimony to City Council by Michael J. McFadden (excerpted)

May 31st, 2000

Councilpeople, thank you for the opportunity to speak today. My name is Michael McFadden and I'm a long-term resident of West Philadelphia. I have no connection to any bars, restaurants, or tobacco companies other than being a good customer....

Antismoking advocates consistently ignore the clear and simple fact that there never has been and very likely never will be shown any threat at all from the microscopic exposures to smoke that might exist in well designed nonsmoking sections.... (T)he Advisor to the Surgeon General herself carefully referred only to "smoky" and "smoke-filled" rooms in most of her testimony. At no point did she indicate that well ventilated smoking and nonsmoking sections posed a threat to the general population.

Most studies that have looked at the long-term health effects of smoking upon nonsmokers have been based on situations where nonsmokers lived and worked closely with smokers, often in poorly ventilated conditions, every day of the week, over periods of up to 40 or 50 years. Even at THOSE extreme exposures only about one study out of 10 has consistently found any statistically significant link between secondary smoke and even small increases in diseases like lung cancer....

Some studies have even come up with NEGATIVE correlations: One of the largest international studies ...by the World Health Organization... showed children of smokers getting 22% LESS lung cancer than matched children of nonsmokers.... There has never been a study linking the incredibly low exposures existing in decent nonsmoking sections and any sort of disease...

(We are not) here today because of a real concern about the health of nonsmokers. We're here because smoking bans are seen as one of the most effective weapons in the arsenal of social engineering when it comes to reducing smoking and getting smokers to quit smoking....

... this is NOT George Orwell's 1984. Our government should **NOT** be in the business of making laws designed to pressure citizens into thinking in proper ways or conforming to a politically correct healthy lifestyle.

Education about the dangers of smoking is fine. Social engineering and behavior modification is not. That's NOT what government in the United States is supposed to be about, and by voting for proposals like this one I believe you will actually be hurting our country and its people a **LOT** more than you'll be helping.

To the President and Members of Philadelphia's City Council

June 1st, 2000

Dear Sirs and Madams,

I am writing to register an official protest over the way testimonies were handled at the Council Hearing on the smoking ban last Wednesday, May 31st.

Prior to the previous Hearing on May 24th I had called and identified myself, upon request, as someone opposed to the bill who wanted to testify on the health effects of secondhand smoke.   At that hearing the only testimony allowed in that category was from SUPPORTERS of the bill. Nevertheless, I sat from 2:30 until I had to leave at 8pm after unsuccessfully awaiting my chance to testify as a "citizen". Most speakers were given free rein for up to 20 minutes or more, though I do not know how the "citizen" testimonies were handled when they eventually came up.

On the 31st, I again found myself listed at the end of the program and waited over three hours for my chance to testify. Again most speakers were given at least 10 minutes of uninterrupted presentation before being urged to close.

When it came time for the "citizens" to speak, most of whom were speaking against the measure, we were told quite sternly and without warning that we would have to restrict our testimony to two minutes! Of course we were welcome to offer our full testimonies in writing, but as the Committee in its preferences toward the bill was fully aware, citizen testimony is often partially extemporaneous or from handwritten notes concerning earlier testimony.

In sum, after sitting in Council Chambers for over 8 hours, I was allowed 2 minutes to read my 6 minutes of testimony. In that time period I read aloud the first and last few paragraphs of my prepared testimony. At this point I have no idea whether the rest of my testimony will receive its proper official place in the record: it certainly did NOT get anything like the "public hearing" given to the opposing point of view.

This is particularly disturbing since my testimony was fairly unique in nature. Aside from one or two other "citizens" who had their testimony chopped from beneath them, there was very little questioning of the science and the rhetoric about science that was being often misused in support of the bill.

I enclose my written testimony since you may not otherwise have access to it. Please take just two minutes to look it over and I believe you will agree that despite its brevity it calls into serious question some of the "science" that was constantly repeated to make quick passage of the bill seem vital to the public health.

Sincerely,

Michael J. McFadden

Summary of Efforts to Participate in City's "Task Force"

Subj: A Concern ....
Date: **11/7/00** 2:15:20 PM Eastern Standard Time
From: Cantiloper@aol.com
To: healthdept@phila.gov

I am concerned because I have not received any further response from you. In our first conversation you recommended that I send the documentation and request for the Task Force papers and information via email. In our second you confirmed they had gotten through. In our third you indicated that Commissioner Tsou had been given my communications and was considering them.

It has now been almost two weeks and I have still heard nothing. This is exactly what I heard from Michael Nutter's office as well. If this is indicative of the approach that the Commission/TaskForce has taken in responding to those critical of its position I believe that a serious breach of the public trust has occurred.

I am not sure of what avenues are open to me in following this up, but I will certainly be investigating. In the meantime, under whatever legal rights I am entitled to as a concerned citizen who offered formal testimony with regard to the matters under consideration by the Task Force on Smoking in Bars and Restaurants I would like to ask once again for the relevant documents.

Sincerely,

Michael J. McFadden

The Nutter Proposal: A Disgrace to the Democratic Process

There is a side to the controversy about the proposed smoking ban that's gotten very little hearing… literally.

Back in May when City Council was first holding its hearings on this matter I called up Michael Nutter's office to submit my name for testimony at the hearing. I was asked if I would be testifying in favor of the proposal or against it and with a somewhat simplistic faith in the fairness of the political process I indicated I would be testifying against.

I found myself listed at the very end of the itinerary at the first Council hearing and after six hours I had to leave before my name came up. I resubmitted it for the second hearing and after close to three more hours of listening primarily to fairly long presentations by paid lobbyists for various Antismoking groups my turn and that of my fellow "citizen testifiers" came up. However, for us simple voters, the solid majority of whom were there if my memory is correct to testify against the bill and question and rebut the "facts" that had been lengthily presented by the other side, we were informed that we were limited to **TWO MINUTES APIECE** of testimony. So much for the value of "citizens" and their testimony as compared to that of paid lobbyists in the eyes of City Council.

At the end of the hearing Mr. Nutter declared that a task force would be formed to develop recommendations reconciling the various points of view. I went home and waited for further information to come about this task force and heard nothing. A call to their office produced a vague promise that "the task force was being worked on" and that I would be contacted. I heard nothing more, nor did I get any response to my testimony or a written complaint about the process in which the voice of opposing citizens was so effectively silenced, until four weeks ago when radio station KYW announced that the task force was about to present its final report.

Further calls to Mr. Nutter's office resulted in my being referred to Commissioner Tsou's office. Dr. Tsou's secretary indicated that in all likelihood the Commissioner had never been apprised of the substance of my testimony and had not even considered my participation in the task force. I was however advised that I could submit my testimony and request for consideration and receipt of relevant materials via email. I proceeded to send them three emails containing testimony, documentation, and eventually, a follow up memo of concern indicating that I'd heard nothing in response. Follow up phone calls had confirmed not only that my material had arrived, but that it had been given to the Commissioner himself. To this date I have still heard nothing in response.

If you examine my testimony you will find that it indeed raises credible points with regard to the types of "propaganda science" that were presented by the lobbyists pushing for Nutter's bill. Despite this, and despite other credible testimony by citizens against the bill, our position was completely and totally ignored in the charge by City Council to the Task Force. The task force was told to ignore any evidence that might serve to mitigate the argument that secondary smoke was the most deadly thing to hit the public since World War II nerve gas and to simply assume that their job was *"preventing, to the greatest extent possible, second-hand smoke from drifting or recirculating from restaurant bars to indoor smoke-free areas of restaurants."*

By ignoring the question of whether microscopic quantities of tobacco smoke actually posed any threat at all to nonsmokers in normally ventilated and separated sections of restaurants the task force was obviously given only one real choice in *"preventing...to the greatest extent possible"* the chance that even a few molecules of smoke might somehow move against ventilation streams to a nonsmoker yards away. That choice is of course reflected in their decision, reached unanimously by the Antismoking groups, and unanimously rejected by everyone else on the Commission, that the only practical solution was to totally ban smoking in restaurant areas.

The "compromise" put forward by the Antismoking groups (allowing smoking inside of sealed, biohazard airlock style chambers) is not really a compromise since the expense involved makes such accommodations wildly impractical for all but the highest priced and most profitable establishments. Thus, the **real** objective of the Antismokers in these hearings was achieved: to put smokers out of sight and make it so difficult for them to smoke that many of them might decide to quit instead.

The voice of the citizens received very little hearing by the City Council. The voice of those who question so much of the purported science presented by Antismoking groups received even less hearing in the task force set up to arrive at this "compromise." And finally, the reactions and response of the formal bodies of the Council and the Health Department in ignoring written, emailed, and oral testimony and concerns of citizens in this matter is disgraceful and unworthy of a city where freedom of speech and discussion, and the free exchange of thought was first declared paramount in this country.

Testimony and documentation attached.

Michael J. McFadden

(The preceding was printed out as a one-page handout and distributed to City Council and the media along with the Summation that follows just before the final vote was scheduled. The vote was then tabled! Sometimes you CAN fight City Hall and win! To be totally fair however, the efforts of people like Georges Perrier, Mike Driscoll, Debbie Garvin, and others in the Restaurant Association went a long way toward sliding us into the winning column: no one works in a vacuum.)

Summation of Efforts with Philadelphia City Council

Date: 11/16/2000
(Date of the final hearing)

Response to date:

Phone response: None.

Email response: None.

Fax response: None.

US Mail response: None.

Total real response to date:

NONE. *

*At some point I did indeed get a generic "thanks" from a Councilperson. **During** the final hearing itself, **after** I had handed the above summary out to the Council and the media, the health department had someone scurry to a computer and quickly email a generic "Thanks for your input" response.

Appendix H

Communicating With Antismokers

One of the most frustrating aspects of being an activist on the wrong side of a money issue is that it's hard to get as much media coverage as one's better funded opponent. Those unfamiliar with such a political struggle will often say, "Why don't you simply challenge their lies?" The problem of course is that such challenges don't usually get much news coverage and are almost universally ignored by those they are aimed at; thus, to all intents and purposes, they have no existence. In the previous section I cited an example of my effort to communicate with the Philadelphia City Council and the routine way in which it was ignored.

The examples cited below are mainly from personal experience. I've heard anecdotal tales from other Free-Choice activists who have had similar non-reactions to their efforts, but I'll stick mainly to reporting two that I was involved in myself and can verify from my files.

I make one exception however, and share an effort made by a wonderful and very intelligent woman I enjoyed meeting several years ago: Martha Perske, has been vilified by Crusaders because she dared to write to a tobacco company several times seeking information and advice in fighting Antismoking efforts. That simple act of communication has given them a handle to discredit her research and critical work by saying "She describes herself as a 'smokers' advocate,' but industry documents show that she stayed in close contact with Philip Morris...."

(Derek Yach et al. "Junking Science...." *AJPH*   Vol. 91 #11. November 2001).

Writing a letter to the wrong people asking for advice or help is evidently not a wise move in today's America. I am more than proud to share some hard-hitting letters she wrote a few years ago in trying to get a newspaper to take responsibility for correcting a blatantly biased piece of reportage.

Email Exchanges

The emails cited below have had the repeated earlier copies and primary email addresses deleted but nothing of substance has been left out or altered. The email addresses have been deleted because, although I feel these figures have a public responsibility for their statements and actions I do not wish to subject them to possible cyberharassment. It should be noted that it is not unknown for individuals to send emails that never reach their destination... just as sometimes "the check was lost in the mail" is also true. Personally, I believe the latter is more often true than the former.

Tom Rankin

To start off we will look at an example of a questionable claim made by Tom Rankin, President of California's State Federation of Labor, and distributed around the world in a paid press release. In an attempt to see if Mr. Rankin was simply misled or mistaken, or if perhaps he actually knew something that I did not, I sent him several polite emails. None received a response. To make sure the emails were not simply being misdirected, I finally sent a query to him with copies to several of his associates. Again, he gave no response, although one of his associates indicated it was indeed proper to email Mr. Rankin himself with my concern. In all, I sent five emails spaced over three months, asking him to clarify his statement. Five queries, no responses.

1st email:

Subj: Source question...
Date: 12/13/2002
From: Cantiloper@aol.com
To: trankin

Dear Mr. Rankin,

In the Business Wire press release of November 20th on smoke-free workplaces you were quoted as saying "We know cigarette smoke contains over 4,000 chemicals, including dozens of known human carcinogens."

While I know the original source for your figure of 4,000 chemicals (it's a tobacco industry journal article containing a seat of the pants estimate by a "flavoring expert"), in my reviewing of Surgeon Generals Reports I have only been able to find six known human carcinogens as being listed for tobacco smoke.
There are of course several dozen substances that rank as suspected animal carcinogens and such, but those are many of the same ones found in our coffee, food, and water so I don't imagine you were referring to them. Could you please share your source for the "dozens of known human carcinogens"?

Many thanks.

Sincerely,
Michael J. McFadden

Response: NONE.

2nd email:

Subj: Source?
Date: 12/30/2002
From: Cantiloper@aol.com
To: trankin

Dear Mr. Rankin,

I sent the below to you about two weeks ago and have not received a response. I understand that with the holidays these things can sometimes be shuffled out of sight mistakenly, so I'm resending it.

I hope your holidays are going well.

 :)

Michael

Response: NONE.

3rd email:

Subj: Source Question?
Date: 1/12/2003
From: Cantiloper@aol.com
To: trankin

Dear Mr. Rankin,
I sent the original email below roughly a month ago. It's possible that you have filed it in your backlog while checking the source and it has passed out of sight. To make a response easier I am copying the emails below.

Many thanks for your attention.

 :)
Michael

Response: NONE.

4th email:

Subj: Mr. Rankin?
Date: 2/21/2003
From: Cantiloper@aol.com
To: trankin

Dear Mr. Rankin,

It has now been slightly over two months since I sent my original inquiry below to you. Many thanks for your attention.
<Previous emails reproduced in original>

Response: NONE.

5th email:

Subj: Tom Rankin?
Date: 3/13/2003 7:46:46 PM EST
From: Cantiloper@aol.com
To: milkman, polney,trankin

Three months ago I sent an initial query to Mr. Tom Rankin regarding a claim made by him with regard to banning smoking in workplaces. I followed up the initial inquiry twice since then <<Note: it had actually been thrice, not twice.>> but have received no response. It is possible that he is no longer with you, but I still have interest in the source for his comments. Can you help me?

Please see below. (Copies of earlier emails here deleted.)

Thank you.

Michael J. McFadden

Response: only from polney, suggesting that I email Mr. Rankin.

Total Responses from Mr. Rankin to 5 Emails:

NONE.

Andre Picard

My experience with Mr. Rankin is regrettably not that unusual. I reproduce below the experiences of Martha Perske in her attempts to correct some grossly inaccurate information in a newspaper article. The lack of proper response in this case is even more reprehensible than in that of Mr. Rankin's since the press has a special responsibility to be accurate in its reportage and should be greatly concerned about such errors. The text of the following emails were supplied to me by Martha Perske from her records.

1st Email to Andre Picard. July 16th, 2001

From: Martha Perske
To: Andre Picard

Dear Mr. Picard:

I am writing about the article you wrote, "Second-hand smoke can triple risk," pertaining to the new Canadian study on secondhand smoke.

Could you please let me know if you read the study, yourself, or did you get your information from other sources? The reason I ask is because you state that the "new research found that when the number of 'occupational smoker years'…reaches 26, the risk of lung cancer has doubled." But then you say "When researchers looked at the upper third of workers – those exposed to the most second-hand smoke – they found the lung cancer risk was more than tripled."

I have gone over and over the study and can find no "tripling" of the risk for the upper third of workers. Where does it state or show a tripling of the risk?

In fact, Table III of the study shows the results (odds ratios) for "occupational smoker years" which you refer to, and the reported risk for those exposed to the most secondhand smoke (64 or more smoker years) is LESS than for those exposed to 26-64 smoker years. For example, Table III shows an odds ratio of 1.98 for 26-64 smoker years of exposure, but the odds ratio for 64 or more smoker years is 1.58.

Did you know that?

Also, I'm not sure where Dr. Roberta Ferrence, director of the Ontario Tobacco Research Unit, got her information that "this research demonstrates a dose-response: The more exposure you have, the higher your risk." That's certainly not true for the majority of the findings presented in Table III of the study. In fact, when it comes to years of exposure for "residential plus occupational years" the odds ratios show a consistent DECREASE in risk with increased exposure. For example, the odds ratios for 1-24 years, 25-45 years, and 46 or more years are, respectively, 1.46, 1.40, and 1.35.

The only subset in Table III to show a statistically significant "trend" is "residential plus occupational smoker-years." However, not one of the results in this category is statistically significant, and in fact, the odds ratio for exposure to 1-36 "residential plus occupational smoker-years" shows a REDUCED risk of 0.83.

I would be most appreciative if you would respond to my concerns, especially the claim that this study shows the risk "more than tripled" for the upper third of workers, since I can't find it anywhere.

Thank you.

Martha Perske

1st "Auto-Reply" from Andre Picard. July 16th, 2001

I will be back in the office on Thursday July 19. I will reply to your message at that time – or sooner. Or you can call me on my cell phone.

Thank you.

Andre

Email to Neil Campbell. July 22nd, 2001

From: Martha Perske
To: Mr. Neil A. Campbell, editor, Globe and Mail

Dear Mr. Campbell,

I hope you are as troubled as I am over Andre Picard's alarmist article of 7-12-01, "Second-hand smoke can triple risk," in that he appears to have seriously misrepresented findings from a Canadian study.

I've submitted the attached letter to the editor, which I hope you will see fit to publish. I have a copy of the Canadian study and will fax it to you at your request, so you can see for yourself that Picard did not disclose all relevant data.

I have emailed Picard regarding this but have received no response.

Sincerely,
Martha Perske

Email to Neil Campbell. August 8th, 2001; published by Martha at JunkScience.com

From: Martha Perske
To: Mr. Neil A. Campbell, editor, Globe and Mail

On July 22, I emailed you information about Andre Picard's alarmist article, "Second-hand smoke can triple risk," published in the Globe and Mail on July 12. I said I hoped you were as troubled as I was over his misrepresentation of the Health Canada study, and that your paper would see fit to publish my letter to the editor, a copy of which I sent you.

I also emailed Andre Picard with questions about his article.

Since I received no response from you or Mr. Picard, and since to my knowledge my letter to the editor was not published, I am taking this opportunity to make public what the Globe and Mail apparently would not.

I can only surmise that Mr. Picard, your "public health reporter," did not read the study before he reported on it. Either that or he knowingly misled your readers. In either case, he is a sorry excuse for a "public health reporter."

For example, he claims that the Canadian study "provides some of the most compelling scientific evidence yet for a total ban on workplace smoking, including bars and restaurants," yet not once does he disclose the fact that this study found no statistically significant increased risk from secondhand smoke.

He claims that the study "found that the more people smoke in a workplace, the greater the risks to non-smokers." On the contrary, if he had read the study he would have seen that it found just the opposite when it came to "occupational smoker-years." It shows that nonsmokers who worked with smokers for

64 or more smoker-years had a LOWER risk than those working with smokers for 26-64 smoker years.

The study further found that the longer nonsmokers lived or worked with smokers, the more their lung cancer risk decreased. A most unlikely thing if secondhand smoke really is the culprit Mr. Picard portrays it to be, and one has to ask why he made no mention of this decreased risk with increased exposure.

According to Picard's article, Dr. Roberta Ferrence of the Ontario Tobacco Research Unit hopes that this "strong new evidence will prompt strong new action" to expand smoking bans in the workplace. Oh really? Findings that are not statistically significant are "strong evidence"? I don't think so. It appears, also, that Dr. Ferrence didn't read the study or she would have seen the authors' cautionary statement that the small number of cases "precludes drawing strong conclusions."

Only one subset in this study found a significant "trend" for increased risk with increased exposure to secondhand smoke. However, not one finding in that subset reached statistical significance, and in fact it shows a reduced lung cancer risk for nonsmokers living and working with smokers for 1-36 smoker years. Again, a fact not mentioned by Picard.

In my letter to the Globe and Mail, I suggested that you publish a more objective follow up article to Mr. Picard's, one in which all relevant data from this study is reported to the public.

To my knowledge you have not done so, and that does not speak well for your paper. It suggests that in your zeal to advance the antismoking agenda, you have no qualms about misleading the public, and that is reprehensible.

Sincerely,

Martha Perske

Response From Mr. Campbell. August 8th, 2001

From: Neil Campbell:
To: Martha Perske

Mr. Campbell responded to Martha Perske in an email she no longer has on file, indicating that he dealt primarily with the online version of the Globe and Mail and that she should actually contact a Mr. Richard Addis, the main editor.

Martha's Email to Mr. Addis. August 8th, 2001

From: Martha Perske
To: Richard Addis

Dear Mr. Addis,

It is a sad state of affairs when no one at the Globe and Mail will respond to my repeated efforts to hold Andre Picard accountable for his misrepresentation of a scientific study.

Thus, my letter published today [to Neil Campbell] which I thought you'd be interested in: http://www.junkscience.com/aug01/perske-ets.htm

Perhaps now you will see fit to respond as to why you let Picard's article stand, despite the fact that you were informed that it was most misleading? And why you saw fit not to publish my letter to the editor?

Sincerely,
Martha Perske

Response from Mr. Addis. August 9th, 2001

From: Richard Addis
To: Martha Perske

No problem. I'll ask Andre to reply to you. He is probably away on holidays but he will get back to you when he is in the office next.

2nd Email to Andre Picard w/cc to Richard Addis. August 9th, 2001

From: Martha Perske
To: Andre Picard

Dear Mr. Picard:

Regarding your July 12 article, "Second-hand smoke can triple risk," Richard Addis tells me that he has asked you to reply to me. I hope you will.

In order to refresh your memory, I'm forwarding an email I sent you on July 16 (see below) that went unanswered.

Since I could get no answers from anyone at the Globe and Mail (including you), I took the opportunity to make public my concerns about your article in a letter to Neil A. Campbell. That letter, a copy of which I sent to Richard Addis, appears here: http://www.junkscience.com/aug01/perske-ets.htm

I hope to hear from you.

Sincerely,
Martha Perske

2nd Email to Richard Addis. August 10, 2001

From: Martha Perske
To: Richard Addis

Regarding my request that you provide a date as to when a response from Andre Picard may be expected, please know there is a degree of urgency in my request in that the Globe and Mail, as well as Mr. Picard, could be held responsible for damages resulting from bans based on dissemination of misleading information.

The questions asked of you and Mr. Picard are not unreasonable, and more than a few people are interested in the answer.

Once again, I would appreciate your indication of a time frame for Mr. Picard's reply.

Sincerely,

Martha Perske

3rd Email to Richard Addis w/cc to Andre Picard. August 19, 2001

From: Martha Perske
To: Richard Addis

Dear Mr. Addis,

In light of Andre Picard's article published today, "Secondhand smoke main cause of death in the workplace, study says," I hardly think he is away on vacation as you suggest.

How is it that Mr. Picard has time to sensationalize a report, "Deadly Fumes," published by Airspace (an anti-smoking organization), but has chosen not to respond to me, even though you assured me in the below email that he has been instructed to reply to me?

Please explain why I have not heard from Mr. Picard.

Thank you.
Martha Perske

2nd "Auto-Reply" from Andre Picard. August 19, 2001

I will be back in the office on Thursday August 30. I will NOT be receiving e-mail messages during my absence. But I will attempt to reply to your message upon my return. Or you can call me on my cell phone.

Thank you.
Andre

4th Email to Richard Addis (6 months later). January 1st, 2002

From: Martha Perske
To: Richard Addis

Dear Mr. Addis,

Attached is your email to me dated August 9, 2001, in which you say that Andre Picard will respond to me regarding his apparent misrepresentation of a Health Canada study on secondhand tobacco smoke.

It is now five months later and I have yet to hear from Picard.

Could you please let me know when I can expect a response from him?

Kind regards,
Martha Perske

Almost Two Years Later:

No Further Responses from Mr. Addis.

No Actual Responses at all from Mr. Picard.

Nurse Clay-Storm

The following example may not seem as serious as irresponsibility among reporters and newspaper editors, but is arguably much more troubling than the case of a mere President of a Labor Federation. The following email exchange was with a nurse at a major University who is in charge of the health and health guidance of the students and who should certainly be open to defending and justifying her Antismoking efforts insofar as they will affect the health and well-being of those students.

Near the end of 2002, the Associated Press ran a story about the efforts of Crusaders to enact ever-widening smoking bans on campuses in an effort to manipulate student behavior. These bans, even when extended to the outdoors, are often superficially justified as being intended to protect the health and welfare of the nonsmoking student population. Of course, as we've seen earlier, the strong subtext behind such bans is always a desire to make smoking itself so uncomfortable and "denormalized" that people will simply quit.

The University of Southern Maine banned smoking in all its dormitories in September of 2002 and implemented a rule requiring smokers to stay at least 50 feet away from any building if they were carrying a lit cigarette. Pamela Clay-Storm, a USM nurse and former head of a task force that created the rules was not content with this situation however. Smoking students were still visible, and even on a cold winter's night the 50-foot trek from a dormitory was not enough of a hardship to successfully force the student smokers to quit.

Thus, in the fall of 2003, thanks to the efforts of Ms. Clay-Storm and other USM Antismoking activists, students will be forced to trek much further than a mere 50 feet in order to enjoy smoking outside in the snow. The new rule will call for smoking students to be isolated in designated smoking zones, likely far away from the sight of "normal" students. Whether there will be any extra security provided in these areas at night is not known, but such concerns may not be so high on the University's list of concerns.

Below I reproduce an exchange of emails with Nurse Clay-Storm. In response to my first email she sent a fairly standard canned type message outlining the standard Crusading sound bite responses to questions about bans. When I sent her a more detailed question, challenging some of the assumptions in those sound bites, she responded by saying that my questions were "great" and affirmed that she did indeed have "well researched and thought out replies" to them, but wanted to know who I was and why I was asking such "confrontational" questions.

I then responded politely and honestly, waited, and heard nothing. So I sent a follow up email two weeks later, and a follow up to the follow up two weeks after that, and then finally, a follow up to the follow up to the follow up two months after that. At this point the good nurse once again sent me a request for my credentials and once again I sent her the same polite response as before. And yet one more time, once again my efforts were for naught: her "well researched and thought out replies" to my "great questions" never materialized. After six emails, spaced over three months, all of which were painstakingly polite, my request for Nurse Clay-Storm's justifications for the persecution of smokers at the University of Southern Maine are **still** unanswered as of the publication of this book in September, 2003.

For a person of responsibility in the academic arena, and clearly active in attempts to dictate the lifestyles of students, to simply refuse to communicate with those who question the wisdom of such dictation should be unacceptable at any institution of higher learning.

As of this writing I do not know the plans for smoking bans on the campus of the University of Southern Maine for the academic year of 2003/2004. Hopefully *Dissecting Antismokers' Brains* will help students raise some questions about whatever the policy may be and help them be listened to more seriously than they might have been.

1ˢᵗ Email to Nurse Clay-Storm.
December 13ᵗʰ ,2002

From: Cantiloper@aol.com
To: Nurse Clay-Storm (email address deleted here)

Dear Ms. Storm,

Hello! :)

In a recent article that was carried by the Associated Press there was a discussion about extending the current "50 foot ban" on smoking near campus buildings even further afield. You were quoted at the end of the article as saying:

'This is not smokers vs. nonsmokers," said Clay-Storm. "It's about trying to create an environment that is healthy and safe for everybody."

I am aware that the dangers of secondhand smoke are becoming more widely publicized and accepted but was wondering if you could clarify that statement in terms of what might be considered unsafe or unhealthy about smoking 50 feet from a building? This is for some writing I am doing in association with my work with a community group and your information could be most helpful.

Many thanks!
 :)
Michael

1st Response.
December 16th, 2002

From: claystorm
To: Cantiloper@aol.com

Hello Michael,

I believe what the statement refers to is the University of Southern Maine's Policy. The smoking policy adopted by USM this past summer removes secondhand smoke exposure from all indoor areas, including residence halls, and addresses outdoor exposures by creating designated areas for smoking. The intent of the policy is to reduce exposure to secondhand smoke, reduce the environmental impact of cigarette litter, promote tobacco-free lifestyles, and reduce the risk of fire. On our 3 campuses the common areas for secondhand smoke exposure included entryways to buildings and through open windows around perimeters of our buildings. The task force assigned to address smoking on campus felt a specified distance "i.e. 30 or 50 feet" was not a very effective message. Many people do not have a visual understanding of specific distances, furthermore, in some cases any distance would place individuals smoking in parking lots. Considering our four objectives and the layout of our campuses it was the task forces recommendation to designate areas where smoking would be allowed. Presently, we are in the implementation phase and hope to have designated areas created by the start of the Fall '03 term. In the meantime we are focusing on promoting cessation services and providing positive educational messages regarding tobacco-free lifestyles. The USM policy addresses a variety of issues related to tobacco on our campus and is consistent with both the American College Health Association and the American Cancer Society's recommendations for a comprehensive smoking policy. You can view the policy at the following web address.

http://www.usm.maine.edu/hrs/policy/10112.html

I hope this information is helpful.

Sincerely,

Pamela
Pamela Clay-Storm, RN
University Health Services
University of Southern Maine

2nd Email to Nurse Clay-Storm. December 16th, 2002

From: Cantiloper@aol.com
To: claystorm

Thank you for a prompt and courteous response!

I must confess to still having some lack of clarity about the new policy as it relates to most of your objectives however. While promotion of tobacco free lifestyles is certainly well served by setting up ghettos where smokers are forced to huddle out in the snow and elements, particularly during the cooler months of the school year in Maine, I'm not clear on how the other 3 objectives are met by the expansion of the 50 foot rule.

1) exposure to secondhand smoke...
It is possible that I'm not familiar with the particular studies indicating serious health problems connected the secondhand smoke exposure in the open air beyond the immediate perimeter

of the smoker but I would be very interested in examining them. May I ask for the references on this? I'm familiar with concerns about entryways but they are usually quite close to the actual doors of the buildings involved. Many thanks!

2) I live a few blocks away from the University of Pennsylvania campus where smoking is generally still allowed in dormitories and have seen very little evidence of a litter problem as concerns cigarettes. The primary problems on that campus in that regard seem to relate more to flyers, newspapers, and fast food detritus. Is it possible that this aspect of your campus policy would be better served by having dormitories where smoking was allowed, or at least providing indoor facilities for such? Granted, this would remove the value of stigmatization and segregation arising from a designated ghetto policy, but perhaps the value of addressing the litter concern might make it worthy of consideration.

3) Risk of Fire... Definitely a problem worth taking into account, particularly in dormitories that house students who are allowed to drink alcohol off campus and then return in impaired states. I'm not familiar with USM's policies with regard to suspension/expulsions for students found to have used alcohol but the risk of fire from smoking tobacco or marijuana or using electrical equipment or candles is probably far better reduced by a zero-tolerance policy for alcohol among students and staff than by simply banning smoking. One problem with such bans is obviously that students "sneak" smokes in areas that are out of sight and will often improperly dispose of smoking materials when "authority" is thought to be approaching. Such improper disposal can be a prime source for loss of life in fire.

I believe that in our own area a few years ago there was a problem of this type at Seton Hall University (I'm not certain I'm thinking of the right one here) in a dormitory where smoking had been banned. After the fire there was no change in the smoking policy despite its consequences or suggestions on the internet that the policy could render the university legally liable. Perhaps the best approach here would be the designation of smoking lounges within dorms that were supplied with properly safe ashtrays and furniture that was not conducive to fire. Granted, such provision would have less behavioral engineering impact upon the student lifestyles than exile to the far outdoors, but it might well be safer overall.

A final question ... the policy page that you referred me to seems to be well written and thought-out but there were two points on which I also had some question. One, the second paragraph mentions an intent to respect the rights of smokers, but succeeding paragraphs don't seem to address this point or enumerate/define those rights. Can you address this? And second, the policy notes that campus organizations are prohibited from accepting support from those engaged in tobacco sales. Does the same policy apply to those engaged in alcohol sales? I know that MADD has been concerned about the policies of some schools with regard to their relations with off-campus alcohol vendors, particularly since most students are below the legal age for drinking (as opposed to the situation with smoking age and college students.) Some colleges evidently even allow "college bars" in the neighborhood to advertise in school newspapers and such. Can you tell me anything about USM's policies/plans in this regard?

I appreciate whatever you can tell me about the points above. I realize you have many other duties but the impact of these policies on student populations can be substantial and your attention is appreciated.

Many thanks again!

 :)

Michael

2nd Response.
December 16th, 2002

From: claystorm
To: Cantiloper@aol.com

Michael,
You ask great questions all of which I have well thought and researched replies to. I will be happy to respond to your questions/concerns but I would like to ask you to please explain your intent for this information. You appear to have a slight confrontational tone to your rebuttals. I would just like to be clear on your background and desire for these details.

In pursuit of truth,

Pam

Pamela Clay-Storm, RN
University Health Services
University of Southern Maine

3rd Email to Nurse Clay-Storm.
December 16th, 2002

From: Cantiloper@aol.com
To: claystorm

(reproduction of body of earlier Clay-Storm email deleted)

I'm active with an informal internet discussion/community group that is primarily concerned with the problems and difficulties inherent in some of the current regulations and government policies that seem at times to unfairly impact smokers. I apologize for any sense of a confrontational tone that you may have perceived in my email... I am aware that you are supportive of policies that I myself may not be, but try to maintain an open mind: thus the detailed nature of query since it is quite possible that the areas I addressed have indeed been considered and addressed by USM already.

<<In pursuit of truth,>>

As am I... :)

Thanks again for your attention.

 :)

Michael

4th Email to Nurse Clay-Storm.
December 30th, 2002

From: Cantiloper@aol.com
To: claystorm

Dear Ms. Clay-Storm,

I realize with the holidays my email response to you below from a couple of weeks ago may have gotten shuffled out of sight so I thought I'd send it again. I hope things are well with you and wish you a happy New Year's! (I know... New Year's for ANY medical person is usually far more busy than happy, but nonetheless... :>)
 :)
Michael
(Earlier emails reproduced for Ms. Clay-Storm's convenience but deleted here.)

5th Email to Nurse Clay-Storm.
January 12th, 2002

From: Cantiloper@aol.com
To: claystorm

I have not heard back from you and thought that perhaps it would be helpful if I copied my original email of questions and concerns below.
Many thanks for your attention...

 :)
 Michael
(Earlier emails reproduced for Ms. Clay-Storm's convenience but deleted here)

6th Email to Nurse Clay-Storm.
March 29th, 2003

To: claystorm
From: Cantiloper@aol.com

Dear Ms. Clay-Storm,

I believe I sent you several emails in December and January with regard to some questions I had regarding your thoughts on University smoking policy. As far as I'm aware I have not heard back from you, perhaps because my emails were misfiled during the holidays and such. I really would appreciate a response to them....
Thank you.
Sincerely,
Michael J. McFadden
(Previous emails again reproduced but deleted here.)

3rd Response. March 31st, 2003
(Basically a repeat of Nurse Clay-Storm's 2nd Response)

From: claystorm
To: Cantiloper@aol.com

Michael,
You're "rebuttals" have a strong defensive tone. Please remind me of you're interest in this information. I sense you have a hidden agenda.

Pamela Clay-Storm, RN
Pamela Clay-Storm, RN
University Health Services
University of Southern Maine

7th Email to Nurse Clay-Storm
March 31st, 2003

To: claystorm
From: Cantiloper@aol.com

Dear Nurse Clay-Storm,

I attach below the original request you made similar to the above and my response to it (not answered) as well as a follow up email I sent as a reminder...

Thank you again for your attention.

 :)
Michael
(Previous emails attached for Ms. Clay-Storm's convenience but deleted here.)

No Further Responses from Nurse Clay-Storm as of August 13th, 2003 .... eight months after the first of my seven emails.

~*Summation*~

After five follow up emails extending over a four-month period I have still not received any of the "well thought out and researched replies" promised by Nurse Clay-Storm. To the best of my knowledge The University of Southern Maine is proceeding with its poorly based smoking ban and ignoring all information or argument that conflicts with their plans. The "pursuit of truth" evidently has its limits. Tom Rankin and Andre Picard have never, to the best of my knowledge, engaged in **any** communication with anyone who has challenged their misrepresentations of reality on this subject.

The responses, or lack thereof, of these three Crusaders are not at all atypical. If I went through my email files of the last five years I could probably pull half a dozen or more similar stories out for reproduction, but I think the three above make the point sufficiently.

Those in power, and those who have power over or access to the media and money, generally have no need to respond to those who confront them with their falsehoods in the private arena. It is ultimately up to each of us as citizens to follow up on such behaviors and publicize them until at last it can be seen that the emperor indeed has no clothes.

Appendix I

Truth, Lies,
and Ice Cream

Let us suppose that I earn $500,000 a year as a fast-talking lawyer. I then go on to run for public office, and to boost my image I proclaim that I believe in the importance of giving to those less fortunate. I adopt an earnest and heartfelt look and state that I give regularly to both organized charity and to the poor and homeless I encounter on the streets. I go on to emphasize that I maintain my giving year in and year out, no matter what my financial situation or pressures may be, and that I will carry similar dedication and selflessness to my career as an elected official.

In truth, my "regular contributions" consist of my dropping a shiny new penny into a Salvation Army bucket each Christmas, and then tossing a somewhat grubbier one at a homeless guy who's sleeping under a blanket (while being careful not to get too close).

Did I tell a lie with my above proclamation? Technically, no... I **do** contribute regularly, and I said nothing about the amount. However anyone in their right minds and with a sense of fairness would certainly argue that I had not been truthful.

A great number, perhaps even the vast majority, of the statements made by Crusaders in pursuit of smoking bans are of roughly the same quality when it comes to truthfulness as our lawyer's statement above. David Kessler, past head of the Food and Drug Administration, in commenting on claims about drug effectiveness, drew the distinction between a statement being "Accurate" and being "True." This distinction applies perfectly to our pseudo-philanthropic barrister, as well as to much of the material present in the ads and public statements of Crusaders: his statement would indeed be accurate, but in the wider sense of the real meaning of truth, it would not be true. (Gina Kolata, "Stung by Courts..." *New York Times* 10/15/02).

I consider myself an honest person. I feel that the information I've presented in this book is not only accurate, but also true in the sense of not being misleading. I would call the lawyer's claim a lie, pure and simple. Personally, I feel comfortable taking Kessler's distinction a step further: the self-promoting shyster noted above is a **liar**, despite the fact that he technically told the truth.

In much the same vein, I feel quite comfortable in calling many Antismoking Crusaders liars even though they could squirm and scramble and say that by the strict letter of the law they have not actually perjured themselves any more than the Big Tobacco executives with their carefully worded statements on Capitol Hill. This Appendix will examine 24 different "lies" used by Antismoking Lobbyists to frighten and intimidate people: one for each hour of the day in honor of a deceased and sorely missed Free-Choice activist on the Internet's alt.smokers newsgroup, Cliff Roberson. Cliff liked to end his carefully crafted essays with the statement "**ALL** Antis lie, **all** the time." Technically, that may not be an accurate statement, but nonetheless it's pretty true.

The first few lies will be explored in some detail, but to avoid needless repetition many of the later ones will simply refer readers back to parts of *Dissecting Antismokers' Brains* where the lies have already been examined. The very first lie to be examined is the one that provided the inspiration for the title of this Appendix. It comes from one of the multitude of misleading statements made by the misnamed Crusader group, "Truth. com," in their many expensive television spots.

- **Lie #1**

The TV ads show an ice cream truck marketing cigarettes to kids in playgrounds. The voice over of the ad claims that the secret papers of the tobacco industry revealed they had been considering such a thing as a marketing strategy to children.

It took me a while to track down the basis for this claim and when I did find it I was not really surprised to see its context. This plan to "reach the children" was one of hundreds of items in an 18-page list clearly aimed at marketing to 18 – 24 year-olds. There was a heavy emphasis on advertising in bars and to the college generation and a random mess of wacky/silly ideas like creating a cigarette brand national monument like Mt. Rushmore, setting up public photo booth services to make fake college ID cards, having female pissing contests in taverns, associating a brand with rattlesnake pizza-toppings, and indeed, having ice-cream style musical trucks. There was no plan, hint of a plan, or ghost of a hint of a plan to market to children in playgrounds by using ice cream trucks.

Antismokers presented this claim as "The Truth."

I call this claim a **lie.**

- **Lie #2**

Lie #2 comes from a public statement by an activist with the Ohio Antismoking youth group known as STAND. As 52 members of this group "stormed" MTV headquarters in New York the activist spokesperson to the press claimed they were there because "Most of the shows on MTV are filled with smoking and tobacco use…." (*PRNewswire*. "Ohio Kids Storm MTV…" 06/19/03).

For any reader who might still harbor a suspicion that I am somehow being secretly paid by Big Tobacco to write this book, what I am about to say should remove any doubts. On July 10th of 2003 I watched **twenty-four straight hours** of MTV simply to put the above claim to the test. Fortunately the technology of TiVo® helped speed things up, but there is **no** amount of money that Big Tobacco could **ever** have paid me to be worth that task!

Twenty-four hours translates to 1440 minutes.

If we assume that ...

1) the average number of reasonably sized human beings portrayed on the TV screen at any given time was two (it's probably greater, but I'm giving the Antismokers the benefit of the doubt here),

2) the normal American smoking rate to be at about 25% (quite reasonable, particularly since most of the people on MTV are aged between teens and forty years or so), and

3) the average smoker would smoke for about 10 minutes an hour

... then the amount of smoking needed to correctly portray reality would be roughly 120 minutes of that 1440. To claim that MTV is "filled" with smoking, or that it grossly over represents smoking in the real world, we would expect to see at least double that amount... 240 minutes out of 1440.

What did I actually find however?

1) **Three minutes and thirty-six seconds** of actual human smoking with a full two minutes of that occurring in a single video featuring a takeoff on a smoking, singing Frank Sinatra.

Another 40 seconds came from four plays of a Mya video that opens with a ten second shot of her taking a puff from a cigar. **There was less than one minute of actual smoking in all the other shows combined!**

2) One third of a minute total of a cartoon bear with a pipe in its mouth in a multi played commercial for Pay Per View.

3) One quarter of a minute of puppet squirrels with pipes in a Tolkeinesque tree house.

4) About one minute of characters holding cigarettes or a cigarette pack but not actually smoking.

5) About five minutes of two videos where pimpy looking "gangsta" types were holding unlit marijuana blunts.

6) **Ten full minutes of Antismoking commercials** from Truth.com that collectively showed over 10,000 teenagers dropping dead in the streets from smoking.

Note: the important figure here is the first one: the amount of actual smoking being shown. Three and a half minutes is a far cry from the 120 "expected" minutes or the 240 "claimed" minutes. Even just using 120 as our base, the Antismokers' claims are off by almost a factor of 40, or, to use the percentages Crusaders often like to use to magnify reality, we could say they exaggerated by almost **four thousand percent!**

Antismokers claim that MTV is "filled" with smoking.

I call this claim a **lie.**

• Lie #3

Lie #3 lie is a generic lie, variations of which have been repeated hundreds of times by Crusaders in statements and articles around the United States. In its simplest form Antismokers simply claim that any groups or individuals opposing the Crusade or its ideas are on the payroll of Big Tobacco. The claim used to be made by labeling groups like FORCES.org or Smokers Fighting Discrimination as "Big Tobacco Front Groups." More recently, perhaps out of fear that they might actually get sued for defamation, Antismoking spokespeople now commonly refer to such groups as "Big Tobacco Front Groups or Allies."

Since anyone supporting **any** goal of Big Tobacco could be considered their "ally" in some sense, the Antismokers are on reasonably safe legal ground. However, as noted earlier in the chapters on Language and Fallacious Argumentation, lumping the word ally into the same phrase as "front group" ties the two together in the listeners' minds so as to give a very deliberate false appearance.

When I first started researching the subject of secondary smoke on the Internet, I was careful to avoid joining any activist groups. I assumed, just as most people do, that these groups were fronts for Big Tobacco and that any information from them would simply be parroting the Big Tobacco Line. I believed my own arguments about the relative harmlessness of secondary smoke to be true and demonstrable, and I did not want to take a chance on them being discounted with Ad Hominem arguments.

As time went on though, I engaged in emails and chat rooms with a number of activists in these groups and came to know them as people. I saw and participated in discussions about funding and it quickly became clear that there was **no** funding coming from Big Tobacco to any of these present day groups with the exception of openly admitted funding to the British based group known as FOREST. Suggestions that any funding beyond such basic things as accepting web-page ads to support Internet costs might be of help were usually quickly quashed by those of us who pointed out that the total independence of activist groups was one of the most powerful weapons we had in fighting the hundreds of millions of dollars spent by the other side. Anything less than an equivalent level of funding from Big Tobacco would do far more harm than good.

This insistence on "purity" has hurt in many ways. Free-Choice activists rarely get together for conferences because all expenses have to be paid by the individuals involved. Free-Choice activists virtually never take out newspaper ads or put out paid press releases: at $1,000+ a pop such releases are penny-ante to Crusaders, but out of reach for true grassroots activist groups. Free-Choice groups can't afford to fly in "experts" to testify at City Council hearings, nor can they give away thousands of T-shirts at rallies, distribute slick brochures, or pay research-ers to do honest research. While many Antismoking Crusaders are paid or comped for their work, such luxuries just aren't available to those who seek to fight them. And as far as trying to pay for ten one-minute spots a day on MTV... the option is so laughable that it's not even funny.

This is a price worth paying though: it keeps Free-Choice groups clear of obligations to corporate policies and positions with which they often disagree and it gives them a solid pedestal to stand upon when presenting information to the public. Over the past three or four years, as I've gotten to know and even occasionally meet activists from various Free-Choice groups my fears of being "contaminated" by insubstantial or outright imaginary contact with Big Tobacco have lessened to the point where I have now joined and become an active member of a number of several such groups. Most of the people I've met who are active in this cause are often plain working class people or loving grandparents giving their time and effort out of concern for disappearing American freedoms.

Antismokers claim that Free-Choice groups are "fronts" for Big Tobacco.

I call this claim a **lie.**

- **Lie #4**

Antismokers claim that smokers cost society money and that nonsmokers pay extra taxes to support sick smokers.

This claim is fully refuted in Appendix C.

I call this claim a **lie.**

- **Lie #5**

Antismokers claim that nonsmokers are being "poisoned" by tobacco smoke.

This claim is fully refuted in Appendix B.

I call this claim a **lie.**

- **Lie #6**

Antismokers claim that ventilation and air cleaning technology cannot produce air that is safe to breathe in environments where smoking is allowed.

This claim is easily proved false, unless we want to lower our standard of "air that is safe to breathe" to the point where virtually **no** air exists that is safe to breathe.

A restaurant or bar, even one that allows unlimited smoking, can always produce a mixture of ventilation and air cleaning technology that will produce air that is actually cleaner than the air outside and cleaner than the air inside would be without smoking and without such ventilation and technology.

The air might not meet the Crusading standards of "100% smoke-free," but it can certainly be cleaned to a point where it is cleaner of poisons and particulates than average un-cleaned, un-conditioned, and smoke-free air in a restaurant or bar would be. In particular, the treated, cleaned, and changed air in a Free-Choice establishment might actually be far more free of disease-causing airborne fungus and bacteria: remember the increase in fungal colony forming units in the air of airplanes that banned smoking that was discussed in the chapter on Smoking Bans.

Antismokers argue that such air treatment is too expensive, but if this were true then they could simply mandate that bars and restaurants meet reasonable minimum air quality standards and drop their push for smoking bans. If those standards were too expensive to meet then bars and restaurants would have to ban smoking. Crusaders never support such standards because they know they can be easily met and because, in truth, clean air and workers' health has never actually been their real goal.

Antismokers claim that the air in a smoking venue cannot be made safe to breathe.

I call this claim a **lie.**

- **Lie #7**

Antismokers claim that tobacco smoke is more addictive than heroin.

This claim is fully refuted in the chapters on Language and on The Ex-Smokers.

I call this claim a **lie.**

- **Lie #8**

Antismokers claim that nonsmoking service people in bars and restaurants inhale up to 80 cigarettes per shift.

This claim is fully refuted in Appendix B.

I call this claim a **lie.**

- **Lie #9**

Antismokers claim that Big Tobacco is still an all-powerful big money lobby.

Actually, Crusading groups today are far more powerful than Big Tobacco. In addition to the emotive power supplied by images of threats to our children, the power of hundreds of thousands of kids working for them in school programs powered by scholarships and prizes, and the power of TV ads, they also have the pure raw power of money beyond a drug-lord's wildest dreams.

As noted in Appendix F, Crusaders placed ads in Florida newspapers condemning Big Tobacco for spending 1.5 million dollars over the past 10 years to influence Florida's politicians on issues like smoking bans, taxes, and Antismoking funding. This is again a prime example of what Dr. Kessler referred to in speaking of something being "accurate, but not true."

Big Tobacco may well have spent $150,000 a year on political lobbying in Florida but the lack of truth comes in when one realizes that the Antismoking Crusade spent over **thirty times** that amount in just a single year in their efforts to pass a statewide constitutional amendment to ban smoking in most public places. (www.no-smoker.org/ANRF_13_(florida_ad).pdf; www.ballot.org).

Antismokers claim Big Tobacco is a Goliath of a Lobby while they are a David.

I call this claim a **lie.**

• Lie #10

Antismokers claim that having a non-smoking section in a restaurant is like having a non-pissing section in a swimming pool.

As pointed out in the chapter on Secondary Smoke, this claim is off by a factor of at least 15,000 air/water changes. In percentage terms the Antismokers are exaggerating by **one million, five hundred thousand percent.**

I call this claim a **lie.**

• Lie #11

Antismokers claim that secondary smoke is a Class A Carcinogen.

This claim would seem to be almost irrefutable. The designation of "Class A Carcinogen" is established by a respected international body, the International Agency for Research on Cancer (IARC), and any element designated as Class A by them is, by a matter of definition, Class A.

However, I feel that this claim is another example of what Dr. Kessler would say is "an accurate, but not true" statement. A review of IARC's 9th *Report on Carcinogens* reveals that the basis for that definition was drawn largely from the equivocal studies reviewed in Appendix A, a far weaker, indeed, **uniquely** weaker standard than IARC has applied to **any** other element it has identified as a Class A carcinogen.

Almost 95% of the substance of secondary smoke consists of such elements as oxygen, nitrogen, carbon dioxide, water, carbon monoxide, and other elements that bear no relationship at all to cancer. The total weight of the six Class A carcinogens in ETS is less than one half of 1/1000th of a gram per cigarette; less than 1/1000th that given off by a standard alcoholic drink in an hour. These are the elements that, in sufficient quantities, could cause cancer, not the entirety of secondary smoke itself.

If one were to examine the smoke from candles, the reflected wavelengths of light from a full moon, the dust in the air at a horse show, or the impurities in an ordinary glass of tap water, and apply the same sort of reasoning and examination to these, one would be forced to classify **all** of them as Class A Carcinogens. In these other cases though, it is correctly recognized that it is the individual components, and the concentrations of those components, which determine carcinogenicity. Only in the case of tobacco smoke does the IARC abandon such scientific determination in order to classify an overall compound of elements as carcinogenic with the specific goal of mass behavior modification.

Antismokers claim that secondary smoke as a whole is a Class A Carcinogen, without any regard or concern for concentrations of exposure.

I call this claim a **lie.**

- **Lie #12**

Antismokers claim that California's extreme Antismoking efforts have brought about a 14% drop in the state's lung cancer rate.

This claim is refuted in the chapters on Secondary Smoke and Fallacious Argumentation. The "kicker" in this argument is that the study the Antismokers are referring to was completed two years **before** they banned smoking in bars: it could not possibly reflect the results of such a ban! (op.cit. *2001 Master Plan for a Smoke-Free California*)

I call this claim a **lie.**

- **Lie #13**

Antismokers claim 85% of smokers "want to quit." While there seems to be no single source for this statistic it is still one that is repeated often and loudly to buttress the claim that smokers want higher taxes and more smoking bans. Even if one accepts the statistic as technically valid and not biased by smokers' desires to simply agree with their interviewer in order to avoid prolonged questioning, one has to accept that much of the motivation for the response lies not within smoking itself, but within the environmental conditions brought about by the Antismoking Crusade.

Many people want to quit because they feel they spend too much money on cigarettes. Why are they spending so much? Because Antismokers have tacked taxes of several hundred per-cent on to the base price of cigarettes. If those taxes were allocated fairly to reflect the medical and economic cost of smoking, a pack of cigarettes would cost less than a dollar and many smokers who desire to quit for this reason would no longer "want to quit."

Many others want to quit because they have absorbed exaggerated fears about the effects of smoking on their own health or upon the health of those around them. If the Antismoking Crusade had actually spent the last 30 years spreading truth instead of lies, many in this segment of smokers would no longer say they "want to quit."

Some want to quit because of the social stigma and restrictions surrounding smoking that have resulted from the Crusade. Again, without the Antismokers, many of these folks would no longer "want to quit."

Some want to quit because they've been led to believe, both by Antismokers and by Big Tobacco, that smoking many unpleasant, smelly, and unsatisfying low-tar-and-nicotine cigarettes is safer than smoking fewer regular cigarettes. The choice of safer higher nicotine brands has been denied to them by Crusaders. Yet again, without this situation, many smokers would enjoy their smoking more and would no longer "want to quit."

Finally, some will always say they "want to quit" simply because they have been overwhelmed by the massive media message that anyone who does **not** want to quit must be stupid, not to mention terminally evil for killing all those around them.

Something Antismokers never want to admit, and something that even some smokers have pushed to the back of their consciousness, is that many smokers often actually **enjoy** the act of smoking. It doesn't matter whether they enjoy it as a fulfillment of an addiction, or as a means of relaxation, or as something to do when they are bored or in the depths of thought; what matters is that there are many times when many smokers **do** enjoy smoking and have no desire at all to quit outside of such external pressures as are put upon them.

Antismokers claim eighty-five percent of smokers want to quit smoking.

I call this claim a **lie.**

- **Lie #14**

Antismokers claim that the studies indicting secondary smoke as a cause of lung cancer are "unanimous and unequivocal." A quick look at Appendix A quickly shows the falsehood of this claim.

I call this claim a **lie.**

- **Lie #15**

Antismokers claim that there is "a strong societal consensus" in favor of universal smoking bans. However, when actual polls are taken that offer such alternatives to total bans as separate and well ventilated smoking sections, most folks vote in favor of such accommodation rather than outright bans. Most people who have not been falsely led to believe that even the smallest, most invisible, wisp of smoke is deadly are primarily concerned about smells, comfort, and the avoidance of outright smoky surroundings. They have no wish to see smokers and their friends thoughtlessly consigned out onto the streets.

I call this claim a **lie.**

- **Lie #16**

Antismokers claim that smoking causes over 400,000 premature deaths a year.

As noted earlier in the chapter on The Spectre of Death, roughly 200,000 of those "premature" deaths occur after the age of 70 and over 50,000 of them occur after age 85. And the overall number itself is likely to be greatly exaggerated by the use of double counting, confounding of causes, lowering of scientific standards, and bias in the assignation of formulas from data that may be biased upward to begin with.

There could well be many tens of thousands of deaths caused each year by smoking, and those deaths are sad and terrible. But there is good reason to believe that the actual number is far less than claimed; although any death, from any cause or at any age, is sad and terrible. To appreciate this lie in its proper context it's worth remembering the 900,000 "Deaths Due To Eating" examined earlier. Smoking is something that many people choose freely to do and to continue doing and the individual should always have the freedom to choose and weigh the risks of life's enjoyments.

Antismokers claim that 400,000 premature deaths are caused each year by smoking.

I call this claim a **lie.**

- **Lie #17**

Antismokers claim that for every 10% increase in the price of cigarettes there will be 7% fewer teen smokers.

This is a very important claim because it allows Crusaders to push for tax increases far beyond anything that would ever be tolerated without the "Save the Children" flag waving from the front of the charge.   In New York City, smokers actually swallowed a tax increase of 1,700% that followed quickly upon the heels of several other large increases. The Boston Tea Party occurred with **far** less provocation.

In 1991 the average price of a pack of cigarettes was 92 cents and the average youth smoking rate was 12.7%. In 2001 the average price of a pack of cigarettes was $3.73. That's a 305% increase in the per pack price which should have brought the youth smoking rate down to well below 5%. (http://www. geocities.com/madmaxmcgarrity/PRICEVSYOUTHSMOKING.h tm).

So was the 10%/7% claim shown to be true? Did the youth smoking rate drop from 12.7% to 5%?   No. The smoking rate among youth actually **increased** to 13.8%. And this increase occurred not only in the face of the 305% price hike, but also in the face of the most incredibly massive enforcement and media-intensive program of behavior modification attempted in human history.

Antismokers claim reasonable tax hikes substantially reduce the number of children smoking.

I call this claim is a **lie.**

- **Lie #18**

Antismokers claim that secondary smoke is worse than the smoke the smoker inhales.

This could be argued to be true in a very limited sense: if one positioned a straw right over the burning end of a cigarette and then snorted that smoke directly into one's lungs it would indeed be "worse" than the smoke the smoker inhales from the other end of a cigarette.

     In reality of course, as noted in Appendix B, no one does that, and the actual exposure of a nonsmoker is likely to be on the order of $1/1000^{\text{th}}$ that of the smoker: the secondary smoke a nonsmoker is actually exposed to is **not** "worse than firsthand smoke," as the Antismokers claim.

I call this claim a **lie.**

- **Lie #19**

Antismokers claim that if you smoke around pregnant women you are killing their babies.

There is absolutely no credible scientific evidence to back this claim up. While there is a reasonable basis for claiming that heavy maternal smoking itself can significantly increase the frequency of medical conditions that might harm a fetus, there is no sound basis for concern about casual exposure to secondary smoke. As far as I have been able to determine, there is not even any reasonable basis for concluding that working or living on a regular daily basis in a smoking environment causes any measurable increase in conditions that could kill a developing baby. To claim that an individual who lights a cigarette in an area with a pregnant woman without first asking is guilty of anything beyond lack of consideration is clearly false.

Antismokers claim that smokers are killing the babies of pregnant women with their smoking.

I call this claim a **lie.**

• Lie #20

Antismokers claim that "tornado like winds" would be needed to adequately keep smoke out of nonsmoking sections in bars and restaurants.

The theoretical basis for this claim seems to rest upon the observation that molecules of gas and submicroscopic particles leaving the burning end of a cigarette may have a short-term velocity of several hundred miles per hour. However, as almost anyone who has taken freshman college classes in physics and chemistry knows, such molecules and particles are slowed down within nanoseconds by collisions with other molecules and particles in the air.

Experimental studies as well as casual observation both clearly indicate that a regular air movement of just several miles an hour is more than enough to move any measurable quantities of smoke quite effectively toward exhaust vents.

Antismokers claim such directed ventilation cannot work without winds that would instantly kill smokers and nonsmokers alike.

I call this claim a **lie.**

- ## Lie #21

Antismokers claim that smoking needs to be banned from public parks and beaches because infants are being poisoned by cigarette butts.

While such a claim obviously has power because of both the "Save the Children" factor and the outright disgust factor, it is fully refuted in the chapter on "Saving The Children."

Antismokers say smokers are killing others' babies with butts.

I call this claim a **lie.**

- ## Lie #22

Antismokers say smoking bans will actually be good, rather than bad, for the bar business.

They base these claims on studies that often include such confounders as areas where bans are not actually in place or have been rescinded, areas where ban enforcement is lax, profit figures that ignore wider economic conditions, and mix-ups of bar business with such things as restaurants and fast food franchises.
    The lie of this claim is shown clearly by the Crusaders' constant cry for "a level playing field." If smoking bans were good for bars and restaurants there would be no need for a level playing field since businesses would rush to increase their profits with smoking bans of their own. Instead we see such bizarre occurrences as bars that comply with smoking bans suing other bars that don't on the basis of "unfair business practices" (M. Hall. "Owners can be sued..." *Union Tribune* 02/24/01).

According to a spokesperson for the Vancouver Coastal Health Authority, a single noncompliant restaurant in one area met with such outrageous success that smoke-free restaurants nearby were actually forced out of business and had to close! Research conducted by Otto J. Mueksch, the President of Californians For Smokers Rights, indicates that during a time period when the economy was generally booming, over 1,000 California restaurants and bars went out of business without being replaced.   In Waterloo the government is considering sending bar owners to jail, claiming that the 1% of noncompliant bars are stealing too much business away from the other 99%! (CBC News British Columbia 01/14/03; Otto J. Mueksch. "Smoking Ban Impact...." FORCES.org 03/01/01; Jeff Outhit. "Bar Owners May Get Jail...." *Waterloo Record* 06/18/02)

Antismokers claim that smoking bans will be good for both the bar and the restaurant business.

I call this claim a **lie.**

• Lie #23

Antismokers claim that they are pushing for smoking bans out of concern for the health of workers exposed to secondary smoke.

For anyone who has read this far into *Dissecting Antismokers' Brains* there is no need to refute this claim further.   The motivations for bans and for engendering unreasonable fears of secondary smoke have been fully discussed, and concern for the "health of workers" ranks far down the list for most Antismokers pushing their ban agendas.

I call this claim a **lie.**

- **Lie #24**

Antismokers claim that their motives and research are pure, that there is no reason for anyone to have any doubt as to the truth of all they say or the purity of their motivations.

Examination of the first 23 lies should sufficiently expose the falsehood of that.

I call this claim a **lie.**

~ Summation ~

So much of the Antismoking Crusade is based on lies, exaggerations, and premises that twist reality into otherworldly convolutions that it's hard to imagine that it could ever have achieved the success it has, much less serve as a model for anything in the future. Amazingly however it **has** achieved an incredible level of success, and even more amazingly, as we'll see in the following and last Appendix, it **is** being used as a model for future attacks on our freedoms.

Appendix J

Beyond Tobacco...

We are not unlike the laboratory frog that, when dropped into a pot of boiling water, quickly jumps out. But when placed in lukewarm water that is slowly heated, the frog will remain there until it is rescued.

-- Al Gore

Those people who seek to restrict and limit the freedoms and lives of others are found outside the arena of the Free-Choice vs. Antismoking battle as well as within. What may be surprising to those not familiar with the behind the scenes politicking however is the extent to which different "Nannying" movements are inter-connected.

Before tax money became so easily available one of the powerful early players in the Antismoking Crusade was the enormously wealthy non-profit Robert Wood Johnson Foundation. With a nine billion dollar punch RWJF shaped the direction and strategies of many of the modern Antismoking efforts and is now looking to the next victim in a drive toward a government controlled, moral, and healthy world.

The article below is an excerpted summary of a Special Report put out by the Center for Consumer Freedom. Before reading it you should be aware that the Center has been criticized because it is partially supported by money from Big Tobacco. However the points made in the report rang with enough credibility to my ears that I wrote them and asked if I could reproduce portions of their summary in an Appendix to this book. James Bowers wrote back with gracious permission and I wish to thank him and them for that: I believe that the message they are imparting, even with the motivational bias that may lie behind it, is one that's both frightening and worthwhile.

The writer of the report itself, Dan Mindus, did an excellent job of research and presentation. The parallels between today's Neo-Prohibitionist Antialcohol movement and the approaches taken over the last few decades by the Antismoking Campaign are truly hard to believe and I highly recommend that those with access to the Internet read the entire piece.

(Excerpts from summary)

SPECIAL REPORT: The Robert Wood Johnson Foundation's Neo-Prohibitionist Agenda

[T]he *Philadelphia Daily News* warns that "The anti-alcohol forces are out there" and wonders: "Are we facing a return to Prohibition?"

A new report from the Center for Consumer Freedom answers that question in the affirmative, and details how the new temperance movement is conceived, coordinated, and funded by the $9 billion Robert Wood Johnson Foundation (RWJF). Follow the money, the report demonstrates, and you'll find that nearly every study disparaging adult beverages in the mass media, every legislative push to limit alcohol marketing or increase taxes, and every supposedly "grassroots" anti-alcohol organization leads back to Princeton, New Jersey, where the RWJF is head-quartered.

The most famous organization in the neo-prohibitionist cabal is Mothers Against Drunk Driving (MADD). The group's name has become a misnomer, as MADD no longer dedicates its energies to tackling the scourge of drunk driving. MADD now assails drinking of any kind. Its new slogan "impairment begins with the first drink" is carefully crafted to position alcohol as a drug for which there is no such thing as moderate or reasonable consumption.

A television spot produced by MADD depicts heroin being boiled in a spoon and sucked into a syringe while the voice-over intones about the dangers of alcohol. The effect... -- as MADD well knows -- is to promote the image of alcohol as a destructive, addictive, and abnormal drug that American society should not abide. This report shows that MADD has received more than three million dollars from the RWJF since 1996....

The RWJF's neo-prohibitionist agenda becomes as clear as day when it funds groups that link alcohol to prohibited drugs like heroin. Shortly after one anti-alcohol organization produced an advertisement depicting a bottle of beer as if it were a syringe, the RWJF made one of its directors a "Developing Leadership in Reducing Substance Abuse" fellow, which carries a $75,000 cash award. The Center for Science in the Public Interest (CSPI), meanwhile, is pushing for alcohol's inclusion in the federal government's anti-drug media campaign. "Don't forget beer, the king of drugs," the group says. The RWJF gave CSPI $750,000 for its anti-alcohol project in 2001 alone.

The RWJF hardly limits itself to linking alcohol with illegal drugs. Many of the neo-prohibitionist activist organizations and leaders that the Center for Consumer Freedom has reported on over the years are funded by the RWJF. That includes: ...

The Center on Alcohol Marketing and Youth (CAMY), which exists for one purpose: to accuse the alcohol industry of "targeting" underage drinkers. The RWJF established CAMY with a five million dollar grant.

The Department of Education's Higher Education Center for Alcohol and Other Drug Prevention (HEC), which argues for "changing people's knowledge, attitudes, and behavioral intentions regarding alcohol use." ...

Jim Gogek, an editorial writer for the *San Diego Union-Tribune*, who wrote an op-ed in *The New York Times* accusing the Governors of Maryland, New York and New Jersey of being bought and paid for by the alcohol industry because they oppose even higher "sin" taxes. Gogek is paid $25,000 a year by the RWJF.

Richard Yoast ... argues there are two kinds of people: those who abuse alcohol, and those who abstain. The former shouldn't have access to it, the argument goes, and the latter won't care if you take it away.... The RWJF has given nearly six million dollars to Yoast's office since 1995. ...

The RWJF's family of anti-alcohol warriors can't advocate prohibition directly, so it seeks instead to make alcohol prohibitively expensive through higher "sin" taxes, or prohibitively hard to come by through restrictions on where and when one may drink. The RWJF funded campaigns to ban alcohol from airports, parks, cultural events, sports stadiums, and even golf courses. It funds efforts to restrict the hours bars, restaurants, and liquor stores can stay open. And it has never met an alcohol tax it didn't like. Taken together, these efforts have been called prohibition "*drip by drip.*" ...

The RWJF seek[s] to drive adult beverage consumption underground, away from mainstream culture and public places. Restraining the availability of alcohol, combined with linking it to illegal drugs, will marginalize drinking to such an extent that Prohibition will have been achieved by stealth.

The RWJF has put in place all the elements required for such sweeping change. From 1998 to 2002 it spent more than $265 million cultivating a vast network of anti-alcohol community organizations, centers for technical support, a compliant press, and a growing body of academic literature critical of even moderate alcohol consumption. The next highly-publicized study or angry local movement may now reach the "tipping point" where the RWJF-funded anti-alcohol agenda snowballs into the kind of orchestrated frenzy that culminated in the 18th amendment.

<End of Excerpted Summary>

As noted earlier, the Center for Consumer Freedom has critics who call it "a front group for the restaurant, alcohol and tobacco industries." But as also noted earlier, a classic Crusader propaganda trick is always to use an Ad Hominem link to Big Tobacco as an argument no matter how weak that link may be, how far in the past it occurred, or how valid the opposing argument might be. I chose to reproduce their article because I felt their points were valid and showed the striking similarity between the emerging approach to the War on Drinking and the already successful model of the War On Smoking. The current activities of the RWJF are well reflected in a compilation of their grants documented by Wanda Hamilton on the FORCES site at http://www.forces.org/ evidence/money/rwjgrant.htm.

As if to quell any doubts I had about including the preceding analysis here, one of Delaware's two major newspapers, *The Delaware News Journal,* ran a major editorial in its Sunday edition, May 18th, 2003 headlined "**PEOPLE WHO LIVE UNHEALTHY LIFESTYLES PENALIZE THE REST OF US.**" The *News Journal,* known as a staunch supporter of Delaware's contentious smoking ban, urged its readers to understand that:

> *It's time that government, which has an enormous stake in the cost of health care, and insurance companies join forces with the medical professions to establish guidelines for healthful behavior that can be enforced.*

They were not just editorializing about smoking, but rather, as other paragraphs made clear, about eating and drinking habits as well. The concept of these three gigantic forces in our society, Big Pharma/Health, Big Insurance, and Big Government, all coming together to rule the minutiae of our lives is scarier than any other thought that could possibly close the Appendices to this book.

Epilogue

As *Dissecting Antismokers' Brains* was approaching its final revision, the debate in New York heated up as a bouncer at a bar became the first casualty of the smoking ban. His brother blamed the "stupid cigarette law," since the altercation began as the bouncer was trying to throw two smokers out of the club. The mayor, the person ultimately responsible for the situation, simply said that his "thoughts are with the family" of the slain bouncer. His thoughts are probably also with the smokers who are now being pelted with eggs and garbage from the upper stories of houses near bars, and when one of them responds someday with a gunshot his thoughts will then be with the family of the unfortunate neighbor (Jeane MacIntosh. "Quality of Life..." *NY Post* 05/27/03).

SARS also began hitting the headlines. Although its major outbreaks have thus far been confined mainly to Toronto, Beijing, and Hong Kong, the nightmare vision outlined earlier of an epidemic spreading in the closed and recirculated confines of smoke-free airliner cabins or even hospitals may become a reality before this book is even fully published.

I'd like to close with a final thought and note of appreciation.

I first became aware of the "fake science" involved in the Antismoking movement back when it was still easy to see it for what it was. I was blessed (although at the time I saw it as far from a blessing) with a housemate in a non-violence training community I was involved with who came home one day with a fistful of pamphlets from ASH, GASP, and the ALA. These pamphlets had frightened him into believing that we, his smoking housemates, were killing him!

That was way back in the mid 70s, long before there was even a decent facsimile of real science out there to support those views. Because the claims were so patently false it was easy for me to see their errors and to see the techniques being used to whip up fear in people. If I had remained unaware of the Anti-smoking Crusade until the 90s it's quite possible I would have been as fully taken in by it as many of "The Innocent" described earlier in this book.

However, armed with that early skepticism I knew that whenever new claims or studies came out purporting to show the dangers of smoking and secondary smoke I needed to carefully examine them for fakery and bias rather than simply accepting them at face value.

I was put in mind of this recently upon reading F. Paul Wilson's new book, *The Haunted Air* (Forge Press. 2002). In that book he does a wonderful job of debunking a spiritualist con game known as the "one-ahead." Any reader who remembers Johnny Carson's "Incredible Karnak" routine has seen a similar, though more transparent, reenactment of this scam.

The spiritualist in question will ask members of the audience to put questions to the dead into sealed envelopes that are dumped into a container and pulled out one by one. As each is chosen, the spiritualist will raise it to his or her forehead and deliver the "answer from the spirit world" before opening the envelope and apparently reading the question. Since there is seemingly no way for the spiritualist to know which question is coming up, the answers appear to have a genuinely supernatural origin. Anyone who generally believes in this stuff will sit there and be happy with this "proof" of the spirit world's existence.

Of course, it's not "proof" of anything: it's a scam based upon some sleight of hand in which the spiritualist, even before pulling the first envelope out of the container, has already seen the question "one-ahead" (a single envelope in the container is secretly and deftly opened and the question exposed before the readings begin) and in each case is merely making up answers to questions he or she has already seen.

To a believer, it's proof. To an unbeliever, even if they don't know just how the trick was done, it's nothing more than another example of clever fakery. Even if the "scam" can't be immediately uncovered, the skeptic will know that there **is** one, somewhere, somehow, hidden away – Behind the Curtain.

This is a good analogy for the situation that many of us "skeptics" of the Crusade find ourselves in. We've seen so many instances over the years where the public has been lied to and bamboozled in order to achieve the goal of a smoke-free world, that we know that each new study and each new claim that comes up is likely to be built upon very shaky foundations, even if such shakiness is not readily apparent.

So in closing, I would like to thank that old housemate, who was sincere though misguided, and also thank the early scam artists of ASH and GASP who made such blatantly over-stated claims that even I, dense as I was, could see through them and learn to doubt the better financed and more sophisticated lies to come.

As nightfall does not come at once, neither does oppression. In both instances there is a twilight where everything remains seemingly unchanged. And it is in such twilight that we all must be aware of change in the air – however slight – lest we become unwitting victims of darkness.

– Supreme Court Justice William Douglas

Remember: they are not just after smokers. Giving up our freedoms to those who would control us in exchange for a little extra comfort or security is the single most dangerous legacy any of us can leave to our children.

Recommended Bibliography

The selections below are by no means exhaustive, but they do provide a basic introduction to the other resources that are out there. My descriptions and opinions about them are obviously purely personal.

Books:

Best, Joel. *"Damned Lies and Statistics"* – While this book says almost nothing about smoking it provides a readable and fascinating introduction to the ways statistics can be misused by those pushing an agenda upon the public. Anyone who's intimidated by the idea of criticizing the "statistical truths" presented by the media should read this book cover to cover.

Colby, Lawrence. *"In Defense of Smokers"* -- Larry Colby is a longtime smokers' rights advocate who tackles not just claims about secondary smoke, but those connecting smoking itself to cancer and other diseases. While most Americans will have a difficult time even conceiving that there could be serious questioning of whether smoking is a primary cause of lung cancer, Mr. Colby strongly attacks that belief as largely arising from a few early and poorly designed studies and raises some very good questions. The one drawback for some folks is that the book is not generally available in hardcopy: Mr. Colby has released it over the Internet for either online reading or for downloading and printing out. It is freely available at: www.lcolby.com/colbyl.htm

Nickles, Sara, ed. *"Drinking, Smoking, and Screwing"* – This is a wonderful collection of short articles and essays by writers ranging from Dorothy Parker and Mark Twain up to Fran Liebowitz and Erica Jong about America's love of "naughty" pleasures.

Oakley, Don. *"Slow Burn: The Great American Antismoking Scam (And Why It Will Fail!)"* – Don wrote the book that I had wanted to write for years, but he had the courage to go for it while I diddled around being too daunted by the magnitude of the task. In an extraordinarily readable and comfortable style he outlines the political and social history of the modern American Antismoking Crusade and fires scathing broadsides at those who have attacked our freedoms.

A retired editor, Don Oakley brings formidable organizational skills to the task and backs up his contentions with close to a thousand carefully footnoted references. Without Don's book in the background I could never have found the focus on psychology and science that allowed me to write my own book. Of all the books in this area I think Don's is probably by far the best in terms of combining readability and information --. just be ready for some real reading: it's 600 pages long!

Snel, Jan. *"Permission to enjoy"!* – Jan is a psychophysiologist from the University of Amsterdam in the Netherlands. In this book he takes a view diametrically opposed to that of the Puritan mentality: if you enjoy doing something in your life, even if it's bad for you, make a decision as to whether you really want to do it anyway. If the answer is yes, then go ahead and do it without feeling guilty! As Jan points out, some of the things that are "bad" for us may in fact actually be "good" for us in terms of the relief of stress and the addition of pleasure to our lives.

Sullum, Jacob. *"For Your Own Good. The Anti-Smoking Crusade and the Tyranny of Public Health"* As pointed out in my chapter on Ad Hominem arguments, Mr. Sullum has been strongly attacked by Crusaders because he once wrote an editorial critical of their position that was later picked up and reprinted by a tobacco company after they paid $5,000 for the rights. In the Antismokers' bible, that allows them to forever discount anything Sullum might say, because he is "in the pocket of the tobacco industry." In *For Your Own Good* Mr. Sullum strikes back at them strongly, freely and honestly addressing the incident in the very first paragraphs of his book and proceeding from there to expose the manipulative efforts of the Antismoking community to control the rest of us "For our own good."

Free-Choice Web Resources

Most Smokers' Rights groups use the Internet as their primary communication tool. Web pages, email lists, and message boards have served to tie together a community that largely lacks the financial resources for such luxuries as international conferences. There are dozens, perhaps hundreds of groups and web pages, far too many to list in any detail here, so I have decided to simply highlight two or three of the most active and then provide two links that will open the door to over a hundred others!

FORCES.org – FORCES provides an incredible resource through its web pages. News, editorials, archives that stretch into the thousands of pages, and links to people who believe passionately in what they are fighting for... all that and more can be found on Forces' pages. Forces was really the first Free Choice group to note the importance of Big Pharma and its lobbying power as a support for the Antismoking Crusade, and it has gone on to successfully educate many European legislative bodies about the lies of the Antismokers.

While the home pages of FORCES International provide a treasure trove for activists around the world, those pages also link to dozens of local chapters and affiliates in countries all around the world, bringing together activists from East and West, North and South, providing a basis for the sort of unity and communication that has made the Crusaders' movement so successful.

NYCClash.com – CLASH (Citizens Lobbying Against Smokers' Harassment) was started just three years ago by Brooklyn police officer Audrey Silk. I've had the good fortune to meet Audrey when I went to New York for a City Council hearing and was amazed at amount of energy I found. She's built CLASH from absolute scratch up to the point where today it is regarded as a vital voice of opposition to bans and taxes whenever New York or nearby media are covering smoking stories. While CLASH's web pages are not as exhaustive as those of FORCES, the material they highlight can form a base for anyone seeking an introduction to actually fighting smoking bans and taxes on the local legislative fronts. Together with NYCTUFF (Taverners United For Fairness), CLASH is spearheading the opposition to Mayor Bloomberg's Puritanical vision for New York City.

Smokers United – http://www.geocities.com/CapitolHill/ Parliament/4061/Index.html -- For a long time my annoyance with Antismokers had remained a bit unfocused. I posted on internet boards and wrote a few letters to the editor, but didn't do much else: I felt like I was alone on a raft in the middle of an ocean: NO ONE seemed to agree with me! Then early one Friday evening I wandered into the Smokers United Chat room and found Spinner (SU's host), Gabz, John Jacoby, Boomer, and a bunch of other friendly folks who were ticked as hell and weren't gonna take it anymore!   The energy and support I found there spurred me to become more active and provided the foundation upon which *Dissecting Antismokers' Brains* was built.

Founded by a loving grandmother known by the screen name of Spinner who divides her time between smokers' rights and cooking up ceramic gargoyles in her backyard kiln, Smokers United is an inspiration. It provides far more than mere chat: its pages contain lots of excellent analysis of Antismoking lies, clear and graphic representations of Free Choice positions, and hard hitting exposures of some of the hate and harm caused by Crusaders. And if you bump into Spinner while you're there, ask her to make you a gargoyle! :>

Smokers Fighting Discrimination — http://www.geocities.com/ sfd-usa/ -- Founded in the mid 1990s by Dave Pickrell and several other Texans, and fueled by his constant dedication to fighting injustices aimed at smokers, SFD has long provided a cornerstone for U.S. activists fighting smoking bans and taxes. Dave has been published in dozens of newspapers and regularly makes himself heard in legislative debates in Texas and its surrounding states. SFD has a very active mailing list and provides many valuable links and resources on its site.

Dave Hitt's "The Facts" at http://www.davehitt.com/facts provides an excellent summary of rebuttals to Antismoking lies and has a flavor unique to a web icon in his own right: Dave's "Hittman Chronicles" have long been an internet favorite.

And, for something of a contrary view, you might want to check out Carol AS Thompson's page at http://ourworld.compuserve. com/homepages/CarolASThompson/ Carol presents a very critical view of FORCES and some other smokers' rights activists while arguing that the Antismoking Crusade is the ongoing creation of a group of Big Health interests that she refers to as The Lasker Syndicate. While I may disagree with her view of some things, it's certainly a view worth looking at and considering: her points about pushing the blame for diseases caused by infections on to the back of smoking are certainly worth some serious thought.

Finally, two links that will lead you to over a hundred other freedom-loving sites, and one site that anyone who's read this far will certainly want to visit.... :>

Samantha Phillipe's SmokersClub.com site has a members' links page with links to about 50 sites of various groups and also provides hundreds of issues of her weekly newsletter... VERY well worth signing up for while you're there. Samantha, as is true of so many smokers' rights activists, puts an enormous amount of energy into her work for freedom and her newsletter provides an essential weekly summary of Free-Choice supporting news, articles, and commentary. Her links page can be found at http://www.Smokers club.com/mbrlks.htm

Smokers Web Ring provides the option for the browsing activist to move through a world of a hundred or so web sites that support smokers' rights in various ways and forms. Some of the sites are very radical, some are very conservative, some are very politically oriented, and some are not. Well worth spending an evening exploring: http://k.webring.com/hub?sid=&ring=pro smoker&id=&hub

www.AntiBrains.com is my own site, created for this book. The site will grow and change as this book spreads and as Antismoking tactics change. I plan to reproduce two or three of the more important chapters and appendices there, and may also extend several sections with updated material (I'm thinking most specifically here of additions to "Communicating with Antismokers" and "Truth, Lies, and Ice Cream.") Activists who wish to order multiple copies for fundraising or just to distribute to their local politicians will find significant quantity discounts on the page, and at some point I may even add a message board for open debates.

In Peace, Freedom, and the constant search for truth, I hope that *AntiBrains,* my original and very fondly remembered title, has proven a worthwhile reading experience for you.

Michael J. McFadden,
Cantiloper@aol.com
Antibrains@aol.com

Now that you know their lies...

... Spread the truth.

About the Author

Michael J. McFadden grew up in Brooklyn in the 1960s and graduated cum laude and Phi Beta Kappa from Manhattan College with a degree in both Peace Studies and Psychology. He went on to study statistics and propaganda analysis under a doctoral fellowship at the University of Pennsylvania's Wharton program in Peace Research.

He left the University after two years to host a Quaker training center in non-violent social change and has worked at various levels in the areas of peace activism and social change ever since. His activities have ranged from public transportation advocacy to being commissioned by the Queen of England to conduct training workshops in Canada. Aside from writing, his recent endeavors have included such diverse activities as canvassing door-to-door for SANE/FREEZE and coordinating educational conferences in the cyberspatial environs of America Online.

Mr. McFadden currently lives and bicycles in West Philadelphia where he shares a small row house with a very noisy cat and a very quiet squirrel.

Printed in the United States
135136LV00002B/32/A

9 780974 497907